THE
VAUDEVILLIANS

BILL SMITH

THE VAUDEVILLIANS

Macmillan Publishing Co., Inc.

New York

Macmillan Publishing Co., Inc.
866 Third Avenue, New York, N. Y. 10022
Collier Macmillan Canada, Ltd.

Library of Congress Cataloging in Publication Data
Smith, Bill, 1903–
  The Vaudevillians
  Includes index.
    1. Vaudeville—United States. 2. Entertainers—
United States—Correspondence, reminiscences, etc.
I. Title.
PN1968.U5S4   792.7   75–28477
ISBN 0–02–611890–4

First Printing 1976

Printed in the United States of America

Book Design by LIBRA *Graphics, Inc.*

To Ro, whose secretarial skills, driving force, and love got this book off the ground.

ACKNOWLEDGMENTS

My thanks and gratitude to Bill and Roger Littleford (publishers of *The Billboard* when I was there—they're publishing tycoons today) for giving me the opportunity to catch and review performers in theaters and night clubs.

It was through them that I became part of an exciting scene that gave me the opportunity to meet performers professionally as well as socially.

Also, a low bow to Leonard Traub, the then editor of *The Billboard* (he's now with *Variety*), who hired me. There were times when he boasted about me. There were also times when he would have gladly thrown me out the window.

CONTENTS

THE
VAUDEVILLIANS

INTRODUCTION

MY LOVE affair with vaudeville began during World War I, when I was growing up in the Williamsburg district of Brooklyn. We were surrounded by movie houses, some of which played small-time vaudeville. There were Fox's Folly, Loew's Broadway, the DeKalb, and the Halsey. The magnet that drew us was the movie serials *The Perils of Pauline* and *Mysteries of Myra*. Vaudeville was an extra special. But it was vaudeville that had us singing the popular songs of the day, like "It Ain't Gonna Rain No More," "When You Wore a Tulip," and "You Made Me What I Am Today."

Admission to those theaters was eleven cents. The odd penny was the war tax. Later, whenever I could accumulate twenty-five cents (which wasn't easy), I'd go further afield to Keith's Bushwick, a real vaudeville house. It was there that I first saw the big-time headliners Gallagher and Shean, Ted Lewis, Fanny Brice, Sophie Tucker, and others.

I never thought that one day I would meet and talk with some of them on a familiar basis or that my work would entail writing reviews of their acts or that some of them would even seek me out. Their stories of "When I played the Palace . . ." fascinated me. This all began when in 1943 I joined the staff of *The Billboard*, a show-business weekly magazine, as an editor covering vaudeville and nightclubs. Now I no longer "saw" or "watched" performances, I "caught" them. I was no longer a "civilian," but rather a part of the show-business scene.

When I got to know performers better, I listened to their stories either at the Friars Club or at the various eating places actors frequented. In pursuit of my professional duties, I spent many hours at places like Lindy's, the Gateway, Gus and Andy's, and Hanson's drugstore.

Lindy's, on Broadway and 51st, was especially popular with performers late in the evening. Protocol was scrupulously observed: music-business

1

people sat to the right of the entrance; small-timers sat to the left; head-liners held court in the center. Tourists—and this category included all nonprofessionals—were relegated to the rear of the restaurant.

The Gateway was on the street level of what was then called the RKO Building—1270 Sixth Avenue—next door to the Radio City Music Hall. This building housed the William Morris Agency, General Amusement Corporation, and scores of independent talent agents. Between two and four in the afternoon the Gateway was crowded with performers on their way to or returning from their agents.

Gus and Andy's, a few steps from the stage door of the Palace, was a favorite with those playing that theater. Many an actor was carried on the tab at Gus and Andy's restaurant.

Hanson's drugstore was more than its name implied. It was a drugstore with a lunch counter, but it also had tables and chairs in the back where performers would spend hours discussing their acts. At times it became an impromptu rehearsal hall. I saw Sammy Davis, Jr., then part of the Will Mastin Trio, test out some of his imitations and impressions at Hanson's.

When I started "catching" vaudeville it was no longer a major factor in the amusement world, having been replaced by the "talkies." The world that Joe Laurie, Jr., and Abel Green, then editor of *Variety*, had written about in their book *Showbiz* no longer existed. It had been replaced by the big movie houses, the so-called presentation theaters. Every major city had at least one such theater. New York had several: the Paramount, the Strand, the Capitol, the Roxy and Loew's State. These were movie houses which put on five or six live stage shows a day. By 1932 the Palace had fallen from its pinnacle and was mostly a movie house. Every now and then it would reactivate itself with headline acts, then go back to straight movies.

The big move by performers was into radio and the movies. Night-clubs were also important buyers of talent, though only a few vaudevillians could tailor their acts for nightclub audiences. Those vaudevillians who played clubs usually got their chance because they had achieved fame in radio. Later, television fame would provide the entry.

The headliners of an era, vaudeville that millions had seen, were gone. A theater that was *the* entertainment of the masses from the 1880s to the 1940s existed only in the memories of performers like those who tell their stories in the following pages.

Along with vaudeville, many stage shows, nightclubs and restaurants have disappeared. When vaudeville and nightclubs vanished from the entertainment scene, *The Billboard* gave up these departments. I was the last editor covering these fields—a position I had held for a decade or more. The thought of doing a book on vaudevillians wasn't mine. It came from Jay Williams, an old friend and Connecticut neighbor. He got the idea from Tim Seldes, his literary agent, who in turn got it from a Macmillan editor. In the months that followed, there were times I wished all concerned had kept their mouths shut. Locating old-time vaudevillians was a job for the FBI. Some I found in New York; many had landed in California; some were living in Florida. Still others, their names mostly forgotten, were living with children and grandchildren in various other parts of the country. Of these, only a handful were willing or able to talk. Some were writing, or thinking of writing, their own books and for this reason were reluctant to talk to me for publication.

I was aware of the obstacles, but having committed myself, I mailed off notes requesting interviews to those performers I once knew, hoping they would remember me. While waiting for replies I continued having lunches with a group of former vaudevillians: Sammy Berk of the team of Berk and Saun, now a manager; Percy Oakes of Oakes and Delour, now an agent; Harry Levine, former Paramount booker; Phil Offin, an agent; Benny Kuchik and Jimmy Schure, formerly agents with Music Corporation of America; and sometimes Sim Kerner, another ex-performer. This group met at least twice weekly, and when I told them of the book I proposed to write, they jumped in eagerly. Over the months their memories, discussions, and arguments could be heard all over whatever restaurant we were lunching in.

Jack Benny—how did he really start? The group agreed he was "just a number-two act" who played fiddle in the pit of the local theater in Waukegan, Illinois. They also remembered that Benny could not use his real name, Kubelsky, because there was a concert violinist around at the time—1914 or so—whose name was Jan Kubelik and the similarity would be too confusing. Benny played some small-time vaudeville with various partners and then joined the Navy. After the war he bought an act from Al Boasberg, a well-known writer of vaudeville material, and then he began moving up. When Benny played the Palace in 1927 he was a hit.

Talk about the old comics brought a consensus that Frank Tinney (no one knew if he was still alive) was the first to use a classic routine that was copied by many. Tinney would lean over the footlights and whisper to the audience, "The leading lady is stuck on me." He would look to the wings, then back to the audience, and confide, "It's kind of sad. I met her coming out of the stage door last night and I said hello to her, but she's so crazy about me she couldn't answer." At this point the lady (nobody remembered her name) would cross the stage. Tinney, put-

3

ting a finger to his lips to warn the audience not to give him away, would greet her: "Hello, Gorgeous" or "Beautiful" or whatever (there were arguments here). She would look at Tinney disdainfully and walk off the stage. "See—what did I tell you?" Tinney would say, facing the audience. "She's crazy about me."

Replies to my notes began arriving, mostly from California. They carried addresses and some even had phone numbers. So I set off for California, armed with these and some additional phone numbers given to me by my lunch companions. Most of the numbers proved useless. One of the things Hollywood actors do regularly—about every month or so, it seems— is to change their unlisted numbers. I turned to the talent agents, who provided me with a new set of numbers—cautioning me not to tell where I got them. You know what? These too had been changed.

The greatest help came from William Morris's head man, Abe Lastfogel. Morris was the talent agency that had represented at one time or another most of the people I sought.

Equipped with my revised list of numbers, I started calling. I got an awful lot of "He's out of town," "Won't be back for six weeks or so," and "Sorry, he's in Australia." Later many wrote sorry-I-missed-you-we'll-get-together-next-time-you're-here notes to me.

Back in New York, I sought out others. I had planned to talk with Sid Gary, a former vaudeville partner of George Burns, and an old friend. I discovered that Gary had died while I was on the West Coast.

Then there was Jack Pearl, the "Vas-you-dere-Sharlie" of radio, who would talk on the phone endlessly, but in whom the prospect of a personal interview set off a nervous reaction.

If all this sounds like a journey into futility, it wasn't so. I did interview over thirty former vaudevillians. We met in grand houses in Beverly Hills, luxurious hotel rooms in New York, retirement homes in Florida, drab furnished rooms off Times Square and equally dismal quarters in downtown Los Angeles that reeked of stale cooking and cats.

With few exceptions most of the performers are close to eighty; one is over ninety. Yet their voices seemed to grow stronger as they reminisced of the days when they were on top. If their versions of what happened to them and their contemporaries occasionally seem at variance with facts, it was the truth as they saw and remembered it. One thing they all claimed —they were all show-stoppers. And with the possible exception of one or two, all played the Palace in its heyday. The only editing I have done of their stories is to eliminate my questions, to prune repetitions, and to cut out excursions into nonvaudeville matters.

4

In the main, vaudevillians were simple, easygoing people. Without extensive formal education, most of their reading was limited to the show-business periodicals; *Zits, The New York Clipper, The Billboard,* and *Variety*. Their knowledge of geography was mainly limited to their booking routes, particularly those places where they had been hits. In many ways they were childlike, always ready for a laugh or a practical joke. But there was nothing immature about their professional work; on stage they brooked no nonsense or interference. The baggy-pants comic may not have known anything about geography or politics but he knew his act perfectly.

I once attended a convention of vaudevillians and nightclub performers—a meeting of the American Guild of Variety Artists (AGVA). It was nonsense atop nonsense. Though the members constantly referred to Roberts' Rules of Order, they seldom followed or even understood them. If a member got the floor by claiming a point of privilege—whatever that meant —another actor-member, well aware of theatrical billing precedence, would call for special privilege, and another would claim extra special privilege. And so it went for the whole meeting.

Between sessions of the convention the vaudevillians put on impromptu performances for themselves that were gems. Once John Bubbles sat at the piano and began tinkling. Immediately he was joined by dancers, singers, and then magicians, all attempting to outdo one another. Suddenly, the show was on—full swing. They were professionals who knew their craft even if they couldn't run a convention properly.

Today? Well, those who played vaudeville in its heyday have long left showbusiness, or at least the stage aspect of it. Some keep their hand in as agents or managers or in some other aspect of the business. Others have put their vaudeville days behind them and perhaps regale their grandchildren with tales of "when I played the Big Time. . ."

HISTORY

THERE IS a widespread belief that the terms "New York Palace" and "vaudeville" are synonymous, but this has no basis in fact. Vaudeville flourished before the Palace was built in 1913 and continued to exist after that theater had given up its two-a-day policy. From the turn of the century until its death vaudeville was dominated by the Keith organization and its successors, Keith Albee and Radio-Keith-Orpheum; the Palace was the most important theater in the chain, but by the first decade of the century San Francisco had the Orpheum, Chicago had its American Music Hall, and in New York there were Tony Pastor's, Koster and Bial, and Hammerstein's Victoria. All were big time.

Vaudeville was splintered into big time, small time, and small-small time, somewhat like New York's Broadway, off-Broadway, and off-off Broadway. Big time meant two shows a day in good theaters with good dressing and toilet facilities for performers. Music was furnished by a large orchestra of musicians who could read music. The big-time performer enjoyed a higher salary as well as better traveling, living, and working conditions. He was also closer to the possibility of being tapped for a part in a musical comedy or revue, which in turn could mean a permanent home and only eight performances a week, even though legitimate theater salaries were lower than earnings in vaudeville.

Small time and small-small time ran the gamut. It could mean four or five, even six shows a day. It could mean theaters with seats, lodge halls with benches, storefronts with standees, Mom and Pop operations, riverboats, or wagon shows. Music was provided by a pianist and a drummer, sometimes augmented by a violinist. In one Midwest town the music was furnished by the local milkman and barber. The former delivered milk in the mornings so he was always available for performances, but if the barber had someone in his chair the show had to wait till he finished. Such waits might be filled by song slides flashed on a white sheet or by vaude-villians who could perform without music.

Small time and small-small time were where the performer served his apprenticeship, where he perfected his craft. It was here that performers Ed Wynn, Eddie Cantor, Smith and Dale, Al Jolson, and Eddie Leonard, to mention but a few, got their education. Some well-known movie actors also learned their trade in this school: Charlie Chaplin, Cary Grant, Jimmy Cagney, Martha Raye, Walter Huston, Buster Keaton, and Joe E. Brown.

Unlike a dramatic actor, the vaudevillian faced his audience unaided by directors, scripts, and prompters. His act might be a series of jokes or a monologue interspersed with songs or a dance routine, but it was polished by constant use and exposure to scores of different audiences. The performer learned by direct experience how to tell a joke, how to build a story toward the punch line, where the laughs belonged, and how long each might take. He learned, too, that some stories or songs would do well in one part of the country but poorly in others. Entrances and exits were important and constantly practiced. Dancing acts were honed to precision and new techniques were constantly incorporated. Acrobats worked ceaselessly to perfect their art.

Vaudeville became one of the most highly disciplined entertainment arts. Experienced vaudevillians knew to the fraction of a minute how long each routine would run. When required to do four minutes, they knew just which routine or a part of one they could lift from their stock. If called upon to do ten minutes, they could perform, as skillfully and professionally.

Dramatic actors appeared in vaudeville, attracted by the larger sums they could earn compared to their salaries on the legitimate stage. Star attractions, the Barrymores for instance, could command salaries two to three times more than those they received in legitimate theater. Such actors would play vaudeville for only one or two seasons, and when a "legit" vehicle was offered, returned to their original medium. The legitimate theater was considered "class" entertainment, as opposed to vaudeville, which was considered "mass" entertainment. The legitimate actor tended to patronize the vaudevillian as crude, ignorant, and lacking in culture. The vaudevillian regarded the actor with mingled feelings of envy and disdain and brushed him off with the curt "legit." He was envious because the legitimate stage actor represented "class," but he was also disdainful because the stage actor knew nothing of the camaraderie that existed among vaudevillians.

Some Broadway stage plays, before being produced in their final form, were sliced into small segments and performed on vaudeville stages to gauge audience reception. If the segments passed muster, they became part of the legitimate stage production; if not, they might be changed or eliminated entirely. In later years the Marx Brothers tried out bits and pieces from their proposed movies before vaudeville audiences. *Animal Crackers* was previewed this way before being produced in its film form.

The act was everything to the vaudevillian. Into it he poured all his knowledge, hard work, skill, time, and money. It was his bread and butter, which he always hoped to transmute someday into steak and potatoes. Whatever the length of his apprenticeship in the small and small-small time, it was a hard school. First there was the immediate problem of getting work, sometimes accomplished through an agent but more often by direct replies to classified ads in the show-business trade journals, *The Billboard* and *Variety*. Then came the jumps, the long journeys from one job to another, sometimes overnight, often in freezing trains. On stage the performer would strain every fiber to please the theater manager. He was painfully aware of the backstage sign that read "Do not send out your laundry until after the first matinee." Most performers knew the sick feeling when a manager came backstage after the first matinee, handed them their publicity photographs which had been displayed in the lobby and in front of the theater, and brusquely uttered the fatal word "canceled." Cancellation could mean being stranded with no money and days away from the next job. Agreed-upon salaries sometimes were not paid, and the early small-time vaudevillian often had nobody to turn to in the towns where he may have been cheated. He couldn't appeal to the law; it was not uncommon for theater owners to be in league with the local authorities.

The small-time performer worked under primitive conditions. Cellar dressing rooms were common. Often his only source of water for washing was a faucet in the yard. He had his meals in greasy spoons and often lodged in vermin-ridden boardinghouses. But all these hardships were disregarded if the act was a hit. Even if the house policy called for six or more shows a day, the grind was inconsequential if only the act was successful.

All small-time performers believed they would break into the big time. Meanwhile they took whatever jobs they could, learning and perfecting their craft. This faith in one's skill and talent was necessary to go onstage, alone, night after night, months on end, before audiences of every manner and receptivity. The reality was that of the thousands of vaudevillians performing all over the United States between 1920 and 1930, only a comparative few made the big time, perhaps 800 out of 10,000. Yet in small time there were so many theaters or other places where acts were presented that there was enough work to keep performers busy the year round.

Vaudeville performers sometimes obtained their material by imitating more successful acts, sometimes developed their own material, and sometimes bought it. Special writers produced material on order; others just wrote, hoping their material would sell. Material was paid for either by a flat fee or, in the case of top writers, a percentage of the performer's income. Inasmuch as the material was the lifeblood of an act, it was closely guarded by various methods. Some would send, by registered letter, a sealed description of their material to *Variety* and *The Billboard*. The letter was to be opened if a dispute arose about ownership of material. Similar letters might be filed with the Vaudeville Managers Protective Association, headed by the renowned Pat Casey, who was the arbiter. If a claim was verified, Casey would notify the offender to cease using the disputed material. It is doubtful that any vaudevillian receiving such a letter ignored it. The Association was an arm of the United Booking Office (UBO), the Keith-controlled booking agency, and an offender could be refused bookings.

The birth of the name "Jack Benny" was the result of such a letter. Ben K. Benny appeared in vaudeville from about 1910 until the early 1920s and had achieved enough recognition to cause Ben Bernie, a famous band leader, to complain that the two names were similar enough to cause confusion. Benny got a Pat Casey letter, and substituted Jack for the Ben K.

Some vaudevillians never filed formal complaints, choosing to take more direct action. To make his point to a new comic at the Palace about 1928, W. C. Fields hired two strong-arm men, who met the offender in the backstage alley. He never used the disputed material again.

Benny Rubin, in his book *Come Backstage with Me*, wrote of a comic, Harry Breen, who wrote his own material. One day Breen met a fellow comic, who he believed had stolen his best joke. Breen greeted him, "You make a living talking, don't you?"

"Yeah, what about it?" was the reply.

"Okay, try doing it with a lisp," said Breen, and punched the man in the mouth, damaging some expensive dental work.

Some theater owners, familiar with one performer's material, would

Harry Rose, the "Broadway Jester," had a platform built across the orchestra pit; when he announced offstage, "Here's Harry," he would dash out and mount the platform. At Loew's Paradise (N.Y.), stagehands forgot the platform, and when Rose dashed out he fell into the pit. He hurt himself badly and was unable to rise. The orchestra leader looked down: "You want me to play your entrance music again?"

11

stop another from using it, under threat of cancellation. Other owners, however, preferred the imitator because he usually could be hired for less money than the originator.

But even good material and long experience did not guarantee success. The vaudeville terms for success or failure were succinct and colorful, and are still used today in other branches of entertainment. A performer never did so-so—he "died." If he was just fair, his fellow performers would say he "bombed." He was never just a success with an audience, he "killed them." Heavy applause was translated into "I fractured them." If he was nervous and doing badly he was covered with "flop sweat."

Many who played the New York Colonial knew only too well what flop sweat meant. The Colonial attracted audiences who didn't hesitate to let performers know what they thought. An act that earned their disapproval was treated to a cadenced applause that became known as the "Colonial Clap." It was a bad storm to weather.

Top vaudeville stars were accorded the same adoration given to movie stars in later years. The real rulers, however, though not well known to audiences, were the managers: B. F. Keith; his chief aide, E. F. Albee; Percy Williams; John J. Murdock; F. F. Proctor; and Martin Beck. These men represented the big time. Keith-Albee virtually dominated vaudeville. To assure control of the industry the Keith empire created the United Booking Office (UBO) in the early 1900s. This many-tentacled organization issued franchises to favored agents who represented top stars as well as standard acts. The franchises were permits that enabled agents to book their acts through UBO. There was no charge, but the franchises could be revoked by UBO at its pleasure and for its own reasons. An agent who lost his UBO franchise was practically out of business; the most important outlet for his clients was closed to him. Theaters outside the Keith empire also booked through UBO because it provided a regular supply of talent, plus occasional big names, at salaries within the budget set by the theater manager.

To the performer, the advantage of a UBO booking was "the route." A route would take in theaters all over the country, arranged in time-saving geographical progression, to keep him busy working for three or more years, without repeating cities. Most of the bookings were in big time. If some small time was included, salaries and working conditions were equal to those in the big time, with UBO guaranteeing salaries. Such routes were worth thousands of dollars. They were so valuable, in fact, that they were accepted as collateral for bank loans. On the strength of a route many performers bought homes—Freeport, Long Island, for some reason, was a favorite area.

At some time or another practically all managers tangled with B. F. Keith. Keith operated on the principle that if you couldn't lick them, buy them out or drive them out. By 1915 he controlled about 1500 theaters in the United States and Canada, either through his UBO hold on vaudeville or through actual ownership.

Originally Keith booked as far west as Chicago. From there to the Coast (and in parts of Canada) the Western Vaudeville Association—of which the Orpheum Circuit, ruled by Martin Beck, was an important part—was in control. Though Beck distrusted Keith-Albee, he came to an agreement with them, so that UBO acts were then booked from coast to coast.

Beck wasn't content to remain west of Chicago. He had ambitions to extend his theaters to the East. In 1912 he bought a site at 47th Street and Seventh Avenue in New York and began building the Palace. Keith was furious. Beck's backers, reluctant to do battle with Keith, withdrew, and when the smoke cleared, it was discovered that Keith had acquired 75 percent of the Palace, leaving Beck with only 25 percent. It became known as Keith's Palace. Later Keith bought the Majestic, an Orpheum house in Chicago, driving Beck out of that city. Ultimately Keith acquired control of the Orpheum chain.

The establishment of the Palace on 47th Street created an ironic situation. Every theater booked by UBO had exclusive rights to Keith acts in its specifically designated area. This applied to large cities like New York, Chicago, and Boston where there were numerous big-time houses. Since Oscar Hammerstein's Victoria Theater in New York had the right to all Keith acts between 34th Street and 59th Street, Keith was contractually prevented from playing his own acts in his new theater. In the end Keith had to pay Hammerstein a reputed $200,000 to waive his exclusivity to allow Keith vaudeville in the Palace.

The Palace opened in 1913 and within a year was the chief ornament in the Keith vaudeville crown. It became the mecca of all vaudevillians. When Keith died in 1914, E. F. Albee became the ruler of the empire. Albee, a shrewd organizer and a merciless opponent, controlled his holdings with an iron fist. His autocratic rule earned him the fear and hatred of many performers. An example was his fighting the White Rats strike of 1916.

For some time performers had been complaining about bookers who switched routes on short notice, sudden cancellations, and sliced salaries. Appeals to Albee were fruitless. At the beginning of the century a fraternal organization of vaudevillians had been formed, which called itself the White Rats (derived from "star" spelled backward). In 1910 the organization had received a charter from the American Federation of Labor. With grievances piling up, the union called a strike in 1916. Albee hit back, using his blacklist as a weapon. Known members of the White Rats were not permitted to work in any of the theaters under his control, which now numbered 10,000 to 15,000. Actors who were only suspected of membership were given unfavorable routes and salary slashes. Albee had spies all over. The White Rats' clubhouse on 46th Street between Seventh and Eighth avenues was deserted. Actors feared being seen entering it. The strike, led by an Englishman, Harry Mountford, collapsed within a year, and the White Rats organization disintegrated.

In 1917 a new actors' club, the National Vaudeville Artists (NVA), backed by Albee, came into being. The NVA took over the White Rats' clubhouse and turned it into a lavish place where actors could live, eat, and relax. Actors were encouraged to join NVA. Those who did received preferential UBO treatment—their cancellation clauses were lifted from employment contracts and new "play-or-pay" clauses were substituted. Under the new clauses, an actor, even if canceled, had to be paid for the full term of his engagement. Albee used this clause like a Ping-Pong ball, batting it back and forth, inserting it at one point, withdrawing it at another, reinserting it when it pleased him.

Ironically enough, even while the struggle for better conditions was raging and managers were battling for theater control, new theaters were opening and more and more work was available. The most desirable theaters were still Keith-Albee. It was in this period that many of the actors who were to become vaudeville legends appeared: Smith and Dale, Frank Tinney, Joe Cook, George Jessel, Nora Bayes, Van and Schenck, W. C. Fields, Benny Rubin, Lou Holtz, and others.

From 1915 to 1920 was also the period when small time spread into what became known as family time. Marcus Loew and William Fox, who owned theaters in the East, were now spreading out over the rest of the country, creating a demand for more and more acts. The Shuberts and Marc Klaw and Abe Erlanger, Broadway producers, were also coming into the vaudeville picture. William Morris, who was to become head of a powerful talent agency, ignored Keith and arranged to find talent for these new theaters. Business was booming. One result of these new enterprises was new confrontations. A suit charging the Keith-Albee combine with violations of the antitrust laws dragged on for years until 1924 when it was dismissed.

One of Albee's most hated opponents was William Morris, who booked these new theaters without using UBO. Morris imported Harry Lauder, an international star, and played him in non-Keith theaters, another heinous affront. Worst of all, perhaps, Morris ignored an iron-clad Keith-Albee rule by booking actors who usually played UBO houses. Keith-Albee was so infuriated that they issued orders that actors were not to accept Morris' bookings under pain of being blacklisted by UBO. Albee offered Morris a high position in UBO. Morris refused.

During this period of conflict the State Lake theater opened in Chicago in 1919. The State Lake was to change the face of all vaudeville. It was the first of the new huge theaters with seating capacities ranging from 3000 to over 5000 (the Palace held only 1800). What was revolutionary about the State Lake besides its size was its lavish appointments as compared to other movie-vaudeville theaters. The State Lake had an orchestra of symphony proportions, luxurious decor, comfortable seats, and a marble lobby whose walls were covered with oil paintings. The theater was manned by a staff of well-trained, well-groomed ushers and had four shows a day (compared to the two-a-day policy of older big-time theaters). Bills were arranged so acts did only two shows a day.

New York followed with its Capitol theater, which had a similar stage show policy. Next came the Roxy and then the New York Paramount, followed by the Strand. Vaudeville houses all over the country began adding movies and equipping for talkies. Some theaters dropped vaudeville entirely and played only movies. The panic was on and by the late 1920s big-time vaudeville, with its two shows a day, was drawing to a close.

The Albee-Morris fight continued. Albee kept expanding. He bought a half-interest in the B. S. Moss chain and acquired the huge Hippodrome in New York as well as the Canadian United Theaters. As always, he was on the lookout for new attractions but refused to use those that were coming out of radio, the new entertainment medium. In fact, the word "radio," unless used derisively, was forbidden on Keith stages. (In later years the N. Y. Capitol similarly forbade the word "television" on its stage.)

New interests were coming into the entertainment field. Joseph P. Kennedy moved into vaudeville when he acquired enough Keith stock to control the company. By 1927 a merger of Radio-Keith-Orpheum, Pathé, and Kennedy's small film company took place. The Keith vaudeville houses became the RKO theaters.

Talking movies were now the number-one medium. The big movie houses, with their huge seating capacity, booked the famous radio names, while big-time vaudeville just limped along. Some theaters continued with the small-time operations, occasionally booking headliners willing to work for less money. By the early 1930s vaudevillians were desperately trying to get into radio and the movies. Some, like George Burns, Fred Allen, Jack Benny, Rudy Vallee and Bob Hope, managed it. Most, however, did not and they had no place to go.

Small neighborhood theaters that couldn't afford vaudeville turned to bank nights, dish giveaways, and amateur nights. Out of these amateur nights came new performers. Some moved on to the resort areas—the Borscht Belt—and others received exposure on a Major Bowes radio show and from there went into nightclubs.

During World War II an increased demand for acts arose from the USO, which needed performers to tour service installations and entertain the troops. Some vaudevillians stayed with USO for years.

In isolated areas servicemen spent their off-duty hours listening to local disk jockeys who kept spinning records so persistently that the bands and singers became well-known names. Theaters that booked them were amazed at their popularity and draw. Civilians as well as the uniformed personnel flocked to hear the big bands and their vocalists. This period saw the rise of Helen O'Connell, Dinah Shore, Lena Horne, Frank Sinatra, Perry Como, and others. Many comedians who were part of such band packages were graduates of the neighborhood theater amateur nights —Jan Murray, Jackie Miles, Lenny Kent, and Joey Bishop among them. Occasionally a former vaudevillian who had become a big radio or movie name was also on the bill.

By the late 1940s a rash of poor movies cut theater attendance. Band show packages had priced themselves out of sight and were no longer attracting such large audiences. Another era was ending.

Loew's State was the first casualty. It closed its doors on December 23, 1947. Within a year the Paramount, Strand, Capitol and Roxy had also ceased operations. Loew's State and the Warner Strand were remodeled into two motion picture houses. The Paramount became a bank. The Capitol became a high-rise office building and the Roxy became part of the Taft Hotel. Similar closings occurred in all major cities. Some blamed it on the burgeoning new entertainment—television. Others blamed it on the end of the war. But whatever, or whoever, was at fault, vaudeville had come, had flourished, and was gone.

Vaudeville as such doesn't exist any longer in the United States. Occasionally a variety show built around a big-name star is presented at a theater—the Judy Garland and Danny Kaye shows both played the Palace in the 1950s—but there is no big time, no small time, no circuits, no UBO. Vaudeville still exists in a minor way in Australia. You can also see it from time to time at the Olympia in Paris and at the Palladium in London.

BUDDY HOWE

BUDDY HOWE *was the Howe of Carroll and Howe, a comedy dance team. Jean Carroll supplied the comedy—a combination of malapropisms and sophistication that made even standard jokes seem funny. Buddy Howe did acrobatic dancing and acted the straight man to his partner.*

The two met when Howe was part of a team called Bud and Buddy and Jean was a singing, dancing comedienne doing a single. Before that she had been part of several other acts. Dating led to marriage and a merging of their talents. Jean taught her husband, who was strictly a dancer, how to deliver lines as a straight man. He stuck strictly to his learned routine and if she ad-libbed—which she frequently did—he would be petrified, not knowing how to get back to the script.

Today their performing days are behind them. Jean is a housewife and grandmother (see pages 252–259 for her story). Buddy is chairman of the board of CMA (Creative Management Agency).

I started in show business in 1925 when I joined a flash act called Patti Moore and Band with Sammy Lewis and Bud and Buddy. Buddy was Buddy Soloff, sixteen, now out of the business. I, at fifteen, was Bud. We both lived in Brooklyn's East New York in a tough neighborhood, and went to school there. We both took up dancing, planning to become a hoofing team and go into vaudeville. We were rehearsing at Feist Music Publishing. In those days little acts trying to break in would go up there to practice and rehearse. Those were tough times and if we could get free rehearsal space, you bet we took it. While we were going through a dance, a fellow stuck his head through the door and asked if we were looking for work. It was Sammy Lewis who asked us. He took us over to meet Sam Kesler and Patti Moore. We did an audition and they hired us for the flash act.

Patti Moore was a dancer and a singer. She danced more than she sang. She would do a dance with Sammy Lewis and then my partner and I came on to do a dance and do something with Patti. Sammy did something on his own and then we all joined into a finale. We carried our own band, a seven-man outfit.

We played some break-in dates in Poughkeepsie and Newburgh, and then brought the act into New York. We played most of the Fox houses in New York and we were then bought by RKO. We played the RKO time [all the RKO theaters] for two years. We played the Palace within six months of putting the act together. The Palace was still two-a-day, as were all the RKO houses on our route. We played the circuit—the old Palace, Chicago, out to the West Coast, some Western Vaudeville dates, back through the Delmar Circuit into New York where we played the Palace for a second time.

We were pretty good hoofers, Bud and Buddy. The only other young kids of that type who worked like us were the Four Diamonds. Because of our age (under sixteen), we had to have permits from the "Gerry Society" to play in New York, though there were certain cities where we could work without permits. I was in my first year of high school when I went on the stage. My folks needed the money and times were very hard. Out of the $50 a week I got I sent $30 home. We lived very well on the rest. We lived in good hotels—two could live together for $10 or $11 a week. You could get the best meal for 75 cents. Breakfast was 35 cents for eggs and everything else. They paid our fares, wardrobe, etcetera. There was no commission or anything else to pay. The second year we got $75 a week.

On each side of the stage there were annunciator boards into which cards would be slipped announcing the name of each act as it came on. One card would read "Patti Moore & Band." The card on the other side of the stage would read "Sammy Lewis & Bud and Buddy."

When I left the act I became a single playing a lot of theaters. Funny how I got the name Howe, because that's not my name. It was in 1929—I was playing Rock Island, Illinois, where Sam Bramson had booked me. I was working out of Chicago. The emcee asked for my name to introduce me. Emcees were new in the theaters then. I told him my name was Buddy. He said "Buddy What?" I said, "Gee, you've got me." My name is really Zolitan. I wasn't ashamed of it, but it wasn't the kind of name used in those days. So the emcee says, "I'll introduce you—'I want you to meet Buddy.'" I did the first show, the second show, and by the fourth show he introduced me, "Buddy—and how he can dance!" The second or third day he said, "Why don't you use the name Buddy How dances and how—you know, just 'How'?" So I put an "e" on the end and that was my billing from then on.

I was an acrobatic dancer or hoofer. I did a stair dance which was very popular in those days. I guess my act was about twelve, fourteen minutes. I played the Fanchon and Marco time, then the Paramount-Publix Circuit, which included the New York Paramount and all the outlying Paramount theaters. Vaudeville was undergoing a change. The two-a-day days were fading and the presentation type of vaudeville was coming up.

One day I went to the Oak Street beach for a swim and there was a fat guy on the beach clowning around and doing some nice little steps. He was funny. I went up to him, told him who I was, and asked what he was doing, his name, etcetera. I asked him if he was ever on the stage and he said he had been in a sketch. His name was Jack Lubitsky. He changed his name to Jack E. Leonard and we started to work together. Jack died some time ago—a wonderful guy. Anyway, there we were and I said we'd also get a girl in the act because we were going to play Western Vaudeville time and a girl would help dress up the act. I got a girl, Alyce McLaughlin, who later married Charley Corell of Amos and Andy. (She now lives in California.) We did a comedy dancing act. Jack did a song. Alyce did a toe dance. We did a finale together. We played the Western Vaudeville time and then came to New York, played the Roxy and all the Keith houses. We stayed together for three years. During that time I met Jean Carroll. She was then very successful working with Marty May in a very fine comedy act. We started to see each other, go out together, fell in love, and decided maybe we could work together. That was about 1933–1934. So Jean wrote us an act and taught me to read lines. I had never done any lines before. Jean was very experienced. She was also a good writer who knew the business.

We broke in the act on the state fairs. In those days we played eleven weeks for George Hamid. If the state fair wasn't too big, we did the talking act. In others we just danced. Jean could dance, sing, and do a little of everything. But she was essentially a comedienne. We brought the act into New York, showed it, and were immediately bought by all the circuits. We played the Palace a couple of times and every major theater from coast to coast. The Palace was just about to drop its two-a-day. We never played it after that.

The act of Carroll and Howe did very well. Jean wrote many, many pieces, developed them, and performed them, starting many of the things that comics are doing today. She wasn't the first one to talk on the stage, but to my knowledge she was the first woman monologist around. There were a lot of funny women. But I'm talking about a woman standing up there who looked elegant and beautiful and could make people scream with laughter. And all of it with wonderful material, great timing, and everything else.

The thing that was so good about our act was that I was lucky enough to find a girl who could write material that was so distinctive they had to play us. We did material that nobody had ever heard before. All fresh. We seldom, if ever, resorted to an old joke. In fact, it was never a joke, it was always a "bit"; a routine. It was never "Two Jews met on a corner" or "Two Italians met in the street." I think Jean got her comedy out of natural happenings. Even today she has that ability to take a small incident, tell it, embellish it, and come up with a ten-to-fifteen-minute sock routine.

You remember the dress routine? It was first just a one-liner but it turned out to be one of her funniest bits. Here is the way it was born. We were playing Loew's State, just before I went into the army, and Jean went across the street and saw a blouse she liked in a shop window. A woman came out and asked Jean, "Do you like the blouse?" Jean said, "It's nice. What size is it?" The woman said, "Come in and try it on." Jean said she didn't want to try it on, she just wanted to know the size. Now that's all there was to it. When Jean came back and told me about it I said, "Yeah, it must've been a funny incident." Well, Bill, this is true. She went out there and it was the opening thing in the act. She did ten minutes on it and I just stood there with my mouth open. It was born on the Loew's State stage. I didn't know what to say or do.

Me, I was strictly a straight man. If she wrote "When are you coming to dinner?" that's what I said every show, exactly as written. If she changed the words—I was gone. I was essentially a hoofer. Maybe I have the right job now. I've been with this same company for twenty-nine years.

We were married in 1936 and left for England on an extensive tour. We played the Palladium, every major theater in England, and all the provinces. We stayed there until 1939, when war broke out. When we arrived back in the United States, Abe Lastfogel, who was then the head of the USO and also the William Morris office, asked us to go on USO and we did. We stayed on it for two years until I was called up for the army. I spent the next two years in Camp Lee. When I was discharged I was thirty-five. Jean was already doing a single and doing so well it seemed foolish to do a double again. Show business had changed a lot and I was a little older, and to be very honest about it, she was too good. She was playing in Chicago and after my discharge I flew there to be with her.

The Vaudevillians

It was a Friday night and I was out walking when I ran into Bob Weems of General Amusement Corporation (GAC), a talent agency. Weems said, "How about becoming an agent?" I said I'd like to try it and he said come in Monday. So I came in on Monday and I've been there ever since.

Let me go back to Jean for a minute. It was the Night of Stars or one of those things during the war. This one was at the old Madison Square Garden for the United Jewish Appeal. I was sitting out front. Jean was on the show. They had played the Jewish national anthem and the "Stars and Stripes Forever" and everyone was crying. It was the night when Israel was born as a state, in 1948. There were very moving speeches. There wasn't a dry eye in the place. Then the emcee said, "Now, a very funny lady—Jean Carroll."

This is the toughest kind of spot to give a comedian. Well, Jean came out and said, "I've always been proud of the Jews, but never so proud as tonight because tonight I wish I had my old nose back." It was her joke—a solid five-minute laugh. The biggest laugh you ever heard, 20,000 people screaming. That was Jean!

I grew up in what was a tough neighborhood—Brownsville. In my time it was the Jews and the Italians. Many fortunate people came from there—and many unfortunate. But many unfortunate people came from other places too. We had Murder Inc. but we had other things too. I went to school with most of the fellows who turned out bad. So I have to say, there but for the grace of God go I.

I consider myself very lucky. Vaudeville gave me a wonderful life. I think show business is the greatest business in the world. I was very lucky to find and meet the girl I married. It's been a love affair now for over thirty-seven years. We have a lovely daughter and a lovely grandchild. I have a good position with CMA. What more could anybody ask for? I'm chairman of the board of CMA. I'm dean of the Friars. I have my health and I say God has been good to me.

GEORGE JESSEL

GEORGE JESSEL *was basically a stand-up comic "working in one." He was best known for his characteristic phone call to his mother: "Yes, that's right, Momma, this is Georgie—your son—the one from the checks," which became the basis for a series of homilies, witticisms, and jokes, much of which audiences could identify with.*

Between the "phone calls" would be some singing in a strange flat voice which sent audiences into gales of laughter. In his time Jessel was considered one of the great ones.

Today Jessel still performs and gives after-dinner speeches. He is also active in patriotic activities and holds the honorary title of "General." Whenever he travels to entertain American troops in foreign countries he wears his uniform and insignia.

I was nine years old when I went into show business. Show business? What am I talking about? Who knew about show business? I went to work, except what work I did was fun. All this was about 1910—or maybe it was 1909 when I went with Gus Edwards. I know that in 1909 I was the bat boy for the New York Giants and at nights I sang at the Imperial Theater on 116th Street, New York. My partner was Walter Winchell. My mother sold tickets in the box office.

It was while I was with Gus Edwards that I met Smith and Dale and their Avon Comedy Four. They were great people. Joe Smith used to buy me ice cream. I sat on his lap. I guess he liked me. I was a cute kid.

Of course the vaudeville business is long since dead and all of it stopped because of what you're holding now—the microphone. You can't

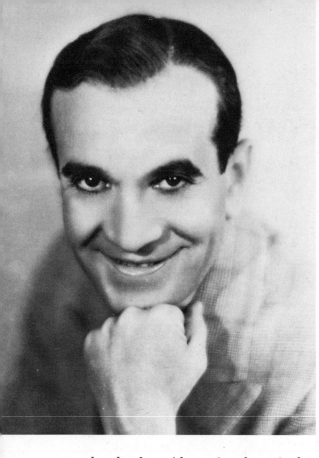

Jolson. "Never an entertainer like him. As a person that's something else."—Jessel

play sketches with a microphone in front of your face. Al Jolson never saw a microphone until he was about seventy. Most of the singers today, outside of a couple, if the mike went wrong you'd have to hug 'em and even then you couldn't hear them. It's a mechanical age without a heart.

Smith and Dale did one act, the "School Room," for thirty years; they did another, the "Hungarian Restaurant," for twenty years. But once mikes came in those sketches were out. All natural acting was dead. The only one who makes you forget is Frank Sinatra. He holds the mike way down in front of him when he sings. His reading of a lyric is so you almost forget he has a mike. He never played vaudeville. Sure, he played the Paramount. That was a five, six shows a day. He's a fine guy—a generous man. One of the few guys who has a heart left, one of the few good guys left in the amusement business.

About Jolson—there never was an entertainer like him. As a person, that's something else. But as a performer, nobody could touch him. And believe me, I worked with him enough times to know what he was onstage and what he was offstage. I buried him.

I didn't become a single until late 1917 and that was only for a couple of years. Then I did a big act called "Georgie Jessel's Trouble." When I was around, there was big-time vaudeville and small-time vaudeville. Big time had eight acts. There was an overture, possibly with the popular songs of the day. The first act would be acrobats or jugglers. The second act would be a boy-and-girl team, maybe singers, or a single singer. The number-three act would be a one-act play—you know, a sketch—which you can't do with a mike sticking up in front of your face. (I'll tell you where you can—never mind. You know what I'm talking about, Bill.) The fourth act, just before the intermission, would be an important kind of act. The headliner, man or woman, would be next to closing—that is, the third act after the intermission. The final act on the bill would be another acrobat, juggler, or something like that—you know, what used to be called "dumb" acts because they didn't talk.

In small time maybe they didn't use all those acts, but there you worked three and four times a day, unlike big time where there were only two shows a day and reserved seats. In the picture houses you maybe played five shows a day. It wasn't vaudeville anymore. People stayed over for more shows, so they knew what was coming next. And if you were a comic, those bands onstage could kill you. For the first show they'd listen and laugh. The second show they'd still pay attention, but not too much unless there were music cues. After that they'd sit there behind you, yawning, picking their noses, fixing music sheets. Laughing? Don't be silly! They'd heard it all. The audience would think, if the musicians aren't laughing, it's probably not funny, so they wouldn't laugh either.

In 1917 I played the Colonial Theater on 62nd Street in New York in a sketch called "A Ray of Sunshine." That was one of the worst experiences I had in my show-business life. For some reason the Colonial always had the toughest audience in the world. They used to throw pennies and other things. And mine was one of those little act-one plays. We opened at the matinee and we were lousy. We went out to eat and we came back for the evening show and there, out in the street, was my scenery, props, and everything. Canceled!

How did I take it? First I wanted to die. Then I wanted to kill somebody. You know what I did? Nothing. I just hoped that not too many bookers heard about it.

I think you once told me that the first time you caught me was at Keith's Bushwick, Brooklyn. Let me tell you what happened there one time when I was playing it. You were in the audience—what would you know. The Yashakawa Japs were on the bill. At that time Arthur Brisbane —you remember him? You wouldn't remember—you're too young. Oh, you do remember! Anyway, Brisbane was the greatest editorial writer in America. He always wrote two things every day. One, that a gorilla could lick any guy in the ring and could be the greatest football player that ever lived. And the second thing—the Yellow Peril and the Japs would attack America. This was in 1920. Well, this one day he was very violent about the Japs. I was next to closing, Yashakawa Japs were closing. They were a lovely family, jugglers. Their only ambition was to get a rolling ball game going in Rockaway Beach. The audience threw things and yelled at them. The head of the act ran to the manager's office.

I was in the manager's office borrowing money and the Jap said, "Mr. Black, please change the billing. Don't say Yashakawa Japs, please. Just say the Yashakawa Company. You don't say 'George Jessel, Jew.' "

A most important thing happened to me when I was just a kid, doing a single. I was playing the Keith Theater in Washington. I was told that President Woodrow Wilson used to come in every Monday night. I was on third. I wasn't very important, and if he came in, it must've been after my act.

I went back to my hotel after the show was over and I got a phone call from the manager to come right back to the theater. Somebody had told the President that I did something talking with my mother and he wanted to hear it. So I came back and did just that portion of my act for President Wilson. Nobody else was in the theater. It was then about 11 P.M.

Which one did I do? Before I go on let me tell you that it was in 1918 that Al White, on the bill with me, suggested I use a phone in my act. My stuff wasn't going over, so I tried it with a phone and you know what happened.

Now let's get back to the routine I think I did for President Wilson. It started with the phone ringing. No, wait a minute. I made the call. I would say, "Operator, will you get me Harlem 1234?" This was before they had dial phones. "Hello, drugstore? Good. This is George Jessel. How are you? Fine. I'm fine. No, nothing wrong. Can you call my mother? That's right. She lives next house from you on the fourth floor, front. I can't call her on our phone. It's not working or something." We didn't have any phone. But why should I tell him that? Then the druggist would say, "I got nobody to send and I'm all alone." And I would say, "It's only a for a few seconds, you can close up the store. What's the matter, you so busy?" Then he would say my mother was just coming in and I could talk to her. And I would say, "Hello, Mom. This is Georgie, your son. Yes, the one from the checks."

Was the President laughing? I'm onstage. He's somewhere out there in the middle of the house but I could hear him. Sure he was laughing. Then I would say something like, "Look, Mom, you oughta buy some-

George Jessel and George Burns at a Friars function. (Photo courtesy of Ross & Weiss Photography Incorporated)

thing. You can't be bothering him all the time to call you to the phone. No, not a stamp. Like aspirin. So tell me, Mom, what's with Anna's feller? They got engaged finally. Good, good. When'll they get married? He has to wait? Wait for what? They've been going together for ten years and—oh, he's waiting for a job. Did he at least give her a ring? He's waiting for me to lend him the money. I see. Look, Mom, what's the hurry, why does she have to get married? She's still a young girl. After all, thirty-eight ain't so old . . . Willie wants to talk to me? Okay, put him on. Hello, Willie. Ya a good boy? Good. How're ya doing in school? Teacher's got a grudge against you. I see. You want my autograph. Only last

27

week I sent you four and a few weeks before I sent you—oh I see, for every six of mine you can swap for one of Eddie Cantor's. Put Mom back on the phone."

That's the way it went. I had a number of those "Hello, Momma" routines. They did very well for me. I would usually end up with: "Yes, Momma, the check is in the mail . . . Good night."

I think when the President was in the house I threw in one with Willie that went like this: "Willie, instead of those jokes you hear other comedians tell, better study your lessons and, who knows, someday you might have a chance to be the President of the United States . . . What . . . You'll sell me your chance for a quarter. Don't be so fresh."

I went to the Coast in 1942. I got a job as a producer with 20th Century-Fox. It's what I wanted. I never wanted to act. I also became the father of a beautiful little baby girl. Lois Andrews, my wife at the time, was the mother. She was beautiful. But then, all my wives were beautiful. You know they were. I was with Fox eleven years and made twenty-four pictures. First was *The Dolly Sisters*. Next was *Wonder Who's Kissing Her Now*. When it opened at the Roxy I came with it and appeared onstage.

You know, they still play those pictures on TV. And I get nothing for it. I'm not entitled—after all, I got paid when the pictures were made. If I sell you a coat for $75 and you turn around and sell it for $90, what's it got to do with me? I had a very good salary when I was a producer. I was happy with it. So that's that.

Did you ever walk down Santa Monica when Georgie Raft and me were in the travel business? Actually we weren't. What happened was that a friend of mine and George's—Barney Puditsky—used to be a great detective in New York. Well, he came into the Friars one night while I was sitting there with Raft. He said he was going into the travel business and if he could use our names we'd get a piece of the action. So one side of the sign read George Jessel and George Raft Travel Agency. On the other side the sign read George Raft and George Jessel Travel Agency. We never got a dollar out of it.

Show business today—well, that's something else. If anybody wanted to go into show business today, I don't know what I'd tell them. If you brought me the most beautiful girl who could sing, I'd have no idea what to do—how to get her started. She might audition for an ad agency who might put her on television—on a Johnny Carson, or Dean Martin or Mike Douglas or Merv Griffin show. Get some exposure and draw somebody's attention to who might give her a job. But outside of those, where would she go? Nightclubs? There's only about four weeks' work in all of America. I don't think there is even four weeks. There's two weeks in

Vegas, nothing in New York, Chicago, or anyplace else. There's a week in Miami—if you play the Diplomat you can't play anything else. Maybe a week in Puerto Rico.

America stays home. New York is pretty bad. But it's that box over there in the corner—the television. Why should people go out? And if you think of vaudeville, there isn't any. Not in this country. Not a week—not a day. Nothing. To think that an industry that gave work to hundreds of thousands on the stage, in back of the house, in front—all the people who made their living off vaudeville—is gone, all gone. It only remains among people who were once part of it. Who lived it and loved it.

I liked working in Chicago best. Those audiences were very loyal to actors. I loved them. It was almost like London. I didn't like Shea's, Toronto, and Keith's Theater, Providence. The manager of Keith's, whenever he heard the audience laugh and he thought it was something dirty, he'd tell the actor to take it out. On every stage door there was a big sign forbidding you to use various words—hell, damn, God. If you did you were immediately canceled. Now these theaters, and many more, are booking *Deep Throat* and *Last Tango in Paris*.

Vaudeville gave us great camaraderie. There were circuits where you played twenty, thirty weeks with the same bill and you became like one whole big family. It was warm and comfortable. You lived by the reaction of the audience. There was something warm and sweet about it. Today you live by a phone call.

BILLY GLASON *was a singing comedian with a talk routine that always got laughs. Between his monologues he sang current popular tunes. His material was a combination of old and new, delivered in a pleasant and ingratiating fashion.*

Glason was from the Boston area, which produced many other well-known vaudeville performers: Benny Rubin, Jack Haley, Fred Allen, Ray Bolger, and others. When he entered show business as a singer before 1920, there were many small-time theaters in and around Boston where a young performer could find work and test his act.

Glason developed his brash and aggressive brand of comedy by watching other performers. He is no longer performing, but writes special comedy material for other performers. He also is a song writer.

I was about ten when I sold newspapers in front of the Tremont Building in Boston. When in later years I played Boston's Keith Theater, nearly all the people in the Tremont Building—they were all customers when I sold papers—came to the theater. I recognized them all. Anyway, at about ten I was selling papers and singing songs. As I became older I sang songs in a publisher's office. They even paid me a little to introduce songs. So I introduced "You Made Me Love You" in Boston's Gray Music Store. Then I plugged songs for Berlin and Snyder, another music publishing firm. I was then about fourteen. I wasn't really a song plugger, I was too young. I was just singing because I liked it. I was about fifteen when I really became a song plugger. I worked for Broadway Music and Watterson, Berlin and Snyder. I went from one to the other. I introduced "They Go Wild Over Me." Oh, there were a lot of songs . . .

In plugging songs in Boston way back then, you went around to the ice cream parlors. They were more popular than the cafés. In these ice cream parlors the windows were out and crowds gathered on the sidewalks. This was all in Revere Beach, which is like Coney Island. Well, song pluggers from the different music publishers would come around and sing through megaphones. That's the way songs became popular. When a singing act played a theater, the publisher would contact Woolworth's so the store would put a display in the window saying that such-and-such a song was being featured at so-and-so theater. So I kinda grew into it, you know, plugging songs. When I got older I would add a couple of gags.

You know that Boston had blue laws. May still have for all I know. On Sundays dancing acts, or any acts that moved to a rhythm, were out. So I was called on. I used to be called on a lot in Lowell, Massachusetts. I stood still while I sang. Later I began to hop around like an Eddie Cantor.

Well, one gag led to another, I added some comedy songs, and before you know it, I had an act and I'm in demand. Abe Montague, who later was a Columbia Pictures vice-president, owned a theater in Boston, the Bay Square, and he booked me to sing with slides. I stayed there for three years. Then I was booked into the Beacon Theater, a well-known vaudeville house on Boston's Tremont Street. They used to book thirty acts on Monday. Ten were always fired. There was no protection. When I first started I was doing a Jew act with the beard and derby. I borrowed my father's derby and a red bandanna handkerchief and I played South Boston, strictly an Irish neighborhood. After my first show the manager came in and handed me my pictures. Murder—I was fired.

I got better. I did one song with slides in the back—"The Chairs in the Parlour All Miss You" or whatever was the pop song of the day. Then I'd do a character song, a comedy song, and so on. Roxbury, Massachusetts —that's where I worked for a year. I was getting $25 a week, living at home, no taxes—and $25 was big money then. When they couldn't use me anymore they broke my heart. "Someday you'll play Keith's," I was told, "and I'll be glad to pay you fifty or seventy-five." It was there I had the opportunity to face all sorts of audiences, use a lot of songs, and I became a comedy-singing-talking act. I did twenty-five, thirty minutes. When later acts were told to cut down, say to ten minutes from fifteen, the gag was born, "It takes me ten minutes to walk out and bow."

But I'm getting ahead of myself. Did I tell you about Lou Walters? He booked me in Boston in those days. He would put me into the Poli Circuit houses in Worcester or Springfield, when they were short an act on account of the blue laws. Well, Lou got me the Globe Square Theater for $50. You know, every time I came to Boston, even when I became a headliner at Keith's, the manager of the Globe would be waiting for me on the sidewalk to tell me, "You owe me a week at the Globe." No matter if I was getting $1,250 at Boston's Keith, he was there. It became a running gag. From Boston my next jump was to Fox's City Theater on 14th Street—it was next to Luchow's. There were about fourteen, fifteen acts on the bill and I ruined them. Every agent in town was after me. But I didn't know from nothing. I was getting $75 a week and all the music publishers wanted me to sing their songs.

I was playing the Fox houses, and there's where I had some bitter words. I introduced a song, "Oh Frenchy," and there was a girl on the bill who was married to Edgar Allen, the Fox booker, and she was singing the song too. But she was number two on the bill, and I was next to closing. I had to give way because she was his wife. I almost quit the bill. We had bitter words. The next job got me $175. It was the Maryland Theater in Baltimore. That's when it began.

Trixie Friganza was next to closing and I was on number four. She couldn't follow me. It was my first week on the big time. From then on word got around—don't follow Glason, he ruins them, he kills the bill. It got so no matter where I worked, acts refused to follow me. I'm on the Orpheum Circuit playing the Orpheum Theater in San Francisco. Elsie Janis is the headliner. She's booked there for three weeks. Her leading singer is a juvenile, Walter Pidgeon. That's the feller who became the movie actor.

Anyway, there were nine acts of vaudeville instead of eight. Now Elsie's got three weeks. I've got one lousy week. I'm seventh, she's eighth, and the usual closing act is nine. I introduce the song "What's Become of Hinky-Dinky Parlez-Vous." She had sung the song also, for a short time, but it was my big song. It was written up in the Sunday Times with the different war songs—"Over There" and "Over The Top" and "Hinky-Dinky Parlez-Vous," with my picture on the cover. It was quite a historic thing. I stopped the show cold. Now Elsie Janis follows me. It's difficult for her. But what can I do, I'm a big hit. I'm energetic and I'm young and I certainly wasn't getting the money or the billing. She's got three weeks and I've got a friggin one week. Her mother, who was her manager and everything, came to my dressing room after the show and praised me with the usual bullshit, the wonderful way I did "Hinky-Dinky." I used to do it in the middle of the stage—about four or five choruses—and walk off to a trumpet Rum-Ta-Dum. I'd take the bows that way, then two more choruses and off again. You know how those choruses go. You go on forever. She couldn't get on. And her mother was saying how wonderful I was doing the number and just as she's leaving she said, 'By the way, tonight you follow Elsie.' I said to myself, Christ, here we go again. And for the rest of the week I had to follow Elsie. It made no difference. Her fercockta act that she did, anybody could follow. She was strictly an international favorite—that's all. But I was sockeroo. A Belle Baker and a Sophie Tucker also wouldn't follow me.

Now I'm playing the Orpheum in Brooklyn. This was a good vaudeville not because it was small, but because instead of being built out and wide, it was built up. The audience was, as they say, practically in your arms. The boxes were almost on the stage. And as big a hit as you were at the Orpheum, you were just as big a flop at the nearby new Albee Theater, because the vastness of the theater took away the closeness you enjoyed as a performer.

Now, Pat Rooney and Marian Bent were breaking in a new act this week. Kerrigan, an old Boston man, was the manager of the Albee. He knew me very well. Everybody came down from the office to see the new act. Edgar Allen wrote the thing. He was the Henry Ford of the sketch writers. Acts that came from the movies, or someone like an Evelyn Thaw, who was all over the newspapers, would get him to write a sketch. Well, Rooney and Bent didn't want to open right after the intermission. I was supposed to close the show. There were only two acts in the second half; five acts in the first part. It went like this. The opening act—tumblers or something—then some singers. The third was a sketch, the fourth was an act in one, and five was a big flash act. Then the intermission and my act. But Rooney and Bent didn't want to close the show following me. So I went to Kerrigan and told him I'd close the show. I closed it that afternoon. Pat Rooney's act was such a big hit too that he said, "Okay, I'll close the show."

A lot of small theaters were taken into the combine that made up the RKO. They were the affiliates. They were the Proctor Circuit, the Poli Circuit, the Butterfield Circuit in the Middle West, and Western Vaudeville. All these little theaters were promoted with the promise they would occasionally get the big-time Palace acts. Now, my act was constructed so I could play Shimokin, Lancaster, Pottsville—every half-assed town. But the Jack Bennys, the Hopes, the Jessels—they couldn't play those theaters. They were strictly metropolitan acts: good for the big cities. We worked fifty-two weeks a year. We used to start from the Kenmore Theater in Brooklyn—that's where the acts showed to go out on the Orpheum Circuit. We'd go to Syracuse, Rochester, Buffalo, Erie, Cleveland, Columbus, Detroit, and into Chicago—all big time, two-a-day. In Chicago we'd pick up our train tickets for the Orpheum Circuit. We'd play Minneapolis, St. Paul, Winnepeg, Calgary, Edmonton, Vancouver, Portland, Seattle,

San Francisco, Oakland, Fresno, Sacramento, Los Angeles, then back to San Francisco, then back again to Los Angeles. Some of these were split weeks and some were three shows a day. After those it would usually be Denver, Kansas City, St. Louis, and into Texas—the Interstate Circuit. You could stay on the road two years. You had to fight to stay home Christmas and Thanksgiving to be with your family.

Everybody worked the small time to get into the big time. There was a booker in New York, Fally Markus. He played the cream of vaudeville. Everyone that had to break in their act, either for the Palace or whatever, went to Fally and said, "Fally, I need three days." And he'd get them. Which meant that Fally got the biggest acts for *bubkas*—peanuts. So maybe it would be Proctor's Fifth Avenue, which wasn't on Fifth Avenue at all. The theater had the lousiest piano player in the world, Harry Ferguson, rest his soul. And an audience of half-assed characters—mostly salesmen who would lay their sample cases on the floor and sit there defying you to be funny or whatever. They were mad because you were working and they weren't. That was a gag, but true. But Proctor's was the stepping stone to the Palace.

Before the Palace I remember playing the Hippodrome. It ran on Sixth Avenue from 43rd to 44th Street. You came down the dressing room stairs on the 43rd Street side and went across backstage to make it to the stage proper. Now this particular act I was following was an animal act—lions. They had them caged up against the wall. Now, I walk on in my new gray suit, almost white, and I feel something warm against me. I looked down and see the lions had peed on me. Here I am ready to go on and I'm all wet with lion piss. I broke all records climbing back to my dressing room to change.

I worked to all kinds of music—from bad to awful. Some bands were really great. For instance, there was the band at the RKO Palace in New Orleans. That band was so good it used to stop the show. Louis Prima was in that band. And when they played an overture—wow! On the other hand, there was the band at the New York Palace. Owen Jones was the leader. They had some women in the band and the musicians were so polite they used to let the women finish first—that's how the music sounded. Every act that went on had to stop in the middle and ask Owen Jones to take the tempo over again. Everybody out front knew what was happening. This bastard was giving every act trouble. He was a musician but he couldn't cut a show. Anyway, one week I closed the show. I think I was the only comic, the only stand-up single, that ever closed the show at the Palace. I remember the picture playing then was Charlie Chaplin's *Shoulder Arms*. Bert Fitzgerald was booked for the closing spot and I was

Billy Glason when he was a headliner.

fourth, but Bert was a lush, and if he got drunk, they would have no closing act. So they put him on fourth and made me the closing act. In those days we had a lot of what we called "dizzies"—disappointments. Monday mornings there were always calls. I played a couple of "dizzies" at the Palace, though I played that house on my own usually about twice a year.

The cream of the Palace usually played the Brighton Beach Theater—that was near Coney Island. It ran for ten weeks in the summer when the heat—no air-conditioning then—closed the Palace and most of the other big-time houses.

Some of the presentation houses had house emcees. The Chicago Oriental had Paul Ash. Later they sent him to the Brooklyn Paramount. In Milwaukee there was Dave Schooler, a great piano player. He was with the Marmion Sisters. This was the bill where I was on with Sophie Tucker's son Bert, and that Charleston dancer who made it big in pictures, Ginger Rogers. Her mother was with her. The whole backstage was full of her friends. It was like one of those Gus Edwards school acts—all those mothers—it was a veritable whorehouse. Not "Chase the children here comes Gus Edwards"—it was "Button your fly here come the mothers."

Ed Lowery was at the Ambassador Theater, St. Louis. It was Lowery and Prince. Lowery was the house emcee and played a little saxophone. It's the afternoon show and I'm a big hit and standing in the wings is Lowery watching to see what material he can take for himself. After all, he's got no act. He has to get enough material for the week so he must see where he can interrupt to make himself part of the act. Otherwise he's a bum. After that first show Mr. Skouras—he was one of the owners— comes up to my dressing room and says he wants me to cut out this and that. I refuse. In fact, I'm ready to pull out—those four or five shows a day were murder. Skouras says, "Oh, please, don't do that. But will you do one thing, will you let Lowery get the last laugh?" I say, "All right, I'll stand there and stooge. But when he gets that laugh and walks off stage, it'll be my stage, see?"

Later on, when I was booked out of Chicago, I was with a unit that was out for forty-five weeks. I was playing the Stanley in Pittsburgh and who was the emcee but this son of a bitch Ed Lowery. After the matinee there's a meeting and he tells me where he's gonna enter. It suddenly becomes a revue. He's telling me and I say, "No, you don't. Get your own

Glason headlining at Brighton Beach Theater in the 1920's.

material." I bawl the shit out of him and walk out. In the alley I stop myself. I say, wait a minute, $950 for a six-day week, don't be a schmuck. So I go back to his dressing room and say, "You son of a bitch, you probably want me to walk off so you'll have the whole goddam show to yourself. But I'm not gonna do it. I'll stay and show you I'm still better than you." I was the hit of the show.

Material was always a problem. Once you got something, you weren't going to let anybody else use it. I came off a show one day and there's a guy sitting on the steps. I ask someone, "Who's this guy?" and they tell me he's the guy who's been doing my gags this past week. It was Dave Vine. That's how I got to meet him. Talk about stealing material. He was the biggest crook, rest his soul. But later we became very good friends.

Now, about material and protection. There was the Vaudeville Managers Protective Association—they protected an act. Anyway, they protected me. I got gags taken out of Jackie Osterman's act, Georgie Jessel's act, and others. We would get notes—"Report to the Office" notes—and be told to take out material because it belonged to somebody else. There was one act—Bob Nelson, later of Truman and Nelson. He was then doing a single and was on right ahead of me. He was my very dear friend but he was doing my whole act right ahead of me. Charlie Freeman was then the booker—he took him right off.

I always wrote songs and put them under my wife's—Helen Smith—name, because actors don't want to use another actor's words. Once I got enough songs together to join ASCAP, I then started to use my own name. So today I write comedy material and service the biggest comedians and writers all over the world.

EDGAR BERGEN

EDGAR BERGEN is a ventriloquist who wrote imaginative material. He was expert at throwing his voice but it was his comic weaving of logical plot lines that made him outstanding. His famous dummy, Charlie McCarthy, delivered outrageously funny lines, sometimes bordering on the "blue," at a time when performers were much more inhibited than at present. But because the lines were "spoken" by a dummy, they were accepted and laughed at.

Bergen was a vaudeville standard act for some time, with occasional dates in the more elegant nightclubs, but oddly enough it was radio and TV that gave him his big jump to stardom. His—or rather Charlie McCarthy's—verbal exchanges with W. C. Fields are still classics of comedy.

He is still active in show business. Candice Bergen, the actress, is his daughter.

started in show business at the bottom. And when I say the bottom, that's what it was. I built fires in the furnace of the local picture theater, and then swept out—the theater, not the fire. I was so good at it I was promoted to also playing the player piano for the movies. You must realize this was when the movies were silent. It was 1914 and the movie house I was in was in Decatur, Michigan. There came a day when the picture didn't start and I went to the office to find out why. I was told the projectionist wasn't there. He had a habit of drinking, I guess. So I went up to the booth and ran the machine. Of course, I'd been up there many times before, fooling with it, so I knew how to run it.

The manager came in and demanded to know why Edgar wasn't playing the piano. He was told, "Because he's the projectionist." "Not my two-thousand-dollar machine," the manager said. Anyway, they brought in an old man who knew about the machine to sit and watch me. He said, "The boy knows what he's doing," so he went home.

I saw vaudeville shows from time to time but not too often. But what I saw fascinated me. I must've seen some ventriloquist somewhere but I don't remember where. I stumbled into ventriloquism in the eighth grade when I used to mimic animals and people. I remember I fooled some people completely.

Somebody said, "You must be a ventriloquist." Not knowing what a ventriloquist was at the time, I agreed. Then I looked it up and bought a book for 35 cents, *Wizard's Manual*. It told how to be not only a ventriloquist but also a magician and a hypnotist. I practiced all three. One night when I was doing a one-man show in Michigan I said I could hypnotize a man who was heckling. But I got nervous with the smart alecs there and I couldn't do it. That was the end of my hypnotism.

After graduating from high school I tried out in different theaters in Chicago. One, the New Maple Theater, paid you $5 a day on weekends if you got by the first show. After my first show the manager came back and said if I cut out the magic I could stay. I didn't give him any argument. That $5 a day looked pretty good. I worked three days in a row. And that was the end of my magician career.

It was in my senior year at the Lakeview High School in Chicago that ventriloquism became an avocation. I tried to make a cocky little character out of papier-mâché. It wasn't any good at all. There was a fresh little newsboy in front of the high school. I sketched his face in my history book and then I took it down to a woodcarver. My first appearance with Charlie was in high school. I was in the school recital group and we were to give a show for the student body on a particular day. But a week or so before I had been told by my history teacher, Miss Angel, not to count on graduating. My marks were too low.

Well, the recital began and I'm up there with Charlie. I say, "Charlie, how are your teachers?"

Charlie: I have Miss Angel for history.

Bergen: Miss Angel—that's a pretty name.

Charlie: Don't let the name fool you. She grows horns at examination time.

Bergen: I see. Do you ever get sent to the principal's office?

Charlie: I've been there so often I have my own desk there. Sometimes we close the door and play checkers. There's only one thing wrong. Square Deal Brown [that was the principal] cheats.

That, of course, was a big hit with the students.

Bergen: I find it hard to believe that the principal is so friendly with
you. And a lot of students here don't believe you.

Charlie: Oh, what do they know!

Bergen: Well, you can prove that he's a friend of yours because he's
sitting in the front row and you can say, "Hello Square
Deal."

Charlie: You're kidding.

Bergen: No.

Charlie: I'm afraid to look. (He looks at the front row—pans from
right to left. When he sees Square Deal, he goes "Yipe" and
falls down in a faint.)

That was a big hit. Next day I was asked to stay after class. Miss Angel
said, "I didn't know you had those talents. The world needs laughter
more than it needs history teachers. If you'll try, I'll help you graduate."
And that's how Charlie made his bow and how I graduated high school.
So I don't put much faith in that old saw that a man is known by the
company he keeps. My closest companion has been a dummy.

Twenty years later I went back to that high school. Miss Angel had
long since died. I told the students of my experience. I told them the
closest friends they had were their teachers because it was their wish that
someday they would shine in their students' reflected glory.

I worked weekends around Chicago in little theaters—that is, little
movie houses. I dressed in cellars, boiler rooms, or wherever there was
room. I played one little theater on North Clark Street, in the slum district,
where I was paid $7 for three or four shows, plus a quarter for carfare.
And you know, that additional quarter was one of the nicest things I
remember. The manager liked my act and I liked him. A real showman.

Summers I would work Chautauqua. I was already known a little
because I was being booked. I also wrote letters applying for jobs. I played
schools, churches, halls, etc. In winters there was the Lyceum Circuit,
sometimes called the winter Chautauqua. I played little towns to small—
occasionally big—audiences. And this was right after high school. Many
mornings I had to get up at 4 A.M., break the ice in the pitcher so I could
get some water, and dash off to catch a train. Often I was the only passen-
ger, so the station agent didn't bother to come down. I had to build a fire
in the potbelly stove. My trunk was on the express wagon and many times
the snow was so deep I couldn't pull the wagon over, so they would back
up the train for me.

In one church the audience was apprehensive about me. They had
never seen, or perhaps even heard of, a ventriloquist or a magician, and

Edgar Bergen with Charlie McCarthy, who received fan mail.

they didn't want to get too close to one. I said there wasn't any danger. If they wouldn't hurt me, I promised, I wouldn't hurt them.

Then I got an offer to play the small-time Orpheum, called the Junior Orpheum. So I went to Northwestern University summer school and played the Junior Orpheum time in winter. I was now in vaudeville. I played all throughout the West, including Chicago and St. Louis, doing four shows a day. I wrote all my own material. I didn't know any writers. Besides, I couldn't afford them if I did. So I played the small theaters, happy for the chance. If I ever thought of the big time, it was only a passing thought. I traveled to Cleveland, St. Paul, Minneapolis, Winnipeg, Calgary, Seattle, Tacoma, San Francisco. I recall once when I was playing the Warfield Theater in San Francisco, and I had a week layoff after that date. And what do you think! At the end of my week the manager asked me to stay over another week. What a thrill to be asked to stay over.

My vaudeville act was onstage in two, sometimes it was in one. When it opened, there was Charlie, dressed as a newsboy, lying on a park bench, moaning. He was a kind of urchin. As I came along, he moaned a little louder. I picked him up. He said he had a sore throat. A girl would come along then and ask, "Is the boy ill?" I'd say, "I'm afraid he is." Then she'd—well, here's how it went:

Nurse: Is the boy ill?

Bergen: I'm afraid he is.

Nurse: I'm a nurse. Maybe I can help. (She takes his temperature and finds he has a fever.)

Bergen: I'm a doctor. We'll take him into my operating room where we can operate. Charlie, you have a temperature of 102.

Charlie: If it makes 104, I'll sell.

Bergen: I'm going to paint your throat.

Charlie: Oh, so you're a painter. I knew you weren't a doctor.

Bergen: I'm going to paint your throat with a silver nitrate solution. (I take out a blue bottle with a swab.) Open your mouth.

Charlie: Do I have to swallow the whole thing?

Bergen: No. It's a two percent solution.

Charlie: Oh no, so the stuff is out. I can get three percent. (He looks into the bottle.) There's a dead fly in there. I guess he's ahead of me.

Bergen: It isn't a dead fly. It's a ladybug.

Charlie: You have good eyes, doctor.

Bergen: Turn over, you little beggar.

Charlie (pointing to a sputum pan): What's that?

Bergen: A sputum pan.

Charlie: I don't think I can spute that crooked.

Bergen: I'm afraid I'll have to cut your uvula.

Charlie: You're not going to cut my vuvulah. When are you going to operate?

Bergen: The operation is all over.

Charlie: Tell me, is it a girl? (That was the finish.)

Vaudeville was kind to me and so were the other actors. It was a nice life. I used to love watching Joe Jackson and his bicycle. And there was Roger Imhoff and his "Pest House." What a scream that was. Then there was Smith and Dale with their firehouse or their Dr. Kronkhite. Just thinking of them makes my sides ache. One of the funniest lines I've ever heard was Professor Lamberti's. Do you remember him? He'd stand behind a xylophone and hold up four hammers—you know, those little things you use to play the xylophone. Behind him two girls would slowly stroll by, supposedly without his noticing them. "I'm now going to play the 'Blue Danube Waltz'—the only man who can do it with four knockers," he'd say, and the audience would scream.

And there was the Great Lester, the famous ventriloquist. First time I saw him he was playing the Lincoln Theater and I was in high school. I took a chance and went backstage. He took me into his dressing room, had me do some of my ventriloquism, and then gave me a demonstration. He was wonderful. He gave me two lessons. I always told myself if I ever make good I'll extend the same courtesy to any amateurs who come back to visit me. The Great Lester was out here when he was about seventy-four, seventy-five years old. I gave a luncheon and a party for him and had about thirty ventriloquists come in with more dummies than you ever saw. Lester was delighted. I also helped him financially in his old age. He was great.

The chief fault with present-day ventriloquists is that some of them think all they have to do is just keep their mouths closed. But their material is so poor!

Yes, vaudeville was something I liked because the audiences were so nice. We had theaters with 2300 seats and no microphones. But people listened better and were attentive. You knew when you had them. Well, we worked full weeks, split weeks, and we had a happy life. We never depended on options, like in radio and television, where if the sponsors run out of money or the ratings fall off, you can be a hero one day and without a job the next. That wasn't true in vaudeville. You worked and you worked, and the audience loved you even if you weren't a big star. I have no regrets. I've had more than my share of good things.

I wish there were places today where young performers could try out to people and not to equipment. I remember when I wrote my acts I would try them out for as long as two months out of town before I would bring them into New York. But now there are no more break-in dates. There is no room for beginning performers.

I remember the first time I played the New York Palace. That was in 1929. Frank Fay was the master of ceremonies. He meant to give me a nice introduction. What he said was, "The next young man never played here before. So let's be nice to him." With such an introduction you're usually in the hole before you open your mouth. Anyway, up to then I had never headlined in vaudeville. I guess I was a bad manager for myself. All I wanted was to have a good act. Anyway, at the Palace I would stand in front—that is, out in front of the theater, in front of the billing—so they would see me. I wasn't the only one. All the other actors did the same thing. Well, after the Palace I played the Keith time and did very well.

At this point I was going to junk Charlie, do something by myself. I'd become a musical comedy man. That's where the future was. I came on as a Swedish lecturer with a dialect. The act was no good. The manager came back and said he was sorry, the act didn't go, but if I wanted to do the old act with Charlie, I could stay. I said, "Charlie wouldn't play a dump like this." It was a small house in New Jersey. I was to do the first show and then Ken Murray was coming out to catch the second show. The act was called the Apple Knockers. But when Murray came out, I wasn't there anymore.

I was booked into the Helen Morgan Club, my first nightclub date. I wanted a different kind of dummy, but there was no time to create one. I wrote to *Esquire* magazine and asked if I might use Esky for my dummy —you know, wine, women, and song kind of thing. They said yes. I asked for a plaster copy so I could follow the Esky style and they changed their minds. They wouldn't give permission—they preferred to keep the Esky character with the magazine. That was one of the nicest things that happened to me. I would have been paying royalties from then on.

So I had to do something to smarten Charlie up. The original dummy was a newsboy urchin and there wasn't time to build another one, so I put a top hat and monocle on him, changing Charlie completely. Now I had to work in tails, because a ventriloquist act needed all the class you could give it.

It was while I was at the Helen Morgan Club that I was booked into a Ziegfeld-Shubert show. That was about 1936. I played two nights in Boston and a week or two in Philadelphia. The show had Bob Hope and

Stan Cavanaugh and was running forty-five minutes too long. As I was the last one hired, I was the first one fired. In all respect to Actors Equity, the union I had joined in order to be in the show, they didn't help me at all. In fact, I wasn't even given notice I was fired. I reported one day and was bluntly told, "You're not working here." I reported it to Equity and they said they would see what they could do. They did nothing. They never even got me the two weeks' salary I was entitled to.

Then I was booked into the Chicago College Inn with Abe Lyman. But I had a contract to play the State Lake theater first. I was told it would be all right, I could play the theater and then go into the All-New York show at the College Inn. But it wasn't all right with Abe Lyman. They had never consulted him. So he fired me before I even started. Now I had been fired twice in a month or so. It was getting rough. I ran into Mike Fritzel and his partner, Jacobs, owners of the Chez Paree, also in Chicago. They had caught me at the Helen Morgan Club and they asked me what I was doing in town. I told them I had just been fired by Abe Lyman and they asked me to come into the Chez and I opened there. I was such a hit there that the Chicago Theater bought me and I was head-lined—for the first time! Can you imagine! I had to become a hit in a nightclub to headline a vaudeville show. Abe Lyman used to come into the Chez to catch the late show and he asked me if I would like to join him in Cleveland for two weeks. I should've asked him why he had fired me, but I didn't. Instead I told him to talk to MCA, my agents at the time.

Then I went to Hollywood, where I played another nightclub—I think it was the Casanova Club. At the Chez in Chicago I was flattered because those famous actors, the man-and-wife team Lynn Fontanne and Alfred Lunt, used to come in very often to catch me. At the Casanova Cary Grant used to come in very often to catch me. He liked my act so much he wanted to sign and manage me. He offered to send me to England and guarantee me $400 a week. I said I can't do that to you, I'm only getting $300 a week here. I talked him out of the deal.

While I was in Hollywood I tried very hard to get writing jobs in the studios. I even offered to work for free. I argued that anyone could see how my stuff was getting laughs at the Casanova. I know now it was the wrong way to sell myself.

I went back in New York to play vaudeville dates and also to do those shorts for Warner Brothers—you know, the Vitaphone shorts that were being played in the theaters. Vaudeville was now dying fast—it was 1934—and I took what dates were offered. I had some Loew dates to play in Rochester, Albany, and Schenectady and I was afraid of cancellations because it seemed that in all the contracts I signed, I was forbidden to do Vitaphone shorts that would play any theater where I was to appear. But I showed up at the theaters as if I didn't know anything. The Warner people had assured me that those Vitaphone shorts weren't going to be released until long after I had played the vaudeville dates. Anyway, I got to Rochester a few weeks after my Vitaphone shorts had played there, and there, in big letters, up in front of the theater, was "Edgar Bergen—In Person." I guess they thought I was important. All those cancellations I was afraid of never happened.

Back in New York I did more Vitaphone shorts when I was offered the *Rudy Vallee Fleischmann Radio Show*. When I first went on, John Reber, who was in charge of radio for the J. Walter Thompson agency, was horrified. He said to Vallee, "You booked a ventriloquist? Well, he'd better be goddam funny." And he was there to watch that I was. They asked me how much I wanted and I said $400. They gave me $350. They asked me how I'd like to be on again. I said I was using up material so I would need $450. I got $400. Then I was asked how I'd like to play for thirteen weeks. I said I'd have to have $500. I got $450.

I got panicky. Where would I get material for thirteen weeks? I learned then that you never know what you're capable of until you have a commitment—a deadline. Then you're amazed at what you can do. I bought up a lot of joke books and ended up not using them at all. You just develop the talent you have. I ad-libbed—and the ad libs were mine. I reread some of my old shows the other day and, you know, I wasn't ashamed of what I had written. It all stood up.

I got a wire from W. C. Fields, who was in a sanitarium, congratulating me on the great comedy and excellent timing. It was decided that when Fields was up and able to work we'd have him on the show.

Looking back, I remember the most exciting day in my life. I got up at 5:30 A.M. to go out to Flatbush to make a Vitaphone one-reeler. Came back to do a Rudy Vallee broadcast—I think it was the second one—and then went up to the Rainbow Room to do a show there. That night I had a club date. What a full day that was! It was the same day they asked me on the Rudy Vallee if I'd like to be on for thirteen weeks.

While everything was so wonderful, I was reminded I had to play the Chez Paree, Chicago, again on the old contract. I begged to be let out because of the Rudy Vallee show, which came out of New York. I offered to play some other time at half the salary, or play the next summer at one-third the salary, if they'd let me out of the present contract.

Well, you know what? The Vallee people liked me so much—or

maybe it was Rudy who arranged it—that they piped me in from Chicago so I didn't have to go to New York to do the show.

Funny thing. Some months before I got the Rudy Vallee show, while I was working my first date at the Chez, I auditioned at NBC for a young man—his name was Niles Trammel, or something like that. He said my work would never go on radio, that my comedy wasn't right for radio. I argued that audiences believed Amos and Andy, and he said that was different. So now when I was being piped into the Vallee show from the Chicago NBC studios I made it my business to pass his office often. Well,

Edgar Bergen with Mortimer Snerd—who had to be "Stupid but likeable—"

he became a vice-president of NBC and I got my own show on the same network.

People used to say you couldn't have ventriloquism on radio. I never argued with them. It all went into one microphone and out the same speaker. It was the material and the delivery that registered. I've gotten mail asking if it was true that Charlie McCarthy was a dummy.

Now came another phase in my career. Sam Goldwyn, or the Goldwyn office, bought me for the *Goldwyn Follies*. It was to be a big picture. So I finally got into the Follies through the movies. They billed me as one of the most brilliant minds to hit Hollywood in many years. And only three, four months before, I would've worked for nothing. Well, that's what makes show business so exciting.

In Chicago I was now a headliner and in personal appearances I was doing encores. But it wasn't right, doing so many encores with just one dummy. I needed another one. So I started with the voice. I wanted something that wouldn't conflict with Charlie's voice. That was the beginning of Mortimer Snerd. Then came the big problem: what should he look like? He had to be stupid, but likable; homely, but very kind. So Mortimer Snerd was born. He is scientifically stupid. He's a lowbrow. He has high arched eyebrows. He's a dreamer and has a low-bridged bulbous nose. He's not nosy or aggressive. He has a weak chin, buck teeth, and little or no determination. But he's likable and there's something very nice about him. He's bashful and afraid of girls, so he doesn't conflict with Charlie.

Now my job was to see that the writing was clean and kept the two as separate individuals. By this time I had my own show so I started to use outside writers. Once I was at an aviation show at the Pan-Pacific auditorium. The man showing the film made a running commentary with jokes that interested me. I asked him if he'd like to write for me. And he said he would. I gave him $35 a page. All I wanted was straight dialogue— you know, Bergen says and Charlie says—no script. I just wanted the meat. No filler. In a month or so I was paying him $50 a page and we worked up to where he got $1200 a week. His name was Zeno Clinker, and when we were thinking of funny names, we couldn't think of a funnier one than Effie Clinker.

When I had my own show I brought W. C. Fields in. I would meet Bill Fields on a Monday and we would talk about what we would do. Fields could write good jokes, but he would forget them. His memory was bad. He'd start reading a joke and he wouldn't know what the payoff was until he got to it. So he couldn't lean on it. He wrote some lovely jokes and we would put toppers on them, which were real good. But he'd try to cut them out because he didn't think they were very funny. Well, if there were any jokes we thought were real funny, we'd say, "Bill, that was one of your own jokes." And he'd say, "Oh, it is?" We never had an argument. We protected him whatever condition he was in. Sure, he'd ad-lib, but Bill never said anything too dirty. We got into a little trouble when we had Mae West, but even that would be dull by today's standards.

I have no regrets today about anything. My manager is unhappy with me because I refuse some of the dates he obtains for me. But I have a happy home. I do what I like.

WILL AHERN

WILL AHERN and his wife Gladys were a fast-moving, fast-talking husband-and-wife team that held audiences spellbound with their novelty act, a combination of singing, talking, and dancing. Will Ahern's big specialty was his rope twirling à la Will Rogers. He was handsome, had a pleasant voice, and was a good dancer.

Gladys was a striking brunette. She helped dress up the act, displaying a grace that insured the attention of masculine eyes. Will's knowledge of foreign languages kept the pair busy working in Europe after vaudeville work in the United States fell off.

The Aherns no longer perform but still have an interest in show business. They have a dance-drama school in downtown Los Angeles and are active in obtaining talent and producing shows for the indigent residents of the Motion Picture Country Home near Los Angeles.

My first vaudeville date was back in 1913 when I was on a bill at the Lyric Theater in Bridgeport, Connecticut. We did a benefit—I think it was for the Dayton flood sufferers. I did some rope spinning, and what I hoped was comedy talk. When that was finished, I worked in circuses and those ranch shows, the Oklahoma Ranch and the 101 Ranch, where I did trick riding and roping.

When the First World War started I joined the Navy and was assigned to the Pelham Bay Naval Installation. There were other performers there— Edward G. Robinson, Jim Crane, Otto Kruger—and we did shows singly and together for the U.S. Navy and for the Liberty Loan drives. When the war ended, Phil Dunning, the chief petty officer who handled all the entertainment, got me and my newly acquired partner, Joe O'Hare, to do

Will and Gladys Ahern performing in Dallas at the Texas Baker Hotel, 1941.

Will Ahern, "Cowboy Wit,"
at the Lyric Theatre in
Bridgeport, Connecticut, for
"Dayton Flood Sufferers"
in 1913.

an act aboard the *George Washington*, the ship carrying the U. S. delegation to Europe for the peace conference. On board were many diplomats and dignitaries, headed by President Woodrow Wilson.

What did we do? Crazy—we did a mind-reading act. I played the mind reader. Before the performance I would go to the radio room to get the names of all the important passengers. O'Hare would be out in the audience asking questions. We had an A-B-C-D code. Never mind how it worked. It worked fine. I was blindfolded and we had that audience oohing with amazement. After one show was over, Charles Schwab, the steel man from Pittsburgh, had us brought to his quarters. He wanted to know where we got the information. I only said that I went by the waves that come to me from my partner. Schwab laughed. He knew damn well there was a code.

Anyway, we did well enough so that in 1919 Blitz Cooper, who had a burlesque show, *Bluebird*, offered us half the billing and good money. We were with him for forty weeks. My partner left to attend to some business in Baltimore and I stayed on doing a single. I opened at the Harlem Opera House on 125th Street, where I was picked up by Eli Sobol of the Sobol Brothers, big agents then. In 1919 I met my wife Gladys and we did an act together. And we still do it today when called on.

52

We really began like many others. We started with amateur nights and then somebody suggested vaudeville. Then we talked to agents until we got opportunities. I was able to spin a rope and my wife was a superb dancer, so we got opportunities. But we didn't have it easy all the way. There were several grades of vaudeville and you graduated from one to another. There was the Gus Sun time, Western Vaudeville, Pantages, Interstate, Orpheum and others I can't think of right offhand. (I'm not giving you these in order of importance.) Anyway, each circuit may have had twenty, twenty-five theaters, and to keep them open they had to use acts. These were the vaudevillian's proving grounds, where he acquired the experience and know-how to handle all sorts of audiences. There was so much work that an act could do the same routine for a long time because it didn't play the same theater again for perhaps three or four years.

Every vaudevillian was an artist—you could say each one was a Rembrandt. Take an act like Imhoff, Conn and Corinne. This was a masterpiece. For thirty, thirty-five minutes Imhoff convulsed audiences. Acts would refuse to follow him. Then take Benny Rubin, who came up the ladder. He was the greatest combination of talent I've ever seen. Or Frank Fay, who did a class act working with stooges (one was Patsy Kelly). Unfortunately his overblown ego, obvious even onstage, held him back. But he, too, was wonderful.

Let me tell you how it worked for most of us. After working most of the circuits you finally came to New York, hoping to play the Palace. If you didn't make it—and there were plenty who didn't—you went back to the other circuits, improving your material. If you were caught by the right people at the right time, fine. Otherwise it was back to the sticks.

It was in 1921, while playing Kansas City, that we got a letter from a New York agent, Louis Borden, who said he wanted to handle us if we came East. He brought us from Toronto to the Greenpoint Theater in Brooklyn. At the opening performance Max Gordon (we didn't know who or what he was) came running backstage. The manager came after him, threatening to put him out (he didn't know who he was either). Gordon asked us to come to his office. He was a dynamic man. He produced so many Broadway plays and he and his partners were great agents. We were with them for twenty-five years. It was a long route—the Palace, pictures, etcetera.

Let me tell you some of the things vaudeville taught you. You remember how there used to be ten best songs in the country. One could be the number-one song in New Orleans or New York, and in Chicago it may have been the number four, and so it went. The singer in vaudeville

Will and Gladys Ahern at the Scala Theatre, Berlin, Germany (1938).

Gladys Ahern in 1929, when she was in Harry Carroll's Music Box Revue and excited Rudy Vallee's interest.

learned the tastes of his public in each area and would give it the songs it liked best. Same thing applied to an even greater extent in comedy. In the South, for example, they were a little slow in getting material. So you had to work slower. In the steel- and coal-mining areas of Pennsylvania and the Virginias, where many of the workers were foreign, you had to broaden and enunciate your material. But in the key cities—New York, Boston, Chicago—you'd do everything with a snap because they were show-wise.

We played the Palace many times. We also played abroad for seven years—the Palladium, the Moss Empire houses, the provinces, etcetera. Because we speak German, French, Italian, and Spanish, working European countries didn't pose any problems. Of course, the rope and dancing were visual, but we always did our talk and comedy in the language of the country we were in. Not that we ever tried to speak the language perfectly. We purposely made mistakes to get more laughs and more hands.

JOHN BUBBLES

JOHN BUBBLES of Buck and Bubbles was the tall, lanky partner, while Buck was short and squat. They came up from the South and made the grade here with comparatively little trouble. Both could dance and play the piano—Bubbles had an unusually good voice—but it was their comedy that set them apart as one of the best teams in show business.

Bubbles lives in virtual retirement near Los Angeles. Buck died a few years ago.

We started as amateurs, Buck and me. We won prizes but our steady jobs were as ushers at the B. F. Keith, Mary Anderson Theater in Louisville, Kentucky, where we worked in the gallery. Following a state fair appearance for Indiana Trucks, for a Mr. Humbolt Collins—a white man who was one of our greatest admirers—we went back to our regular ushering job at the theater.

One day an act that was booked for the vaudeville bill did not go over so good and the manager of the theater, a Mr. George Carter, who had seen us performing at some private party, thought we would be just the act to replace the other act. He sent one of the ushers from the orchestra floor up to the gallery to tell us to come to the office, and when we got there he asked us if we wanted to take the place of that weak act. We said yes and he said, "Go and get your tuxedoes and black hats and come back for the next show."

He had a tutor in the dressing room waiting to help us get dressed. He put the burnt cork on our faces so the audience would not know that we really were Negroes, we being the first Negroes to go on that stage. We

John Bubbles, who not only danced but also sang and played the piano.

also had to wear gloves. We were the hit of the bill and we were held over for another week.

The manager said that a big company called The Kiss Me Company would be on the stage after the vaudeville bill was over and that he would speak to the manager of the show about us. We auditioned for the manager of The Kiss Me Company and he asked us to go to New York. Our mothers had to sign before we could go, and I had to get Buck out of school. I did it by telling his principal that going to New York was the chance of our lives, that if Buck stayed in school the rest of his life he would never learn enough to make as much money as he could right now.

The principal wanted to know who was going to look after Buck if he let him out. I said I would and he said, "Get his mother to sign a paper naming you his guardian and I will let him out."

Our first date in New York City was at the Columbia Theater on 47th Street and Seventh Avenue, on the opposite corner from the Palace. This was September, 1919. We were the biggest hit at the Columbia in seven years. It may be important to know that we were locked in our dressing room. Before we went onstage the house manager told our manager that he didn't want any niggers on his stage. I heard this and wondered. After our first performance that same manager of the theater came running backstage asking, "Where are those two colored boys?"

Only three weeks following our big hit at the Columbia Theater we were booked to play the Palace. You hear me? The Palace for us—Buck and Bubbles! And you know who was on the bill with us? Rae Samuels, "The Blue Streak of Vaudeville," and Clayton, Jackson and Durante. Later we played the Keith's Riverside, on Broadway and 96th Street, where we were billed over Burns and Allen (who complained about it to the manager). At Loew's State we were next to closing and Mae West was on number two.

We played on the same bills with some of the greatest acts in the business, among them Al Jolson, Eddie Cantor, Kate Smith, Danny Kaye. We were the first colored act to be held over at the New York Palace. We were the first Negro act to play the Radio City Music Hall.

Our agent was in bad with some of the offices, including Ziegfeld's. When I went up there to ask for work, Ziegfeld's assistant, Gene Buck, came out. I told him what we wanted. He told me to wait a minute, went in to talk to Ziegfeld, and came out to ask if we were under contract. When I said yes, he told me to come back after our contract was finished. Twelve years later we got together.

Meanwhile we took all sorts of jobs. We were willing to do anything to see that name Buck and Bubbles up there where everybody could see it.

Oh yes, after the Palace we played vaudeville coast to coast. We played the Orpheum time, Pantages, Poli, Gus Sun, Balaban and Katz. Everybody booked us, including the William Morris office.

We were easy to book because we didn't conflict with most acts. Nobody wrote for us or gave us lines. We thought funny and that's the way it came out onstage. We were singers who could dance. We could do funny things. You know—you caught us a lot of times.

In vaudeville all Negro acts worked in the number-two spot. You had to be something special to get any spot other than number two. We played every big-time theater in the United States. Our opening bit—"You pull (the piano), my end'll follow"—was stolen by hundreds. Anyway, by the end of 1920 we were no longer number two on any bill. We were next to closing. We played the Palace about twenty times and each time it was next to closing.

In no theater other than in Louisville did we put on cork. No other place. Did you know we were the only Negro act in vaudeville allowed to

Buck (at piano) and Bubbles (dancing) on stage.

drive our own car from one town to another? Of course, black acts couldn't get sleeping accommodations on trains or in good hotels.

About 1931 we were booked into Loew's State. Though we had played there many times, I had never gone in to see a show. This was the first time. I went in to see the closing act of the bill we were to follow. And who was on the bill but the Ritz Brothers. When they finished, they had to steal a bow! And they were the headliners! Well, I thought, you can bet all the tea in China Buck and Bubbles won't have to steal a bow. We would stop the show.

After the show I went downstairs and asked for the manager. He came out and I knew he was the manager. He wore a tuxedo. I introduced myself and said we were to open the next day. He kind of looked me over like he had never seen me—maybe he hadn't, I think he was new. We spoke about billing, lights, etcetera.

Next day, when I came to the theater, way up there in lights and big signs and lobby pictures was our name, Buck and Bubbles!

After the first matinee I was so happy I cried a bit. I went out for a cup of coffee. When I came back there was Buck on the phone, the one backstage at the entrance, saying to somebody, "Just a minute, my partner's just coming in now." He held his hand over the phone and said to me, "It's the Ziegfeld office calling." And that was just after the matinee on that first day. You hear what I say!

I took the phone and the voice said, "Mr. Ziegfeld wants to know when he can have an appointment with you." I said, "Call my manager." The voice: "What's his number?" I said I didn't remember (I knew it all right). After the next show my manager called to tell me he had had a call from the Ziegfeld office. He didn't know I was the one who had told them to call him.

Anyway, we all went over to the Ziegfeld office. We were shown into an office where Ziegfeld was sitting with Gene Buck and some other people. There's a piano there, so Buck starts noodling on it, very soft but in tempo. I start to move around and talk, also in tempo. I'm listening to the talk between Gene Buck and our manager. Ziegfeld wants us but can only pay $500. My manager says $700. Still in tempo I break in with $800. You hear what I say? $800! I could've said $1000. But we'd have played Ziegfeld for nothing, it was that big. Colored acts didn't play Ziegfeld, and here we had it.

Well, our first show we didn't do so good. So we were told to cut down to nine minutes. We were doing fourteen. You know what a five-minute cut means? Man, do you know? So the next show we cut and when we dance to the side of the stage, the stage manager's there whispering, "Don't go over or I'll put the lights out on you." He shouldn't have said that. Anyway, we finish and we take a quick bow and go down to our dressing room. They're calling "Buck and Bubbles—Buck and Bubbles!" And we don't stir. Harry Richman's on and they're not listening to him. They're yelling "Buck and Bubbles" louder than ever. So Richman makes a joke and says that Buck and Bubbles are in a speakeasy down the street. So they yell up to him, "Well, get 'em back!" So you know what happened? That same stage manager who said he'd put the lights out on us had to beg us to come back on.

Then we toured, and after trying us in various spots, they, too, had to put us on next to closing. There was nobody who could follow us. And you know who was on the bill? I'll tell you: Mitzi Mayfair, Hal LeRoy, Faith Bacon, Gladys Glad, Helen Morgan, Harry Richman, Ruth Etting, Jack Pearl, Frank and Milt Britton's band. We followed all those wonderful people—and all we did was dance and sing—but nobody could follow us. Think about it! All that talent, all those beautiful Ziegfeld girls in those gorgeous costumes—we followed them but nobody could follow us!

Back in 1926 I had a legal battle with my manager and I moved over to another agent. Our salary was then about $750. But I wanted to get out of town so I took a date at the Oriental in Chicago for short money— $375. We get there and discover they never played a Negro act. They claim we made a mistake and they tell us to go over to a theater on the West Side. We had played it before. Now I had the contract in my pocket but we went over to that West Side house.

After our third day there the Oriental people came backstage and asked us to play their theater after we finished on the West Side. There had been "a kind of a mixup." So we moved to the Oriental.

Now we needed our piano in a certain spot. Paul Ash's band was onstage—he was the house emcee—and was there a mixup because of where we wanted the piano. When we finally went on we were told to cut to eight minutes. And we tried. We watched that big clock they had on one side—and you know what happened? The audience wouldn't let us off. We stayed on for fifty-eight minutes and Paul Ash couldn't follow us. You hear that? Fifty-eight minutes!

To go back a bit—or maybe go ahead. After the Ziegfeld show we went back to straight vaudeville with occasional fairs and circuses. I do operettas fairly good and George Gershwin put us into his *Porgy and Bess*, where I sang. I sang at the Waldorf-Astoria with Jascha Heifetz. But all that is past history.

61

The Vaudevillians

We played the London Palladium and all the English provinces. We were on the bill with Gracie Fields. In 1936 we played there again, and on the bill with us were Lou Holtz, Lupe Velez, and Ruth Etting.

Vaudeville was wonderful. You can see it was good to us. Sure, it was hard sometimes. But nothing was easy. For us it could've been harder than for others. But it wasn't.

Buck, you know, is gone. Me? Well, if I get better, who knows . . .

SAMMY BERK

THOUGH BASICALLY Berk & Saun was a novelty dance-team specializing in the wild Russian-type routines highly popular during the early and mid-twenties, Juanita Saun, a striking beauty, was also an outstanding vocalist. She came from a southern family that had played in stock. Her singing was so good that when she reached her teens, W. C. Handy, perhaps the man who gave the blues their greatest impetus, made her his star pupil.

Berk taught his dancing routines to Juanita, who subsequently married him. They retired some years ago. Berk is now a talent agent and manager.

I started in show business as a dancer in my uncle's troupe, the Sokoloff Troupe. I was the baby. We did fancy and Russian dancing. I can't say if I got the idea of doing a single when I won first prize in an amateur cakewalk contest at Tony Pastor's, but I started as a single at the Jardin de Dance, a very swank cabaret that played the biggest. To make a long story short, I was caught there by Mr. Phillips of Stern Music Company, who was friendly with a producer, and I went into a Broadway show, *Lilac Domino*. It was there I met Lillian Broderick, who was a knockout. She was one of the chorus girls. We did a number together, and when the show closed, I decided I'd do a vaudeville act and asked Lillian to join me. She did. That was about 1916.

Well, what can I tell you. We hit it off—but good. We had a very fine act and we worked all around New York, all the Keith houses, and there were plenty. Then the war began. I enlisted in the Navy and Lillian

63

The Vaudevillians

Sam Berk and Juanita, when they played the big time.

Victoria Palace Program

went into a Ziegfeld show. She met Joe Schenck of Van and Schenck, and married him.

When I got out of the Navy I had to get a new partner. I found a toe dancer, a girl named Valda, and we did an act together. We were caught by the bookers and about 1918 we were booked into Henderson's Coney Island and from there we made the Palace. One night I slipped and hurt my knee. We had a lot of work lined up but I couldn't go on. So the act split.

When my knee got better an agent I knew met me at a restaurant near the Palace, the St. Regis—all the acts used to go there—and asked me how the leg was. I said it was better but now I needed a new girl. He said, "I think I have the girl for you. She's working in a nightclub on 39th Street and Broadway."

So we went there to see her. After watching her for awhile I said, "That's the girl for me." So he brought her over and we talked and the next day we met at the agent's office and made a deal. We rehearsed and finally we took one showing date—at the Fox Jamaica, an out-of-the-way place where the bookers could come and see us. They covered us and we got plenty of work. Our act was called Berk and Saun.

Juanita Saun became my wife in 1920. We had a show-business wedding. We couldn't take time off, so we got married while we were at the Orpheum in Seattle (it was then called the Moore Theater). We had a big party that night after the show. John B. Hymer, the headliner, was my best man. He had a great act. His "C'mon Red" was a howl. He's supposed to be selling his soul to the devil, who's all in red. The devil promises that whenever Hymer is tempted, or wants to do something he shouldn't, all he has to do is call, "C'mon, Red," and the devil will appear to remove all temptations. Well, there were all sorts of situations. The audiences would go crazy laughing. They would yell, "C'mon, Red," before Hymer.

Juanita and I played the biggest theaters with the biggest names of the times. When we played with Jack Benny his name was Ben K. Benny. He did a stand-up comedy act. He changed his name because of Ben Bernie, the bandleader, who was much better known at the time. So he became Jack Benny. About Ben Bernie—he was originally in an act called Bernie and Baker. Phil Baker played the accordion. When Phil went into the Navy, Bernie formed a band and became its leader.

George Burns was also a friend with whom we worked. He had many partners before Gracie Allen. The name Burns was a favorite one in vaudeville in those days. There were lots of Burnses, and they all came from the same neighborhood. The original was Sammy Burns of Burns and Fulton, a great act. George Burns' real name was Nat Birnbaum, and when I first met him the name of his act was Burns and José. An agent had asked me to come along with him to take a look at this act. I had nothing better to do, so I saw the act. It was an ordinary act. Later I got to know Burns and he was a very funny guy. But he was funnier on the street than onstage. Yes, George was good for a million laughs, but not when he was working.

About the same time that George was trying to find himself, Jack Benny was handled by an agent named Tommy Fitzpatrick. Fitzpatrick also handled an Irish troupe in which Gracie Allen was doing an Irish jig. There was another act, Ben Ryan and George White. Ryan teamed with a girl, Harriet Lee, and it became Ryan and Lee.

White left to team up with Lucille Cavanaugh as White and Cavanaugh, a fine act. She was excellent, a beautiful girl. It was later that George White produced his *Scandals*, but that's another story. To get back to Ryan and Lee—she became sick, so Ryan hired George Burns and Gracie Allen to do his act. And that's how George and Gracie met. The rest you know.

Vaudeville life was good and bad. It was even not too bad when it wasn't so good. You worked in all kinds of theaters. When you had a week or two open, particularly in the Midwest or in the South, there was always some small-time theater man or booker who'd try to get you to work for them for half your salary. Rather than lay off, you might take the job. In many theaters there were signs backstage warning: "Don't send out your laundry until after the first show." If they didn't like your act, they could cancel you. This was before the pay-or-play contracts.

Jeo Keno of Keno and Green—they're the parents of Mitzi Green—told me of one funny little guy who owned a house performers hated to work in. He used to watch the show, and if an act got a big hand he would come down the aisle, with his back to the stage and face to the audience, saying, "That's a great act, hey? What I had to do to get them to come here. But wait'll next week. I have an act that'll make this one look bad . . ." This made the act already onstage want to kill the man. This guy had a sign backstage. It said, "No dirty jokes!" One time a rube comic onstage had just been fed this line by his straight man: "Elmer, what's the best thing in the world?" The owner rushed down the aisle and yelled up, "Say it and I'll ring down the curtain!"

I worked on a unit headed by Eddie Leonard. Leonard was then a superstar and Keith gave him everything he wanted. He had the right to okay the acts on his bill. On our bill was another dancing act, Stewart and Olive, who did some Russian steps. Now Leonard watched closely every act on the bill ahead of him, and if any act threatened his position onstage, he would have it moved. Nobody was permitted to take the edge off Leonard. We were on third. Our act also had some Russian dancing in it and it got a big hand. Leonard didn't like this because Stewart and Olive, who worked in his unit, also did some Russian steps. So he ordered the manager to move us to close the show. I was furious and threatened to leave the show (I didn't mean it) but the manager said the office had called him after Leonard complained and he couldn't help moving us. Now whenever Leonard finished his act he would walk to the wings for his exit, where his wife, Mabel Russell (a very beautiful girl), always stood with a glass of water in her hand. Leonard would take a drink and go back for another bow. This day I stood there watching him. He was a master. When he saw me, he took that mouthful of water and spat it at me. I was ready to kill him. Apparently he had learned that I had objected to the reslotting of the show, and that was his reaction. But we both got over it and later we played on the same bill many times.

In those days units playing the Orpheum time would stay together until they reached San Francisco. There another headline act was usually added. To show the power of a super headliner: Pat Rooney and Marian Bent were added, but Eddie Leonard and Pat Rooney had words, and Rooney was taken off the bill. Incidentally, Rooney sold or gave his act, "The Newstand," to Jimmy Cagney and his wife and they toured vaudeville with it.

All those people were great. You remember what it was like then, the ones we are talking about, and you say they were gone too soon. But where would they work today? There's no question there's not as much good talent around today as in the past. The small-time acts of yesteryear are the headliners of today. Conditions were different then. You couldn't get in the big time unless you paid your dues. It wasn't a case of making a record and becoming a star overnight. You had to work and eventually you arrived. You had to play a lot of small time. Seldom did an act arrive from left field and play the two-a-day. All the headliners in those days came out of small-time or burlesque. Some developed, some never did. But even those that didn't make the big time found plenty of work in the small time. After all there were thousands of theaters in the small time that needed acts constantly.

MILTON BERLE

MILTON BERLE is a brash, aggressive comedian who seems to take advantage of whatever happens in the audience. He performed at such speed that the audience had to be on its mental toes to stay with him. Much of Berle's material was clever, even if familiar. He was particularly funny when he pretended to join either vocal or dancing groups performing onstage with him, creating a hilarious confusion. His takeoff on Eddie Cantor in blackface was always good for laughs.

A latecomer to big-time vaudeville—it was already in its decline when he became a headliner—Berle made his major reputation in the middle forties and early fifties when he was in fact "Mr. TV." Berle's Texaco Show, in format a vaudeville show, was so popular that on Tuesday nights theaters were half filled and restaurants empty because people stayed at home to watch Mr. TV. Berle was reputed to have sold more TV sets than any advertising campaign. He still appears on TV as a guest from time to time. Once in a while he does a nightclub date, chiefly in Las Vegas or Miami.

Did I like vaudeville? I loved it. And why not? I was brought up on vaudeville. I started in vaudeville in 1916, after working in many silent movies at Fort Lee, New Jersey. In the series I was always the baby who was being kidnapped or something. I appeared with Marie Dressler, Pearl White, Grace Cunard, and the other famous movie stars of the silents.

I began in vaudeville in Philadelphia, not in New York, because the Children's Society—the Gerry Society—wouldn't allow kids to work in

Berle as he is today—a grandfather!

New York vaudeville except under severe restrictions. Same thing was true of Chicago. But we could work outside of these cities.

My first vaudeville experience was as part of a kiddie act, a flash act—three boys and three girls. With us was Bart McHugh and E. W. Wolfe. McHugh was the builder or creator of kiddie acts. I was then in an act called "The Melody of Youth" at the Nixon Grand, Philadelphia, on Ward and Montgomery streets. Also on the bill was an act called Spencer and Williams, a man-and-wife team. He would work with a cigar and had a running gag: "Did you get the idea of that one?" He repeated it after each joke, "did you get the idea of that one?" and the audience ate it up. The Worth Wayton Four were also on the bill. You can see that neither material nor billing was subtle. But the audiences loved it and we loved them.

Of course I loved vaudeville. And I miss it. I started on the small time but I was in it for only about five years, because about 1921 I was teamed with a little girl, Elizabeth Kennedy, in an act written and produced by Milton Hocky and Leonard Green. We did dramatic bits, no comedy. We did scenes from *Romeo and Juliet, Orphans of the Storm,* Frank Bacon's *Lightnin'*. Elizabeth would play Topsy the chorus girl in an imitation of Ina Claire in *The Gold Diggers*.

We broke in the act, Kennedy and Berle, at Fox's Bay Ridge in Brooklyn and followed it with three days at the Crotona in the Bronx. We were such a smash they put us into the Palace right away. We were considered a phenomenon, making the Palace with just a week's break-in. I remember some of the acts on the bill with us: the Ford Sisters—Mabel and Dora; the Watson Sisters—Fanny and Kitty; Jim Toney and Norman, and a little Russian guy who danced and played the mandolin and stopped the show cold—Dave Apollon.

The Gerry Society allowed kids to do vaudeville in New York as long as they did no dancing or singing and were out of the theater by 9:05 P.M. So we were never more than third on the bill. The bills would start with an opening act—an acrobat or something—then there would be a singer, and then the kids, Kennedy and Berle. After the Palace we played the Keith circuit, then went west to play the Western Vaudeville Circuit out of Chicago. It was there that Sam Kahl, a booker, would give us our railroad tickets.

Everything was fine. We lived well and ate well, except by 1924 I was becoming too tall for Elizabeth. I was springing up like a tree. I used to stoop trying to make myself shorter. That's how I became round-shouldered. So we broke up the act and I started to do a single. I was fifteen at the time but looked nineteen.

Now my troubles really began. After playing the big time I was now back trying to break into the small time. I was a lanky, skinny kid, struggling to find myself. I had to start all over again, with the Fally Markuses, Al and Belle Dows, and the others who booked the small time. I worked in Patchogue, Passaic, Paterson, Pottsville, Steubenville—you name it. I worked all the crap houses and flea joints they would send me to.

Elizabeth Kennedy? She's now a grandmother living in Chicago.

Here was a switch that was unique: I began with the kiddie acts—that was small time. In 1921 I teamed with Kennedy and became a child star —that was really big time. Then in 1924 I had to start all over again as a single. I even changed my name three times. Once it was Bobby Baker. (Little did I know that Bobby Baker was going to do a different kind of time.)

I'll never forget when I was playing the Lincoln Theater in Union Hill, New Jersey (now called Union City), as Bobby Baker, and Abe Last-fogel of the Morris office caught me. That was in 1925. I think he was there to look at Frances Arms (he later married her). Anyway, I signed with the Morris office and was with them for forty-seven years.

I suppose one might say that I came into vaudeville as a single at the worst possible time. Sure, there was some prosperity, but then came the bust of 1929. But I just worked where they booked me. I worked with all of them—Owen McGiveney, the quick-change artist; Willie and Joe Mandel; Ethel Barrymore when she was doing the "12 Pound Look." I worked in units in the middle twenties for Paramount when Bob Weitman, now a film producer, was assistant manager of the Paramount Theater and Gene Pleshette was his assistant. (That's the same Pleshette whose daughter, Suzanne, is a movie and television star today.) I worked with Blossom Seeley and Benny Fields in 1920–1921. She eventually married Benny after divorcing Rube Marquard, the ball player. Benny sang through a megaphone—and that was before Rudy Vallee. Fields later played piano for Blossom. I was on the bill with Gallagher and Shean in 1921 at the Maryland Theater in Baltimore. Rose Marie worked with me when she was eleven years old. Years later she was my leading lady in the musical *Springtime in Brazil*.

Did you know Phil Silvers was in vaudeville as a tenor singing in a box, like Sid Silver did for Phil Baker when they were together? About Phil Silvers: My mother used to say of him, "He's a nice boy. You can go out with him." So the first place he took me was to a whorehouse. That's a nice boy, right? So from then on I always went out with him.

After I started all over again in 1924 I gradually moved up. By 1931

71

Milton Berle and fans, 1931.

or '32 I was playing the Loew's Syracuse when I got a phone call to come to New York to play the Palace. The local management had been alerted and were letting me out. Did I grab it? You bet! My big chance came through Benny Rubin's appendix attack.

What happened was this: The Palace had begun a policy of having two emcees who would work together in the next-to-closing slot after working alternately all through the show. The policy started with Cantor and Jessel, then came Lou Holtz and Billy Gaxton, followed by Herman Timberg and Pat Rooney. The Jew and Irishman team had worked out so well they put in another Jew-Irishman combination—Rubin and Haley. At least that was the plan until Rubin fell out and I fell in. At the risk of being called immodest (something nobody ever called me), I can tell you I was a big hit. I stayed at the Palace for eight weeks. I'll tell you who was on the bill with me: George Olson and his band, Fifi D'Orsay, Al Segal with Lillian Slade, the Mills Brothers, and Beatrice Lillie, the top headliner. Two weeks after I closed I was brought back for Pola Negri, a picture star of the period who was making a personal appearance. So it all happened because of Benny Rubin. Incidentally, Earl Carroll caught me at the Palace and signed me for one of his *Vanities*. I got $1300, which in 1932 was a sensational salary.

So vaudeville helped me as it helped so many. It was a training ground, school, and college all in one. It was also profitable. Even under miserable conditions, one learned—and I had my share of them.

Today there are no places for young performers to get started, or to flop in. There's no place for anyone to see young performers except on TV, where you get one shot and you'd better be good. No one wants to book unknowns, even on club dates—that means the resorts like the Borscht Belt, banquets, and one-nighters.

It took monologists like Jack Benny, Bob Hope, Benny Rubin, Frank Fay, and me eighteen months to two years to get seven solid minutes to put into an act. You weeded out the crap, deleted and edited stuff that wouldn't play. Then when you went to Wilkes-Barre, it had to be changed again. And then another town, and still more changes. Where can you get that kind of training today?

The *Texaco Star Theater* was the outcome of my vaudeville experience. It was a vaudeville show. That's the way it was billed—*The Texaco Star Theater Vaudeville Show*—on circulars we gave out to studio audiences. So when that series opened June 8, 1948, you can be sure it stemmed from the deep roots of vaudeville.

When vaudeville died, not too many vaudevillians were able to make the transition into radio and television. There were many reasons. Some were so accustomed to projecting in big theaters that cafés, radio, and/or television escaped them. The intimacy that was required in cafés was beyond them. Lou Holtz tried it and couldn't make it. Neither could Ed Wynn. Maybe I was smart or lucky. Sure, I was brash, raucous, flippant, and aggressive. But it was such qualities that enabled you to move into other entertainment fields when vaudeville was perishing.

BLOCK & SULLY

BLOCK AND SULLY *were a husband-and-wife team with very funny routines. Their crossfire of talk kept the laughs mounting. Eve Sully, a tiny, pretty brunette, delivered most of the comedy lines with hilarious results. Jesse Block played comedian-straight, feeding Eve the lines that enabled her to give the "dumb" retorts that elicited the roars of laughter. Their song-and-dance finale was as expert as their comedy. Miss Sully's querulous "Look at him!" became so familiar to audiences that they anticipated it and shouted it out time and again.*

Neither Jesse Block nor Eve Sully is now in show business. Mrs. Block is a housewife and volunteer worker for charitable organizations. Mr. Block is a Wall Street broker and spends his leisure at the Friars Club trying to prove he's a sharp gin rummy player.

Jessie Block: I started with Gus Edwards in 1915. The name of the act was "Song Revue of 1915." In the act were Georgie Price, Lila Lee, and Arthur Freed, the great producer. I was one of the boys. There was also a fellow—Jack Weiner, he's still alive, he's an agent—who did a trio with Georgie Jessel and the late Walter Winchell. I got the job with Gus Edwards by auditioning.

I lived on the Lower East Side in New York—I still remember the address, 279 Broome Street. We had no phone and we lived on the fifth floor. Well, a few weeks after I auditioned, two fellows came to the house to notify me that Gus Edwards wanted to see me right away, that I had a job. One of the fellows was Dave Seed of Seed and Austin, the other was Walter Winchell of Winchell and Green. I joined the act in Madison, Wisconsin, where they were working.

74

The song "School Days" was part of the act. It was written by Gus Edwards' brother Lee and, I think, Gus Carr. I was with Gus Edwards for about a year. Oh yes, prior to that I worked in an act called "Nine Crazy Kids" with Bert and Howie Gordon, but I was stopped by the Gerry Society because I was only thirteen years old. So I went on the road. When I joined Gus Edwards I was fourteen, or maybe fifteen. We played the Orpheum Circuit. We lived in boardinghouses where we paid $1 a week. Food? Breakfast was 10 cents, lunch—we called it dinner—was 15 cents, and supper was 25 cents. I was getting $18 a week and, believe me, $18 in 1915 was big money. The stars, Georgie Price and Lila Lee, were getting more—I don't know how much. I sent home $10 a week. The punch line is that after being away from home a year and sending home the ten bucks every week, my father and mother (God rest their souls), when they met me at the station, the first thing they asked me was how much did I save. I said I had saved $100. But I didn't tell them I had lost it in a crap game.

After that I did an act for William Friedlander—he produced acts. It was called "Sweeties." I worked with a girl, Lillian Berson—I think that was her name—and three others. Frank McHugh was in the act. I saw him not too long ago, the first time in forty years; he was a great pal of Jimmy Cagney's.

Anyway, Eve and I have been together forty-seven years. Bert Gordon, the "Mad Russian," introduced us. I worked with another girl for a few years. We were called Block and Dunlap. When that broke up and I was looking for another girl, Bert knew it. He arranged that I meet Eve and we went to work together. We quit in 1948. Our last appearance was at Loew's State. I don't think any act played there as many times as we did. We'd go from Loew's State to the Paramount, across the street; from the Paramount to the Capitol, up the block on Broadway; from the Capitol to B. S. Moss' Broadway. We played every theater on Broadway except the Roxy. At Moss' Broadway we played on the bill with Louise Groody—it was Louise Groody and Hal Skelly. The Broadway theater was where the Criterion is now.

Eve Sully: In 1948 they were already trying to break in TV and they took Ginger Rogers and myself to use as models. She was blonde, and in those days my hair was a different color. They wanted to see which would photograph better, they were experimenting. It wasn't released or anything.

We played with Jack Benny at the Palace in Chicago. He was the emcee. We played with Fanny Brice—

Jesse Block: —Yes, that was at the Oriental, also in Chicago. You

75

Eddie Cantor with Eve Sully in his arms as Jesse Block, pretending anger, seems about to enter the fray.

know, there's a wonderful story. We met Fanny many years later in California when she was doing "Baby Snooks"—remember that? She was very absent-minded, she couldn't remember your name. She was close to Eddie and Ida Cantor and she'd even forget their names. Anyway, we came out to California and Eddie gave us a party and Fanny was invited. She went to very few parties but she loved Eddie. And that night we reminisced about how it was. I said to Fanny, "Do you remember when we played together at the Oriental?" She said, "Kid, I don't remember that." So I said, "Sure, don't you remember we went to catch Ben Bernie at the College Inn?" She said, "College Inn? I'll be damned if I remember that." I said, "Fanny, what's the matter with you? We went out—Al Capone gave you a party and you invited us. It was a terrific party!" But she couldn't remember that either. Then I said, "Fanny, I remember the year you got $7500 at the Oriental." She said, "I got $8000." That she remembered.

Sully: When she worked with us at the Oriental she did "Baby Snooks." She was late coming down after our act, so I got into the crib. When she got there, she didn't know I was in it. The curtain went up and the audience knew it was me. They were hysterical. But she couldn't ad-lib. She couldn't say anything. I handed her a lollipop and said, "Take the paper off and eat it." She said "What?" So I said, "You're supposed to take the paper off and throw the lollipop away." It was a joke that we did years ago but she couldn't ad-lib, unless it was written for her.

Block: One story about Jack Benny—I've told it a thousand times, but it actually happened. Jack loves to drive a car. I drove to California with him once—in fact, he bought a car just to drive it out there. Anyway, Eve and I and Jack got to California just about when Jack got a yen to drive back to New York. I said, "We just got out here and it's crazy." Johnny Green said, "If you go, I'll go." So they talked me into it. We got up the next morning and the three of us are ready to drive to New York. Jack was very excited and I was mad and finally I said to Johnny "where do you live in New York?" He said, "I generally stay at the Astor." I said, "Well, I stay at the Essex. So you get in and let me sit on the outside because I get off first." That became a famous story. But it actually happened. In fact, at the Players Club when they honored Benny, I sat on the dais and told the story and Jack said, "That's a true story."

I teamed up with Eve when Bert Gordon—that "Mad Russian" on Eddie Cantor's show—said, "I met a girl at the Morris office. She's the cutest thing." William Morris office was handling me then. Eve was in an act with Jeanette McDonald. She had come to New York to get a job and came to the Morris office.

The Vaudevillians

Sully: I lived with the Jeanette McDonald family in Philadelphia. I was from Atlantic City. They were from Philadelphia. They were looking for a girl for this act. It was a dancing act—Jeanette's sister, Clarence Rock, and McDonald. They later became Rock and White. They were looking for a partner for a short fellow in the act. I was then working on the Boardwalk and they came over and said, "Can you dance?" I said yes, and they asked me to pick up my dress. I was only a kid then—thirteen, I think—and they wanted me for the summer. They were booked in Ocean City and Wildwood for two weeks, or maybe more. I said, "you'll have to ask my mother." So Jeanette McDonald's mother came over and asked my mother. My mother wouldn't let me go alone, so I took my sister. We rehearsed that night in Ocean City and I opened in the act the next afternoon. That's how I got started.

After I played with McDonald two or three weeks I had to go back to school. When we played Philly I stayed at Jeanette's house. I paid her mother for room and board. They fed me very well. They used to churn their own butter. It was the first time I had seen butter made. They got the cream and whipped it and made their own butter. It was very good. Sundays we had chipped beef and cream. It cost me $5 a week. When Jeanette came to Atlantic City she stayed at our house. I think she paid $6 a week for her room and board.

By the following year I was stagestruck—that's when I went to New York, to the William Morris office. The first time I spoke with Johnny Hyde he was a doll. They asked me all kinds of questions: "Can you do this?" and "Can you do that?" and I said yes to everything—even though I couldn't do a damn thing. Do you dance? I said yes. I even said I rode a bicycle and I could roller skate. I was a kid, I looked cute to them. That's all. Bert Gordon called Jesse at the Friars Club and Jesse came over and talked to me. Then he asked me what I wanted a week. I got $125 a week on my first job, including costumes and everything. Jesse was getting about $400.

I wasn't ever scared going on. Just give me an audience and a spotlight, but not in a room and not at a party. At a rehearsal I might blow my lines, but onstage I never ·did. Oftentimes we'd louse up a joke but we'd ad-lib and I'd top it, or Jesse would top it, and it was funnier than it was supposed to be. The audience knew it and the musicians knew it. We always changed our jokes because we played Loew's State three or four times a year. We played the Palace twice a year. In fact, we doubled at the Palace when it was a two-a-day and at another theater that was also a two-a-day—the Coliseum, a B. S. Moss house that had just been taken over by Keith. They gave us a car and a chauffeur. We were number four on the bill. Once we were at the Palace with Harry Richman and Frances Williams—Harold Arlen played the piano for her. We were up there next to closing. We were young and could do four shows a day. When we ate at Lindy's we had the chauffeur stop three or four blocks away because we didn't want the other acts to see us pulling up in a car with a chauffeur.

Block: In those days in vaudeville when you were known there were enough places to play where you could be lousy.

Sully: It's the truth. When we rehearsed the act we got $15 just for them to see what I looked like. I had dimpled knees. I remember somebody said "She's terrific," so we were booked immediately.

Block: We both looked good. We made them laugh. We could dance, sing, there was no trouble getting a job. In the beginning we stayed out of New York to break it in. Jack Benny gave me one of his bits. He told me to use it out of town, and I did. But it fit us beautifully. I asked him to take it out of his act and he did.

Sully: They were great friends, Jesse and Jack. They were kids together.

Block: He knew I had a new girl, so he said use it, but don't use it in New York, because I'm going to use it. You find yourself a new bit.

Sully: After he gave us the joke we were such a big hit that RKO signed us for three years immediately. And we were a new act that had been together only a few months. We went into the Palace and did the joke. Then Jack Benny came into New York and he did the joke. *Variety* said Benny was doing Block and Sully's joke, and it was really Jack's joke.

Block: Rudy Vallee used to do the "Stein Song" so I'd never use it. I'd tell Eve a story, then she'd go to tell that story about a traveling salesman, and I'd break in and say, "Now, the 'Stein Song,' but I wouldn't let her go on. You know—I'd break in.

Sully: We also worked with Jimmy Cagney. He was a big movie star— he had already made two pictures. But he opened in Milwaukee and laid a big egg. And they said, what can we do? They had spent a fortune on his new act and it was nothing. So they called us to work with Jimmy Cagney. I think Jesse was the emcee in those days. Cagney's big part in the bit was to say, "I like your partner—I'd like to meet her very much." After some more talk Cagney would say, "Miss Sully, would you like to go out with me tonight?" and I'd say, "I don't know, ask Mr. Block." Cagney would say, "I'll take you out—we'll go to different places." I'd say, "I can't, I'm married." He'd ask to whom and I'd say to Mr. Block. And Jesse would say, "I'm sorry, Mr. Cagney, I did the best I could."

Block: We originally did the bit with Jack Benny in Chicago and we did the same bit with many movie stars when we were on the same bill and they were doing personal appearances. Anyway, with Jimmy we did a dance afterwards. After that we worked together. He was very good. He was a terrific dancer. We worked with him in a dancing act.

Sully: We were on the bill with the Marx Brothers at the Palace and we did a benefit performance at the Riviera. I'd say to Harry Richman, "What time is it?" and he'd say, "Eight-thirty," and I'd slap him right and left. Then he'd yell, "What's the idea?" and I'd answer, "All day I've been asking people what time it was and everyone has told me different." That was one of our openings and it was tremendous.

You remember in the days of Herbert Hoover, when everybody was out of work, there were breadlines and everybody was blaming the whole thing on Hoover? Anyway, Jesse would come on and I would say to him, "Did you vote for Hoover?" He would answer, "I certainly did," and I'd slap him, break his straw hat, and push him around while the laughs got louder. It was good for a three-minute laugh. After that we were set—any physical thing we could do. We were supposed to do fifteen minutes. We would do a half-hour. As long as they laughed, we'd keep adding.

Block: In contrast to today's obscenities, there were signs backstage— if you used words like "hell" or "damn" you would be canceled. Everything was clean.

Sully: We never did double entendres, no dirty stories. Of course, if you were really big, the cancellation threat was never carried out.

We always did big business. Marvin Schenck of the Loew organization said of us, "I always book Block and Sully because they do business. People get their money's worth." Some of our routines developed because I had fans that would follow me around. They'd go from one theater to another and come backstage and give me a rose or a little gift, and I'd always be nice to them. There were three girls—I think they came from Brooklyn—who'd always make an entrance. At Loew's State they'd come in for the supper show around six or something and they'd walk down the aisle and call out, "Hello, Eve," right in the middle of the act. I would say, "Look at her"—and you never heard such laughs. It was like having a stooge in the act. Any time Jesse'd do something physical or something he shouldn't have been doing, I'd say, "Look at him," and the musicians would fall to the floor. That was my tag line, my identification—Look at him!

At the Palace we did a blackout with Harry Richman. It was like a revue. All the important people on the bill would join in just to do the finish—the blackout. Richman was wonderful. No one worked like him.

He could work with a girl, sing with a girl. He did sketches like a master showman. He and Frances Williams did an act together.

Block: I remember this sketch where this fellow comes onstage and just stands there while Richman and I are onstage doing the act. I walk over to Richman and ask, "Who is the guy standing there?" Nobody knows. Everybody just does their act and there's the guy still standing there. The punchline was, *"Ich denk der man is a spy."* It used to get big laughs.

Sully: In those days we danced like mad. Jesse was a beautiful dancer. (He still is.) We worked with the guy who wrote "Tea for Two" and we'd do a soft-shoe dance.

Block: We were supposed to work with Frank Fay in Chicago but we canceled.

Sully: Because we wanted to be headlined.

Block: It wasn't that at all. It was because they wouldn't give us the billing we wanted that we walked off the show. In those days that's how it was, that's how big we were. We weren't going to let Frank Fay be billed above us. It was also something else. We were on second and I didn't like that spot. Because Fay was emcee they had cut down the show. Instead of eight acts, they had six acts because he had stooges and things. I didn't like second, so we walked out.

Sully: Two weeks later they brought us back and we killed them. And we were in our usual spot—next to closing. We were the first talking act to play the Chicago theater. They had never had a talking act there because the theater was so huge and without microphones, nothing, so they always used singing acts or sight acts.

Nat Kalcheim of the Morris office in Chicago took A. J. Balaban over to the theater where we were working. It was a two-a-day.

Block: Balaban told Nat (he told me afterwards), "I'd love to have that act play the Chicago theater." Nat came back the next day and told me. We were then at the Palace getting $450. He said that Balaban would pay us $800. I said, "The Chicago is too big, and besides, who wants to do five shows a day?" Nat said, "Are you crazy? This could be an important step. It would give you many more weeks and the Chicago never played a talking act before." Anyway, he talked us into it and—

Sully: You left out one important thing. Nat told you that Balaban had a meeting with all the executives from the theater and they bet him that we'd lay an egg there. So he said, "Whatever you're getting at the Palace, I'll double it."

Block: It wasn't that. Anyway, we went in. It was the prime of Greta

Garbo. I remember the picture, *The Single Standard*. She was a tremendous draw—a beauty. They were standing in long lines. On that first show we were nervous as hell, but we were a very big hit. Balaban and the others came back and said, "This is like the weekend. We'll have to ask you to do extra shows." We were doing five already but we did one extra show. The manager told us, "This is confidential," and he gave us $150 more for each extra show. They held us over for the second week and then they sent the whole show over to the Oriental. That was our first experience in a huge theater and from then on everybody wanted us. We were getting $1000 a week, and without a radio show or anything. Just vaudeville.

Sully: They couldn't be nicer to us. They even sent out for food for us. It was "Are you all right, Miss Sully." and "Anything else we can do for you, Miss Sully?" We blazed a trail for all the other talking acts.

Block: Small time or family time in those days was Loew's. But the only Loew's we played was the State—that was the big time of the family time. B. F. Keith, Western Vaudeville, and Orpheum were big time. How the Loew's people went after the big-time acts is another story. They had gotten into the picture business with MGM, and to bring more people in they put stronger acts into their theaters. I think Van and Schenck were the first big-time star act that played the State. They blazed the trail at Loew's State. They got a lot of money. We got $2500 a week, and we were just an act. When we told Nat—that is, George Burns—he said, "Twenty-five hundred—wow! All I want to be rich is to save a hundred thousand"—and look at him now, he's a millionaire. He sold his TV series for $2 or $3 million. We are good friends. It makes little difference who did what first. I always say that long before Block and Sully or Burns and Allen went into business, they had man-and-woman acts.

Sully: In those early days Nat and Jesse would go to the delicatessen and Grace and I would go to tearooms. She was very dainty and I ordered small portions. We weren't big eaters.

Block: Anyway, that's the story. Today I'm a stockbroker. Do I miss vaudeville? Of course. It was a wonderful life.

Sully: Why don't you ask me if I miss it? Yes, I miss it. I was younger, lighter—and besides, I met Jesse. Without vaudeville—well, who knows!

GEORGE BURNS

GEORGE BURNS *is perhaps best remembered as the male half of the team of Burns and Allen. He began in show business as a dancer; later he added singing and talking. He had many partners at different times.*

Gracie Allen was part of an Irish clog dance group. An agent put her and Burns into an act together, but it did only tolerably well. It wasn't until they acquired special material, like "Lamb Chops," that they began to climb until they became headliners. But their true national impact came via radio. Miss Allen's trademark comment to George's dry wit—"Oh George, I'll bet you tell that to all the girls"—beccme nationally known. Miss Allen died some time ago. Burns is a frequent guest on TV programs and is still considered one of show business's greatest wits.

When I started, there was no radio, there was no television, there was only vaudeville. There was big-time vaudeville, small-time vaudeville, and medium vaudeville. Big-time vaudeville meant two shows a day. Small-time vaudeville meant three shows a day, four shows a day, and sometimes five on Saturdays and Sundays. There were burlesque shows and there were stock companies. Vaudeville got to be habit-forming—the same people would go to vaudeville every week and sit in the same seats. Big-time vaudeville was an event—people would get dressed up. In some places, like San Francisco, they'd wear dinner clothes. Vaudeville shows consisted of very, very good acts. The people that were in vaudeville did the same act year in and year out. You had fifteen or seventeen good minutes and you could play for five or six years without changing it, because by the time you got around to the same theater two or three years later, peo-

Burns and Allen

ple would forget what your act was. Someone could take a piece of your act—but they couldn't play it on the same circuit. In those days there was something called the Pat Casey office. You had seventeen good minutes and it was your life savings. You would write it down, put it in an envelope, and put the envelope in the Pat Casey office. If somebody stole a joke, they'd open up that envelope, and if it proved you were the first one to do the joke, they'd make the other actor take it out.

In those days Gracie was a big character and in those days the big jokes were eating jokes. Every girl you took out you knew would want to eat. So how we happened to name our act "Lamb Chops" was a joke. I used to say to Gracie, "Do you like to love?" And she would say, "No." "Do you like to kiss?" "No." So I'd say, "What do you like?" and she would answer, "Lamb chops." So I would say, "A little girl your size, can you eat two big lamb chops alone?" and she would answer, "No, but with potatoes I could." So we named the act "Lamb Chops."

Whenever the Palace Theater in New York City had two headliners on the bill—let's say Sophie Tucker and Blossom Seeley—there was a conflict as to who would get the Dressing Room Number One and who would get Dressing Room Number Two. Nobody minded taking Three, or Four, but between One and Two there was a big difference. One and Two were downstairs and Three and Four were on the first floor. If they had two stars of the same caliber they'd give them Three and Four and the performers would be happy about it. They would paint those dressing rooms I would say at least twenty times a season. This was sort of important in vaudeville.

Songs lasted a very long time then. There was no radio, so a song like Irving Berlin's "Alexander's Ragtime Band" or "You Made Me Love You" would take four years to become a hit and four more before it disappeared. It reached a peak at the end of four years and you heard it for eight years. When a song was very hot, all the acts wanted to sing that song and you had to get to the theater very early on Monday morning to get the first rehearsal check. If you got there early enough to get the first check, you were able to sing "Alexander's Ragtime Band" and nobody else could sing it [on that day's bill]. The headliners—some of the women because it was mostly woman headliners who sang songs—would make sure that their piano players got the first rehearsal check. Let's say at that time there were four or five big hit songs. A headliner's piano player would rehearse all five. Maybe she would do only two, but she wouldn't let anybody else sing the other songs because she had rehearsed them. That way if she wanted to sing them all she'd rotate them—sing one in one show and another in the next and so on. Everybody else had to sing songs which weren't hits at all.

In those days if you did over twelve minutes, that meant you had a good spot on the bill. In other words, if you did thirteen minutes or seventeen minutes, that was a lot of time and it meant you were closing or next to last, and next to last on a vaudeville bill was quite a spot. On a bill of eight acts the seventh act was the tough spot—you had to be awfully good to get that spot. Your time would be fifteen to seventeen minutes or twenty minutes. If you met an actor on the street and asked, "Where are you playing?" and he said, "Fifth Avenue," and then you asked, "How're you doing?" and he said, "Seventeen minutes," you knew he was doing well. If you weren't doing well yourself, you wouldn't walk on the same street that the Palace was on, you'd walk on the other side of the street—with makeup on so that nobody would know you.

Another thing would happen in those days. You went on the Orpheum Circuit, let's say—you started out in Minneapolis and you played fifteen, sixteen, or seventeen weeks. Whatever spot you had in Minneapolis, that would be your spot for the whole time. If you went on number two, which was a bad spot, you'd be there for fifteen to seventeen weeks. Gracie and I played Minneapolis when we were on the Orpheum Circuit.

George Burns, 1974.

We were just a little man-and-woman act at the time—what you call a standard act. We did fourteen minutes, later about seventeen. When we got to the theater we looked at the blackboard to see how the show was laid out. Gracie and I were number two. We couldn't go on because ours was a talking act and the people wouldn't even be seated if we went on that early. For acts one and two, I would say maybe two-thirds of the house was seated. By the time the other third of the house came in, your fourteen minutes were out the window. So I told Gracie to go over to the hotel and take a hot-water bag and go to bed and make believe she was sick. In those days there were play-or-pay contracts. If you didn't play, you had to pay them, and if they didn't play you, they had to pay you. You couldn't say that you didn't like your spot on the bill—the manager had to guess that. I said to the manager, "My wife's not feeling well and she can't work." "Well, can you work alone?" he said. I said, "Oh no. I'm even bad when I work with her. I do nothing. I just smoke a cigar and she talks for fourteen minutes." He said, "What am I going to do?" I said, "I don't know. We haven't got a contract with God. You can get sick in Minneapolis and you can get sick in New York. Sometimes you do and sometimes you don't. She's just not feeling well." Just then he happened to look up at the blackboard and noticed that Burns and Allen were number two. He said, "That blackboard is wrong. The single girl comes out and sings a few songs with a dog—she's number two. Then Burns and Allen. Warwick, he's number four." I didn't believe the manager. I thought maybe he wanted me to commit myself and then I'd have to pay. But he said it was true and he went into his office and brought out a paper that he had got from New York. It was a mistake. The paper from New York said we were on number three. I called Gracie and said, "Put on your clothes and come to the theater. We're on number three."

ALAN CORELLI

ALAN CORELLI's act—labeled a "novelty act"—was a display of feats of muscular control. His muscular skill enabled him to prevent anybody from lifting him, even three or four men. The act was always good for audience participation because there would be plenty of volunteers (called a "committee") eager to challenge his claim of being "unliftable." He taught this technique to his first wife, who also performed in his act.

I got into show business through the U.S. Army—and I'm sure the Army wasn't training me for show business. As a matter of fact, I was an ambulance driver in the U.S. Army Ambulance Corps during World War I. Physical training was always my love. It was during some physical exercises that I fell upon a trick of muscle control that could prevent anybody—or for that matter a few people at the same time—from lifting me. I practiced for hours until I was able to counteract the muscles of any lifter or a would-be lifter.

When I was discharged I went back to the United States but always longed to return to France. I got my chance when I became an advance man for a stock company, which led to my becoming a contact man for the Associated American Retailers, who sent me to France.

I became acquainted with the sports editor of the Paris *Herald*. He liked my billiard playing and particularly my strange muscle control. He would bet on me and I would perform. The American colony—this was about 1922—used to hang around a little book store run by a lady from Maine or Vermont. Her name was Mrs. Beach. Among the regulars were Ernest Hemingway, Louis Bromfield, John Dos Passos, James Joyce, and Floyd Gibbons.

I returned to the United States after I contracted some lung condition, and to help cure it I worked as a sheep herder in the Utah mountains one winter. I also began to play a little semiprofessional basketball and was pretty good.

My health improved and I went to San Francisco where I continued to play basketball. One night there was a party at the Olympic Club and everybody who could sing, dance, or whatever got up and performed. I also got up and showed some of my antilifting tricks. A man came over and offered $75 for three days if I could do the same trick in his theater.

I prepared myself with a white leotard. I did those Grecian poses—the discus thrower, etcetera. That was the first half of the act. I say "act" even though I didn't really have an act. I had nothing but nerve and hunger, and when you're hungry you'll do most anything. So the first half of the act was the Grecian poses. I would then put on a pair of white pants, go out into the audience, and challenge anybody to lift me. I described myself as "the man nobody can lift." Volunteers came up to lift me, and I was in.

I finished the three days and the manager sent me to a manager of another theater and I began working around San Francisco, the small towns, and neighborhood theaters, working my way north into Canada.

In one theater the manager said John Ringling was out front and wanted to talk to me. This was about 1923. First thing Ringling wanted to know was whether the people who came up onstage to try to lift me were mine. I said no, I couldn't afford them. He then said he was coming back that night with four of his razorbacks (those were the big guys who put up the tents and pound the stakes).

When I asked for volunteers that night those four huskies came up. When I finished the act Ringling asked me how I would like to join the Ringling Brothers Circus. I wanted to and said so, but I had another week to go. I was told to join the company in San Francisco when I was through.

In Los Angeles I met a girl, Jeanine, and after three days' courtship we were married. We were in Dallas getting ready to fold for the season. We had only three more days to go when Mr. John—that's what we all called Ringling—called me into his office to meet a revue producer who was in town to open at the Texas State Fair. His name, I think, was Ernie Young. His trouble was that the women of Dallas wouldn't allow his star to open, and he was in a hole. He had caught the matinee and thought I could jump in. Mr. John was all for it and said that if I took the job he'd pay me for the three days.

So that's how I took Fatty Arbuckle's place in the Texas State Fair. While working this date, Young booked me for a club date in the hills. That was the craziest club date I ever had. I was picked up by a car filled with three big guys, all detectives from the Dallas Police Department. After about fifteen minutes we turned off into a dark path and there I was in the middle of a Ku Klux Klan gathering—white sheets, hoods, and everything. I did my act and I got $1000. That, plus what I got for pinch hitting for Fatty Arbuckle, saw me in the money. So I bought a car and we went off wildcatting again. I played the Wacos, the Port Arthurs, the Killeens, Temples, etcetera. I still didn't have a real act. In one spot I was the straight man in a burlesque show that ran six weeks. Then it was back to the joints as a single. I had just worked a show in Vernon, California, right outside of Los Angeles, and I was low, bitter, and discouraged. A few weeks before I was canceled in Pomona, and the way I was going I was a cinch to be canceled here too.

There was a motion picture actress on the bill, Ruth Stonehouse, a silent star of Essanay Pictures. She asked me what was the matter. I told her. She said the reason was that my best trick was to keep four men from lifting me, and I was finished after that, I had nothing that could follow it. She said that should be my finishing trick. She also asked what about that "little filly with you." I told her she was my wife. "Teach her a few tricks, she has a nice figure, make her part of your act." I did everything Miss Stonehouse told me and it worked out fine.

I wildcatted my way East again, stopping in all sorts of towns to show the local theater managers my news clippings and pictures. I offered to work for free if I didn't better the business of a year ago as shown on the manager's books. If I did better, I was to get 70 percent of the overage. This was in the silent movie days when a theater's average daily take was about $40.

I did my own ballyhoo. I gave passes to the storekeepers for free displays; visited the local firemen and police and challenged them to lift me; gave passes to the phone exchange operators who would pass the word about a new big show at the Bijou or whatever. I worked this way all through New Mexico, Arkansas, Mississippi, finally landing in Mobile, Alabama. The manager said that the local Keith house which was playing Paul Whiteman was murdering him. I talked him into gambling with me— no business-no pay—and he agreed. The theater had no stage so we put some benches up front and I worked there. We did better than well.

One day Jules Delmar, who did the Keith booking in the South, called on me and offered me the Delmar time. I took it. My first Delmar job was in Birmingham and we were off and running. Jeanine, my wife, was born in Birmingham so I could play it up big with the newspapers about local girl comes back to play her home town.

I made New York and my first date was a benefit for the Fire Depart-

Corelli with members of Worcester, Massachusetts, Police Department, in 1926, demonstrating his skill.

ment at Palm Gardens. Out of that benefit I got two years of solid work without even showing my act to the bookers. I was put into Proctor's 125th Street to show for a salary and that's all the showing I had to do. It was there that an incident happened that had everybody in vaudeville talking about it.

On the bill was George Whiting and his wife Sadie Burt, Diner and Brennan, a husband-and-wife team, Slim Timblin, and others. It was a warm June day and we were all on the fire escape waiting for the supper show. Next door was a Horton's ice cream factory. The foreman, who had seen the show, offered us some ice cream, which we all had. There was a truck in the alley loading 300-pound cans of ice cream. A big man, about six-foot-four and weighing about 280, was handling those cans with ease as he tossed them into the truck.

The foreman called him over and asked him how he'd like to make some extra money. "All you have to do is pick up that little fellow," he said, pointing to me. "Not here. Go to the show tonight and when he calls for volunteers, you go up."

The big walloper looked at me and laughed. "I pick heem up wid one-a hand."

That night when I called for volunteers he came onstage. He tried to lift me with the "committee." When that failed, he tried it alone. When that didn't work, I whispered to him to take off his coat and roll up his sleeves. He did that and also spat on his hands. After wiping them on his pants, he grabbed me again. He pushed me all over the stage trying to lift me, while the applause got bigger and bigger. Finally he stepped back, gasping and wiping his face. He turned toward the audience and puffed out, "Hey—Joe—dis-a-guy, he no bullsheet!" The howls of laughter must've been heard outside.

Slim Timblin, a shrewd pro, followed me. He started his act with his usual routine, "I'm not going to give you the sermon on the mount," and added "this ain't no bull—" cashing in on what preceded him.

That incident followed me all the rest of my career.

My next jobs took me to Buffalo, Elmira, Binghamton, etcetera. I worked all over the East, including Boston and Philadelphia. When you played Philadelphia, you played the Keith house. But you also had to play the Nixon Grand, the Allegheny, and the Broadway. On Sunday you had to play the Apollo in Atlantic City or you didn't get the Keith Theater.

The same system worked if you wanted to play Shea's in Buffalo. You also had to work Jamestown, Erie, Dunkirk, and all the rest of the towns or you didn't get the full weeks in Buffalo, Syracuse, and Rochester.

My first big-time date was the Maryland Theater in Baltimore. From then on it was all big time. I was being handled by Harry Romm. By this time I was known for getting publicity and the theater manager asked me if I would do some publicity before we opened. I went to the waterfront, taking along a photographer, got some help from the fire and police departments, and collected a number of fine photos. That afternoon all the photos were on easels in the lobby and out in front of the theater.

After the matinee I closed the intermission, a good spot for me. The manager came to me and said he would have to take me out of that spot because the star, Charlotte Greenwood, was complaining that they were still talking about the Corelli act when she came on. I said, okay, I'll close the show, and I did.

Next morning my agent told me that Miss Greenwood had complained to the New York office that my act was interfering with hers and she didn't want me on her bill in the Keith house in Washington, where we were due the following week. So I was taken off and shifted to the Imperial Theater in Montreal. The star there was Miss Ruby Norton.

The manager asked me, "How about some publicity?" I said, "I've just had it in Baltimore and I don't want to antagonize the star." The manager called over Miss Norton and told her what I had said. She replied, "Harry Romm also handles me. You just go ahead and do your publicity. If we do business, we'll both get the credit."

The next theater we played was in Portland, Maine. It was there that a young fellow named Jack Benny joined us. A nice, quiet fellow, a number-two act. He played the violin and told small jokes. There were some three or four similar acts around at that time, you know, stand-up comics who played the violin.

I was playing the Golden Gate Theater in San Francisco, a Pantages house, and Harry Houdini was playing the Keith Orpheum. I was told that Houdini had a blackboard at the Orpheum where people were encouraged to write questions. So I went over and wrote, "Is Alan Corelli, playing at the Golden Gate, a fake?" I returned to my theater and asked the manager to let me know if Houdini came into the house. Sure enough he did and I announced to my audience that I was honored by having the great Houdini in my audience and I invited him on my stage to test for himself my claims. He came on and I ran through my routine.

The next day I went over to the Orpheum and on the blackboard was Houdini's reply to my question: "I have been on the stage and watched Alan Corelli. He is not a fraud."

While working at the Brooklyn Albee I was offered a six-month route in Italy. I grabbed it. I opened in Milano, then on to Rome, Bologna, Genoa, more Italian cities; into France; then London and Germany.

I was working in Paris when Van Horn and Inez, a British roller-skating act on the bill, urged me to find work in London and wired their agent, Henry Sharick, recommending me. Sharick asked me to fly over and talk. When I came into his office Val Parnell was with him. I didn't know Parnell at that time except by reputation. He was the owner and booker of London's Palladium Theater.

They studied my press book and Parnell asked me jokingly if I could lift Sharick. He was a big man who looked like he weighed almost 300 pounds. I lifted him easily. There was laughter and more talk and I was offered the opening at the Holborn Empire in three weeks.

Parnell wired me in Paris that I was to open in Brighton rather than at the Holborn Empire and gave me the date and details. I arrived in Brighton a few days before I was to open. The papers were full of the big dinner that was to be held in the leading hotel in honor of a returning ambassador. It was to be attended by all the big people in Brighton and London, plus all the press.

I went to the hotel manager and told him I was an American entertainer who was to open at the local theater and offered to do a show at that big dinner for free. He welcomed the offer.

The papers the next day gave the ambassador one paragraph. They gave me three columns plus pictures. It boosted business at the theater when I opened. Parnell must've known all about it, for he called me and said I was to open at the Palladium right after I closed in Brighton. Then in rapid order I got most of the other London theaters and the provinces and had more offers than I can remember.

One night I'm ready for bed when I got a phone call from Eric Walheim, an agent, not the actor. He apologized for the late call and said that Sir Alfred Abrams had the Oxford football team at a party in his house and they were all talking about me. Could they pick us up and take us to his house, he wanted to know. They were all waiting and it would mean very much to him. I woke my wife. We got dressed and we were driven to Regent Road, where Sir Alfred lived. (I learned later he was the president of British Paramount.) We were shown into a large room that looked like a gambling house. It was full of well-dressed people playing roulette, chemin-de-fer, and other things. We were greeted and then escorted to another large room with a platform at one end. Then Sir Alfred called for order in the gambling room and told everyone the promised entertainment was about to begin. The big room where I was to do my act filled up and I went to work. I took on the whole football team and anybody else who wanted to try.

After it was all over, one of the guests holding chips in both hands offered them to my wife as a gift. She asked what to do with them. I told her to cash them in. There was $800 worth. We had a bite and prepared to leave. On the way out Sir Alfred's man gave me an envelope. I opened it when I got back to the hotel and there was a check for 250 guineas, or about $1250. I called Walheim immediately and told him I would send him his commission. He refused it and said he was sending me a gift. He'd been trying to sell acts to Sir Alfred for a long time.

After I returned to the United States my wife became ill and divorced me.

I taught two Presidents of the United States how to shake hands without getting hurt. It was at the annual White House correspondents' function. Just before the end of the show the actors all went into a private room to be introduced to the President. That was the gimmick. You didn't get paid, except expenses, but you got to be introduced.

Anyway, there was President Truman rubbing his hand. Dr. Vaughn, the White House doctor, came by and Truman called him and said, "I want you to take a look at this hand. It's so swollen I can't bend it. This afternoon I had about fifty shit kickers [that's what he called them] from Kansas shaking my hand as if they wanted to take it back to Kansas with them."

I said to Truman, "I can show you how to shake hands with a hundred people and never get hurt." He said, "Show me." As I started to, another man came in, put one arm around the President's shoulder and another around mine, and asked, "What're you fellows pumping for?" Truman told him the story. The man said he had the same trouble. I offered to show him also how to shake hands without getting hurt. It was at the point that Merriman Smith, the president of the correspondents' group, came in with a scroll for me and asked Truman to sign it. Truman signed at once. I asked the other man to sign it too. He began to turn it over to sign it on the back and I said, "No, please sign it on the front." He did. And there it is hanging on my wall with two signatures: Harry S Truman and Dwight D. Eisenhower.

I had some club dates and some full weeks in the forties, but vaudeville was on its last legs. I finally decided I'd had it and joined Theater Authority—that's the joint body of all the talent unions that pass on benefits. No actors are allowed to do a benefit unless Theater Authority clears it.

Today I'm happy with the Friars. I'm remarried and my wife and I travel all over the world, and that's that.

JEAN DALRYMPLE

JEAN DALRYMPLE was a dark-eyed beauty who went from a Wall Street brokerage firm into vaudeville, where she became a headliner. Though at first only a supernumerary in sketches, she became such an excellent actress that the Keith office put her name up in lights.

Her real show-business reputation, however, rests on her production of acts for others. She hired unknown actors to tour vaudeville in her packages. Among these unknowns were Cary Grant and Jimmy Cagney.

There was a boy in my life, Don Jarrett, who was in love with me and it was through him that I went into vaudeville and show business. At the time, back in the middle 1920s, I was a secretary for a Wall Street firm of brokers, Dominick and Dominick, and though I was only fifteen, sixteen years old, I was getting $55 a week.

Don Jarrett, who used to get parts in plays that immediately failed, had been out of work for a long time. He finally got a job with a vaudeville act, Thomas E. Shea and Company, that consisted of a series of parts from various plays that Shea had played with great success in the past. Among them were *The Miser, Cardinal Richelieu, Bells.* All the sketches were to be done on a set that would serve as Shea's drawing room when he was introduced. A young girl in the company was to play the maid and all the other feminine roles in the little scenes. The young actress hired for the part got married and her husband didn't want her to leave on a long tour. The company was set for an Orpheum route, opening in Sioux City, and Don was also reluctant to leave me for that length of time because he was in love with me. (I liked him very much too.)

When the little actress withdrew, Don suggested to the Sheas that I be asked to play the feminine parts. The Sheas, who had seen me with Don many times, liked me. Up to then I had never been on a stage, even as an amateur. But they said if I could learn the lines and read them, they would listen and decide.

I didn't particularly want to become an actress. I liked my work in Wall Street, but I also liked Don, though I wasn't in love with him. You see, he was the first man to fall in love with me, and that was quite a thing. Anyway, I read for the Sheas. They liked what they heard and offered me $100 a week.

Though I didn't particularly want to be an actress, I did want to be a writer. So here, I thought, was an opportunity. I could gather material traveling around the country while Thomas E. Shea paid my way plus $100 a week. So I asked Dominick and Dominick for a six-month leave of absence and got it. And late in August, just before my birthday, on September 2, we opened in Sioux City, Iowa.

That was my first appearance on a professional stage, and everybody was extremely casual about it. In fact, we had hardly arrived in Sioux City and gotten settled in the hotel when Don Jarrett, carrying a golf bag and clubs, said, "There's a wonderful golf course here. Leave your stuff alone. Shea's dresser will take care of the trunk and hang your things." Now Don, an excellent golfer, had always wanted me to learn to play golf, so off we went. Me, a bundle of nerves, and Don, cool and calm.

We finally headed back for the theater about 3:30 P.M., though we weren't to go on until that evening. We were a big act, an important act on the bill. We were sixth on the program. It was about a half hour before showtime, when the headliners on the bill, Al Herman and Jack Rose, excellent comedians, came to me and explained that they had to have somebody work with them in an afterpiece, and since I was the only girl on the bill, I was it.

Don, hearing this, flatly said, "No, she can't do it." I said, "Let me hear it. I want to know what this is all about. Maybe I can do it." They asked me if I knew any French. Well, I knew a few words. They said I was supposed to be a French girl and they outlined a short sketch which ended up by my embracing Jack Rose. They would never have allowed me to embrace Al Herman, a black man, or rather a white man in blackface. It was unthinkable in those days. So I was to embrace Jack Rose while I said, "Je t'adore, je t'adore," a few times. At which Al Herman called out, "Shut the door, shut the door, you damn fool! Can't you hear the girl?" And that was the end of the afterpiece. It was fun. The audience laughed and applauded. It was a tremendous pleasure.

The papers the next day were laudatory. One critic wrote, "A very pretty young French girl with a good sense of timing was a very valuable asset. We couldn't find any mention of her name in the program so we cannot identify her better."

The tour took us five and a half months. From Sioux City we went to Omaha, Winnipeg, Vancouver, Portland, Seattle, San Francisco, Bakersfield, Sacramento, Salt Lake City, Denver, and Chicago, where we disbanded. Oh, I've got to tell you about Minneapolis. I got a wire from the Keith home office: "The act is so successful, we are putting your name up in lights as a Christmas present." I couldn't leave the Radisson Hotel soon enough to dash over to the theater to see for myself. And there it was: "All this week—Don Jarrett and Jean Darrwiper"—or something like that. I couldn't wait to get the manager to change that spelling. You see, I didn't know anything about publicity. They had to make up stories about me—the girl with the unpronounceable name—because I never gave them anything, and very few pictures. And Don Jarrett didn't help me.

I went back to my old job at Dominick and Dominick. I had been sending back snapshots and news items, so I was greeted effusively. It seemed that nobody had ever done this in the history of Wall Street.

Don was again out of work and couldn't get a job. I thought he was very witty. He had written a number of things for Hugh Herbert, a well-known sketch writer of the time, but had never gotten any credit for them, though he got paid. I had an idea for a sketch, an act. I could write it and maybe we could play it together. I told him what my idea was and he thought it was very good. But by this time I was getting $75 a week as a secretary and no longer wanted to leave my job. You see, I had a terrific memory, I had total recall, and it was a great advantage to me. I'm sorry I don't have it anymore.

I suggested to Don that he find a suitable girl, try out the sketch, and let me look at it. The act, or sketch, was for three people—two men and a girl. Even though Don was in love with me, he was always a little annoyed, perhaps even a little resentful. Here he was a pro, and who was I—a little girl from Wall Street—always coming up with the ideas. Many times I criticized him and changed the things he wrote. So his resentment was understandable. But I liked this man very much and wanted to keep him in good humor.

Anyway, he finally got a girl, Constance Robinson. She was very funny but completely wrong for the part. But by this time Don had acquired an agent, Max Tishman, and both he and Don wanted her. We got another young man, Al Mathews, who was very nice, to complete the company. The act opened out in Long Island and it didn't go at all. I

Jean Dalrymple. When she finally got headline billing, they misspelled her name.

had previously cautioned them against using a set with a scrim in the middle that lit up when action occurred behind it. Even though I had no technical knowledge, I didn't believe that people would laugh at action taking place behind a scrim. So now they were put to the expense of changing it. The first time the act played without the scrim it went over big.

The sketch played all over the small time and was a big success. Then somebody in the Keith office who had seen me in that afterpiece in Sioux City, and apparently had been impressed, said to Tishman, "If you get Jean Dalrymple in the part we'll back the act on the big time."

We broke the act in in Babylon, Long Island, and it did great. From there we went into Loew's State, a big house, perhaps too big a house for our act. Then came a Brooklyn theater, a Newark theater, and finally Keith's big house in Philadelphia. In the next day's papers we walked away with all the notices; the emphasis was on my comedic abilities. From then on there was no difficulty getting bookings, all big time. The act was now called Don Jarrett and Jean Dalrymple in "Just a Fall."

99

We were always slotted third or fifth on the bill, depending how many other acts were on it.

The act was like this: There's a street scene and Don is out there wheeling our baby when he runs into an old friend of his, Al Mathews, and invites him inside the house for dinner. He then comes inside the house and tells me he's invited his old friend Al Mathews for dinner that night. I glare at him and say, "He's not having dinner here, not while I'm conscious." (By the way, that was the birth of the expression, "not while I'm conscious.") You see, I don't like the Al Mathews character because he had tried to influence Don against marrying me. So we argue and I bring in his family and he brings in my family. We have a big family fight and the audience is howling.

Now Don goes out and tells his friend he's sorry he can't have him over to dinner because the stove blew up and suggests that they go down to the corner for a drink—oh, no, not a drink, because this is during Prohibition—it was go down to the corner for a bite to eat. Now Don wheels the carriage to the door to put the baby inside. When he opens the door, I fall out. I've been listening at the door. When I see Al Mathews

Don Jarrett and Jean (Dalrymple).

Cary Grant, né Archie Leach, got his start as an actor when he was hired by Jean Dalrymple for a sketch.

I say, "Why, Al Mathews, of all people! Am I glad to see you." And the audience falls down laughing. And I turn to Don—"Why didn't you tell me?" So there I am putting poor Don on the other end of the stick and the house is hysterical. There is more—but finally Don looks out at the audience and says, "What must all those people out there think of us?" and I say, "Why, they all do the same thing themselves"—and we go off.

We played that sketch all over, until vaudeville ended. We played the Keith-Orpheum, Interstate, Delmar, and Poli time with it. But let me tell you of at least one theater where we died. It was the Maryland Theater, Baltimore. On the bill with us were Victor Moore and Emma Littlefield in "Change Your Act, or Back to the Woods"; Ruth Etting; and Will and Gladys Ahern. We followed them and they were so funny and so great we just couldn't make it.

Well, having learned that we could write sketches that could play vaudeville, we decided that was what we would do. We'd write sketches and then find actors who could play them and Max Tishman would book them.

We wrote one act that called for a good-looking man who wasn't too brash, who could maybe sing a little, and who could certainly read lines.

We notified the talent agencies and they sent us many applicants. I didn't like any of them. Finally one lad did come in and he was just right. I wanted him but my partners, Don Jarrett and Max Tishman, did not. Don was particularly indignant. "Do you know what his last job was? A stilt walker in Coney Island!" I had to fight with Tishman and Don. I insisted and finally we hired him. The act wasn't exactly big time. It was called "The Woman Pays," with Jack Janistar as the lead name. It played mostly the family time, some of the Junior Orpheum time, some Keith houses, and some Proctor houses. The actor I fought to hire? He went into the movies—changed his name from Archie Leach to Cary Grant.

I was writing a sketch called "In the Park" and was looking for a young man who could move, read lines, and maybe dance a bit. I went to see the *Greenwich Follies* to catch Al Herman, with whom I had done that afterpiece long ago in Sioux City. In that show one of the chorus boys was a short, attractive, fast-moving, red-headed lad, a good dancer who fascinated me. I got word to him to call our office. He did and we hired him. The sketch played the Poli and Delmar time. Later I was told he had bought or acquired an act from Pat Rooney, "At the Newstand," and played vaudeville with it. He later understudied Lee Tracy in a Jed Harris production and then went into pictures. That was Jimmy Cagney.

Once I left Dominick and Dominick, that Wall Street firm, and went into show business, my stepsister and stepmother never spoke to me again. They, like so many others, considered the theater a den of iniquity.

Let me tell you that in vaudeville I found the most family life I've ever seen. Many a performer had his wife and children with him. Entire families would tour. In fact, there were many family acts that played vaudeville. If there were infants, and both parents were onstage, either an older child or another vaudevillian on the bill would babysit. It was pleasant and wonderful. And speak about morality—words used today in ordinary speech were not only barred from the vaudeville stages, but if used, would result in an act's immediate cancellation. Vaudeville was considered family entertainment and nothing that could possibly be offensive to a family was allowed. It was the healthiest life I've ever led.

Later I became more interested in what vaudevillians called the legit —I was associated in producing Broadway plays and today I'm still involved in productions.

Vaudeville? Well, it was part of another era, a very pleasant and rose-colored era.

JACK DURANT

ABOUT SIX-FOOT-FIVE *and darkly handsome, Jack Durant bears a resemblance to Clark Gable. He achieved his vaudeville reputation when he teamed up with Frank Mitchell, an acrobat, who was short, sturdy, and a good foil. With superb timing they did a knockabout comedy act that provoked hilarity from the audience. While their acrobatic feats were noteworthy, it was their comedy slapstick that made the team outstanding. Durant's description of his and Mitchell's experiences, both here and in England, gives a sharp picture of vaudeville in the 1920s and 1930s.*

I was doing acrobatics in school when I was called over and introduced to Bud Aarons [a small-time acrobat]. He wanted to know how much I weighed. I said fifty-nine pounds. He said, "That's great, I want to use you as a top mounter. But how am I going to take you on the road? You go to school, don't you? Can you get out of school?" I said I thought I could, that I would speak to my grandmother. So I asked her. I told her I had a chance for a job if I could get out of school and promised I would send her a dollar a week. "A dollar a week?" she said, her eyes opening. "Where's the school?" Through an interpreter she convinced the authorities that whatever I could earn was needed. Anyway, I was able to get off. I was nine years old.

I went back to this chap and said I was ready. He said, "You know, I'm afraid you're too young to work in vaudeville. I'll have to dress you like a girl." I was outraged. "Don't worry," he said, "we'll fix you up with a blond wig." And he did and off we went to Chicago. I told my grandmother I was in show business but not to tell my parents where I was.

Jack Durant at nine years of age. "They dressed me in girls' clothes so I could work in vaudeville—"

So we got to Chicago and began working in different theaters. It was terrible. I wore tights, but half the time I forgot to pull the strings so the tights would fall down. Aarons would always yell at me—"Pull the strings! pull the strings!" One day we had about fifteen minutes to show time and we were practicing and his pants split. So he rushed to the dressing room and sewed them together again. Only he couldn't sew very well. For part of the act I was on the floor and he would step over me and then reach down to lift me. When I looked up his pants had split again and his things were hanging out. So I began laughing. He growled at me and tried to lift me but I couldn't stop laughing. We finally finished. Oh, it was awful. In the dressing room he started to choke me, calling me all sorts of names, when there was a knock on the door. It was the manager. Aarons said to me—this I remember well—"Stay here, I'll choke you later." We were canned. I forget how many theaters in Chicago threw us out.

I finally managed to remember about my tights and he got his pants fixed and we began to do okay.

Aarons wouldn't let me eat because he was afraid I'd get too heavy. He gave me chocolates for energy but little real food. I had to sneak food when I got away from him. We stayed away for nine months. I got $8 a week. George Hamid saw us and asked if we would like to join his act. He particularly wanted me because I was so light he figured I'd make a good top-mounter. He was going back to New York to open at the Flatbush Theater in Brooklyn and he offered to take us along and pay our fare. By that time I had saved $180.

So I came back to New York. I walked past my house. My father was sitting on the stoop. I said "Hello Pop." He looked up. "You bum," he said—"wait, wait—go into the house—I'll give you . . ." So I said, "Don't get crazy. I got money here." I showed it and he said, "You stole it." I said "No, I'm an actor. I'm working." He took the money and I saw him counting it. "All right, my boy," he said, "come in and eat—eat—when are you going away again?"

So now we worked for George Hamid. When we were working in Atlantic City it was hot and to save money we slept on the sand under the Boardwalk. I remember Hamid pointing to the Steel Pier and saying, "Someday I'm going to own that." And you know, twenty years later he did. And to this day I still work the Steel Pier one week each summer. George Hamid, the father, is dead but his son operates it. You know the Steel Pier? It is the only place left in the whole country that still has vaudeville. They play the biggest stars of that year. Pay $35,000 for two days' work and $20,000 for one day.

Finally I had had enough of this acrobatic tumbling act and said I'd like to try something else. My partner was mad and in one trick he threw me harder than usual and I landed badly and broke my wrist. That was my opening.

I met Frank Mitchell, who was a dancer. We worked out a little and he suggested I put my acrobatics into dancing. I tried it with a time step. It was great. I became fast. I was like lightning. I did splits, wheels, taps—you name it, but very fast. I auditioned for one group, "Dancing Shoes," and the lady who owned it hired me for $45 a week. I was with the act for one and a half years. That was about 1924. We played the Pantages Circuit; all the little theaters, all the dumps. That's how I went from an acrobat to a dancer. I then auditioned for the *Greenwich Village Follies* and got the job but the lady I was working for killed the deal. She pleaded with Rufus LeMaire, who was doing the hiring for the show, that she needed me in her act and asked him not to hire me. Well, he liked her and I didn't get the job.

I was working at Fox's Folly in Brooklyn when some guy also on the bill came to me and said his boss, Mae West, wanted to see me. She asked if I would like to work in her act—she would pay me double what I was getting. I didn't take it because the girl who owned the act I was in liked me very much and I liked her.

One day I hurt my ankle and laid off about twelve weeks. It was then I decided to leave the act. When my ankle healed, I was told about some auditions at the Paramount Theater for a unit that was to go on the road. I went over. The unit was to be called "A Little Bit of Erin." By that time I had acquired a manager, who told me when it came to money to shut up, he would do the talking. And what do you think—I got $325. "Don't worry about it," said my manager. "They're a picture company, they can afford it." That's when Frank Mitchell saw me again. Let me go back a little. When I was with "Dancing Shoes," playing on the West Coast, a boy singer in the unit asked me to go with him while he auditioned for a Fanchon and Marco unit. They booked all the theaters on the West Coast. Well, like Marco said no to the boy, but then he wanted to know if I was the lad who had jumped over seven guys in the dancing act. (They always remembered me for that.) I said I wasn't interested and he told me that if I changed my mind when I got back to New York I should send him a wire and he would pay my fare and give me $300 for the big theaters and $225 for the smaller ones.

That was a year and a half before I ran into Frank Mitchell at the Paramount. Frank said to me, "You remember that guy Mike Marco who wanted to use you on the Coast—he's here at the Waldorf. Why don't you call him?" I did. When I identified myself, he asked if I was the fellow who jumped over seven people and I said yes. He said, "If you want to work for me meet me at the Marcus Loew office," and he mentioned the time. When I got there Marcus Loew and Mike Marco were waiting. Loew said to me, pointing at Marco, "That man will make you a star if you stick with him." I signed. Outside I said to Marco, "I know another guy who works like me." Marco wanted to know where he could see him. I said, "He's working in the Audubon. His name is Frank Mitchell of Moore and Mitchell." So we took a subway up there. Marco paid the admission. I walked up to the box office after him and told the girl we were agents. She said, "Then you don't have to pay," and gave me back the money. I followed Marco and gave him the money, telling him what I had done. He said, "Hey, kid, I like you—we'll get along great."

Marco saw Mitchell. Went back and hired him. But he also had to hire his wife. "That'll be all right," he said. "She sings like a Sophie Tucker and I'll be able to use her. Anyway," he said to me, "you make up your mind what you want, to work with Mitchell or alone. And I'll see you both on the Coast in two weeks."

We got to the Coast and were sitting in the balcony of the Loew's State in Los Angeles when Marco came along. He greeted us and asked if we were ready to go to work. Mitchell said, "Sure," and Marco said, "Okay, you open Monday at the Uptown Theater." I was shocked. I started to yell at Mitchell, "You just booked us and we don't have an act. What did you do?" Mitchell began to phumpha—well, we had to go in. And we did. We did about five or six minutes and we were terrible. But that's all we had had time to put together. We didn't think of working together. It looked like we were dead.

I said to Mitchell, "You know, I have an idea. You're short, I'm tall. We can do comedy. I can do straight comedy and we both can dance, maybe we can put something together. I think we can be funny." He said, "I just closed with a guy on the Keith time. We were next to closing and we got $275—why do I need this?" I pointed out we were each getting more than that now. He said he wanted to talk it over with his wife. Next day he came back. "What did you have in mind when you said we'd work together?" he asked. I told him I would do the act that his old partner Moore had done. Only Moore was sixty years old and I was a young man. We could add some things, and then we'd see. From the first time we tried it we were sensational. A lady came backstage to tell us how much she liked us and how would we like to go into Hit the Deck, which was then playing in Los Angeles. We didn't know anything about shows so I said we were already getting $1500—we weren't. She said she would pay us $1000, and it was only one show a night. A Broadway show.

Fanchon and Marco released us after we made a deal whereby we'd play for them an extra five or six weeks after the show—and we did. We stayed with *Hit the Deck* for a year and a half.

Now it's 1927 and the stories about us being so great are reaching New York. The Morris office comes to us and offers to represent us and get us the Palace. Well, we take it but before we open at the Palace we decide we'll break in the act at the Savoy, a small theater in New York. In *Hit the Deck* we had worked all through the show and it wasn't until the end that we did our knockabout comedy. And we were sensational. But now we wanted to get the feel of an audience. We'd forgotten that we had been adding to our act from time to time and that we really had only ten good minutes. If we went to twelve we'd die. And that's what happened. We went in and did twenty-five minutes at the Savoy and we died. The Palace's Arthur Willi tore up our contract. The William Morris office dropped us. They said we were a Western act, not an Eastern act. So there we were—big stars who couldn't get a job.

Then one day another agent, Murray Fial of Morris and Fial, asked us if we'd sign with him if he could get us out of the contract with the Morris office. He told us he believed in us even if the Morris office didn't. Well, there was a big fight but we got out. First date Fial got us was the Capitol Theater in New York. We did only ten minutes and we were a tremendous hit. The applause was like heavy rain on a roof. That was the birth of Mitchell and Durant as a big-time act.

Word went through the whole industry. Martin Beck gave Arthur Willi orders to get that act for the Palace. Willi explained that we had flopped so they had let us go. But they signed us again. They gave us the big pitch—that the Palace was real vaudeville, two-a-day, not a picture house. It was the big time. They put us on the road to play RKO houses for five weeks to get used to it and then into the Palace.

It was a Monday afternoon and we were next to closing. Bill Tilden, the tennis player, was on ahead of us and Ben Bernie and his orchestra were to close. When we walked off that stage we were a big hit. And if we'd taken one more bow, they'd have had enough of us. Now this was Bernie's second week and he was in a hurry to get on. He ordered the curtain up on our applause, figuring that would get him a good start for his second week. But just because the curtain went up on our bow and applause, the applause for us got bigger and bigger. We had to come back for another bow. In the meantime Bernie was playing one chorus—then another chorus—but our applause wouldn't go down. Bernie was yelling, "Who are those guys? What the hell, they're ruining my second week." And with that he dropped his curtain. We were back in our dressing

Palladium marquee, billing Mitchell and Durant "The Greatest Comedy Act in the World."

room. If Bernie hadn't come in on our applause so soon we'd have been a hit, but not the big smash that we were.

Our reputation now spread all over vaudeville until it reached London. Burns and Allen and Jack Osterman were there. They read the notices and suggested us for the Palladium. At first we didn't want to go. We were already set for a George White's *Scandals,* and with rehearsals and all we didn't want to do the Palladium, but we were talked into going for one week. As we passed the Palladium I was shocked to see the big sign out front: Mitchell and Durant, the Greatest Comedy Act in the World —and I was frightened. Nobody is the greatest in the world. We were just a couple of acrobats and they were killing us before we even started.

Burns and Osterman took us aside and asked us what kind of jokes we did. We told them a few. They were outraged and pleaded with us not to do jokes. We had been brought over on their recommendation, they said, and if we did our kind of jokes they'd never play the Palladium again. When we opened, we followed Burns' and Osterman's advice—we didn't do any jokes. It was only half a house and we got a so-so reception.

The next show we are downstairs getting ready and the two guys ahead of us—Erricson and Brown, I think were their names—were killing the people. Boy, were they getting laughs and hands. We couldn't stand it. We put our hands over our ears. We even turned the water on full to kill the sounds of the big smash that was being registered onstage. Here we were, "the Greatest Comedy Act in the World" according to the sign outside, and these guys were getting the big hands. We began screaming at each other when I suddenly stopped and said to Mitchell, "What're we fighting for? We haven't even been on yet."

We went on and did our act and went off to loud razzing. Well, that was that. The manager ran after us yelling, "Go out there and take your bow." We said, "What do you mean go out and take a bow? They're razzing us." They were yelling, "Core—Core—" something we'd never heard before. "They're not razzing you," yelled the manager, "they're cheering you." And that's what they were doing. "Core" meant encore. But whoever heard that where we played before!

When the papers came out the next day the notices were sensational. We were described as the greatest comedy act to ever play the Palladium.

We came back to New York and went into the *Scandals* and after one year we went back into vaudeville—all the theaters—and then into Earl Carroll's *Vanities*. I might add that in those days, 1928 or so, we could play almost ninety weeks straight in New York. We played the RKO houses, the Loew houses, Fox, and so on. What was great in those days was that every act was different. We had impersonators. The Diamond Brothers tried to do our kind of act and got hurt. The Three Sailors tried to do it and they got hurt. *Variety* said we had more impersonators than Al Jolson.

In the *Vanities*, Will Mahoney was the star. We had a sketch in which we did our act. Now Mahoney didn't want us in the show. (He was getting $5200 a week and was worth it—he was great.) In fact, he threatened to walk out if we stayed, but his manager whispered to him and he calmed down. But he insisted that Mitchell and Durant were to take only one bow—that was all. Just one bow.

The *Vanities* opens and in the scene preceding ours Bill Demarest plays an important producer, sitting at a desk, and in comes Lillian Roth —she was a knockout then—holding a little dog. She puts the dog on the desk and starts complaining about something and the dog begins peeing on the desk. Demarest blows his lines and shrieks, "Get that damn dog out of here!" Lillian picks the dog up—the pee still coming out on the desk and on the floor. I didn't know a little dog could have so much pee in him. Demarest is yelling, "Get outa here and take that dog with you." Now we are to follow that, but how do you follow such a thing? The audience is still screaming with laughter. We come in through the window and tell Demarest we are the writers and emphasize it by hitting the middle of the desk where all the pee is and it splashes. The audience is now laying in the aisles. Then I begin cartwheels all over the stage. I stop and once again hit the middle of the desk and put my hand out to Demarest, offering to shake hands. He refuses so I go back to cartwheels, keeping an eye on the pool of pee on the floor and managing to land right in the middle of it. And wow! Did that audience scream! I get up, again offering my hand to Demarest, and when he refuses, I wipe my hand on the curtain. Mitchell says, "You know you can't do that," and slaps me. I slap him back. We are now right into our act—knockabout. I hit him, he hits me, etcetera. The audience doesn't know we are doing an act and the yells and cheers can be heard outside. Well, we finish and take our one bow. There are more yells so we take another bow. Then Earl Carroll says, "Take another bow," and just then Will Mahoney's voice can be heard shouting from upstairs—"Stop them, stop them. They're supposed to take just one bow." Next day Walter Winchell wrote of the *Vanities*, "What kind of a show can that be when two acrobats run away with it?"

Vaudeville was full of specialists. And each was great in whatever he or she was doing. Vaudeville was great. Let's say you did one show in the morning and you were bad. You said to yourself, I'll try something else in the next show. The more shows you did, the better you got. By the end of the week you had a sock act routined. It was a training ground.

Today there is no place to be bad. Of course comics who work in nightclubs today have it easier than the comics who played vaudeville. In a nightclub, if in the first few minutes nothing happens, nobody gets upset. The people are eating and drinking anyway, so the comic can lose two or three minutes and survive. But in the theater you have to get them in the first minute or you're dead.

Take Will Rogers. He told jokes and spun a rope. If the jokes died, he had something going for him. W. C. Fields, a juggler, also did jokes, and if they missed, he had his juggling. In the meantime he learned timing. Then there was Fred Allen—all these guys had great timing. They learned it by doing all these different things. But today there's no such chance. Today you go out, and bing—

After *Vanities* Mitchell and I went out to Hollywood for Fox to do a picture, *Stand Up and Cheer*. Shirley Temple was in it. We followed that with five or six more pictures. Then I decided that was enough, I'd go back to vaudeville. But Mitchell stayed behind, went into real estate, and is still doing well. I went back to do a single. Herman Timberg wrote me an act for which I paid him $10,000. I would come out in a top hat and a cutaway coat—boy, was I dressed up! I made Frank Fay look like a bum. I opened in Bayonne—and nothing. I was so bad I thought they were coming up after me. I was supposed to talk like Fay—but it didn't work. I then decided I'd do my own act. No more having anybody write for me.

Left to right: Sid Field, famous British comedian; Jack Durant; Bob Hope; Field's manager. "At the time," said Durant, "I knew Bob Hope would never make it."

One day I met Lew Brown on the street and he said I was just the guy for *Yokel Boy*. I took it and went into rehearsal. Brown watched me and said, "Jack, you're doing Gable." One word led to another and I said, "Pay me for the two weeks and let me outta here. What you want is that guy around the corner at the Gaiety, not me." Two days later he hired that guy. It was Phil Silvers.

A few days later I was asked to go back to the Palladium, to open the next Monday. And this was Tuesday. I took a boat to Southhampton, and then a plane to London on Monday. Got to the theater at six o'clock, went on the same night, and was a hit. I guess it was meant to be. Harry Foster, the big agent, came back. I was told if he came back you were a hit. If he didn't—take the next boat home.

I was there for two weeks, then Liverpool, and the provinces. I took a holiday in Paris and came back to London. I was walking in Piccadilly Circus when somebody yelled, "Jack—don't move. Stay there." I waited and Foster came over to me. "What're you doing here?" I said, "I just got in—why?" "Why? You open in Blackpool tonight." "So—I'll be there. What is it? A half-hour?" I thought it was like Brooklyn from New York or something. Foster said, "No, it's five hours away. But never mind, you'll open at the Palladium again tonight." I stayed there for sixteen weeks, broke a record.

Soon a guy comes up to me and says, "Don't you want front-page publicity? They love you here. Can you swim?" "Sure," I tell him. "Well," he says, "we're going to say you're going to swim the Channel." "You're crazy," I say, but agree to practice by swimming in the Thames. And they take pictures and everything.

Now I am doing seven shows a night—at The Hoban Empire, London Casino, Trocadero, Latin Casino. I get around the different places and make it. And who's following me? Bob Hope. He wants to know how I'm doing it, what makes me tick. One night in the Palladium Bob is out in my audience and I bring him on. But nobody knows who he is. Then I introduce his wife, Dolores, and she gets a bigger hand. Next day Bob takes me to eat with him at the Barclay House, where he's staying, and asks me a lot of questions about how I do this and that. By the way he is asking me I know he'll never make it.

One day years later I'm in Bob's house in Palm Springs and I say, "Do you remember how you asked me all those questions?" Hope looks up and says, "If this wasn't my house, I'd walk out on you." But he is a nice guy.

I received a wire from Billy Rose to do a show in the *Aquacade*. He had read the stories about my practicing to swim the Channel and he believed them. Rose's idea was good, but not for me. I'm allergic to cold water. It was October. So I went into Loew's State instead.

The Palace? Mitchell and I closed the two-a-day at the Palace and we played it ten times. We played there every time we had some open time. But you know what happened to the Palace. It became small time and I never played it again.

SYLVIA FROOS

SYLVIA FROOS *began as a child performer who sang popular songs in an audience-pleasing fashion. She learned her craft well and as she grew up it was apparent that she really could sing. More importantly, she could "sell" a song. Between her "straight" singing she did impressions of other better-known stars of the period, chiefly Maurice Chevalier.*

She is no longer in show business but is an active volunteer worker for various charitable organizations.

Bob Martini was putting on a kiddie show, a Kid's Kabaret. I was in the first grade, but I was asked to go into it. I mean, my mother was asked to put me in it.

I was about seven—and somebody told my mother to take me up to Irving Berlin's music company so I could pick out songs. My mother went herself and found songs suitable for me. Our first date was in Baltimore, a split week. I was the youngest member of the Kid's Kabaret company, and I wasn't allowed to appear because I was too young. After that we came back to New York. This was about 1920. I did benefit shows and went to the Professional Children's School. Then I went on the Loew Circuit as a single and traveled all around the country. My mother traveled with me. If it wasn't my mother, it was my sister. It was in 1931 that I appeared at the Palace. The Marx Brothers were the headliners. I was fourth on the bill. I was asked to stay until the end so Zeppo could chase me around the back. They wanted somebody the audience would recognize, so I was it. It was very funny.

For a time I had my own show—that is, a radio show on sustaining*

* Sustaining—an unsponsored radio show.

Sylvia Froos in 1927 in Duluth, Minnesota, as a child vaudeville star known as the "Little Princess of Song."

—and I became a bigger box office name. My vaudeville billing was "Little Princess of Song"—don't laugh, I didn't pick it. When I grew up they dropped the "Little" and I was billed as the "Princess of Song."

I did all the Keith houses, also the Loew houses. At that time Albee was no longer alive, I think, and no one was issuing stern orders to performers not to play competitive theaters if they wanted to play the Keith houses. Besides, they weren't Keith theaters anymore, they were RKO, which I suppose was the same thing.

Later I did a Paramount unit. Incidentally, Vincente Minnelli—Liza's father—was with the Borris Morros Paramount units as a scenic designer.

Then I went to California and was in Shirley Temple's first big movie, *Stand Up and Cheer*. We both had to go to the Los Angeles courthouse to have our contracts approved. Making a movie was occasionally fun, but we had to spend most of the time with our teacher because if you were of school age you had to be coached, or rather taught, by a teacher hired by the studio. Movies were okay but I really liked to see them more than to be in them. For just a little scene—maybe walking to a door and opening it—you sometimes had to do it six or seven times. And it was so boring.

I loved vaudeville—the audiences were so wonderful. They wanted to be entertained—there was no distraction. I played with most of the big acts of the day. I remember a very funny team, Rubin and Haley— Benny Rubin and Jack Haley. We were on the same bill at the Palace Theater in Chicago. They were the headliners, next to closing. I also worked with Buddy Rogers and Paul Whiteman when he had the Rhythm Boys—with Bing Crosby. Usually you got along with all the people on the same bill, but some you liked more than others. Did I know or guess that this Crosby guy would make it so big? Don't be silly. I didn't know, and neither did Whiteman or anybody else on the bill.

I worked with Bill Robinson when I was nine years old. There was Will Ahern and his wife Gladys, both very funny with their rope spinning and fast gags. I knew them well.

I appeared in London and Dublin. In London it was at the Victoria Palace—a wonderful theater with wonderful audiences. In Dublin, let me see—it was a big modern theater, about 1935–36—I can't remember its name but it was comparable to the New York Paramount. They say you never forget the names of the theaters where you were a big hit. Maybe this means I wasn't a big hit in Dublin. But look, it was almost forty years ago and I can't remember everything. In the mid-thirties vaudeville was practically dead here but in London it was booming. The Palladium was packing them in. It was the place to go. I was booked into the London Victoria Palace by the man who owned the theater. He had caught me here in the United States and was planning to compete with the Palladium with top-line American vaudeville acts, and I was one.

As a child I did the current pops. I remember when I was in New Orleans working at the Sutton Theater for the Loew Circuit—I think that was its name. One afternoon some ladies complained that I was dancing onstage—you know, moving around. In those days children could stand up and sing in theaters in New Orleans, but they couldn't dance or even move around. So I wasn't permitted to continue at the theater. I was brokenhearted and frightened. My mother said not to worry and the manager also said everything would be straightened out. After all, I was a child, and I looked up to these grownups. We went to court and the judge wanted to know what I did. And what do you think? He had them put me on top of his desk, right in front of him, so I could show him. And I sang a song. At that time I was doing the mother song from

"Pal of My Cradle Days," which was very touching. The judge said to the manager and the ladies who had complained, "I see nothing wrong in this little lady's song. I only ask if she ever finds a Daddy song that she please sing it for me. Case dismissed."

In a little city in Alabama I was arrested after every performance and the manager had to pay $25 each time. I did three shows a day so it cost him $75, plus whatever he paid me in salary. (I didn't know my salary, my mother took care of everything.) The arrests were again for moving around onstage. In Alabama, too, children could sort of recite, maybe sing a little, but if they didn't stand still, they were breaking the law. The manager didn't care about the fines because the theater was packed for each performance. Not because I was such a sensation, but because the papers as far away as Birmingham were writing up the story and people came to see me. Later the law was changed—I don't think it was because of my case, but maybe it was.

I worked the Paramount many, many times. The Paramount wasn't pure vaudeville in a sense that the two-a-day at the Palace was. The Paramount was a combination of movies and stage show. It was where vaudevillians—the new stars of radio, television, and the movies—now appeared. And it wasn't unpleasant. Sure, we sometimes did four or even five shows a day, but it was either that or nightclubs. And who wanted to fight to be heard above the drunks? So that, or leave the business. Unless you were lucky and made it real big in radio, TV, or pictures.

I was at the Paramount with a unit—a Borris Morros unit—and every time they needed a girl singer on the bill with a name band or something, I'd get the job. I liked it because it meant staying in New York and I had had my fill of traveling. I was at the Paramount with Ben Bernie, Shep Fields, etcetera.

When I came off the Paramount unit, I was beat, so I told my mother I was going to take a vacation. I was in Long Beach swimming when I spotted a bellboy waving and yelling to me frantically. I went ashore and he said there was an important phone call, and the man calling had said it was very urgent. It was Borris Morros. "You have to open here at the Paramount in two days," he told me. It seems they had hired Frances Langford for the spot but they didn't like her material. So I went back again for two weeks.

Later I was on my way back from Europe—I'd been away for four months—and we were about one day out of England or France, when I got a cable from Sidney Piermont, the Loew booker, saying, "You open at Loew's State on the tenth." Now this was like the first of the month. He must be crazy, I thought. What'll I do for material? I got back and called him and he insisted I had to open. So I got some material together. In a few days I had an entirely different act, a brand new act. I went on cold, didn't break it in anywhere. Had five brand new songs. And it was the best act I ever had. This was about 1935. I was on the same bill with Bob Hope in a Proctor house somewhere in Connecticut or Massachusetts. Hope had a funny act. He would wave a baton as if he were conducting an orchestra. And the only other person onstage with him was a man with a saxophone. Hope was conducting him. I was never on a bill with him again.

The Palace theater was my last New York appearance. George Kirby was on the bill; he followed me. He was a much thinner man then. I followed Ray—the fellow who plays the xylophone whose last note is always flat. He's on TV often.

I remember I was about nine years old and I was playing the Tivoli Theater in Chicago, when I got my first fur coat. It was a beautiful thing and I was so proud of it. We went down to the office—Balaban and Katz's office—and Mr. Balaban looked at me in that new fur coat—I think it was squirrel with a kind of lynx collar and I also wore small Russian boots—and he smiled, pinched my cheek, and said, "Well, the way you look, I suppose we'll have to pay you more money."

I played the Chicago Theater on the same bill with John Boles. It was coincidental because we had played together in a picture that was just being released. But neither of us knew we were doing personal appearances on the same bill in the same theater till we met backstage. While I was on the Coast I played many theaters there—the Orpheum in San Francisco, in Los Angeles, and other cities.

Thinking back to Bob Hope, he always had bits but he didn't have an act. A man I know, Lester White, a writer, is now with Hope and sometimes thinks about retiring but Hope always argues him out of it. Says he needs him. Lester worked for Eddie Cantor before.

I also worked on the same bill with Jack Benny. That was at the Franklin. Oh, let me tell you—it was at the Franklin that Dick Powell first caught me. I was fourteen years old. He called me on the phone and asked me to come to Pittsburgh and work with him. Then I worked at the Enright Theater, where Powell originally started.

After the Palace in New York, I decided that was it. I was traveling alone and I'd had it. Vaudeville was dead. When I was in it, it was a great training ground. Out of town I tried all sorts of things, how to come on and get off. That's where I learned. But actually I came into vaudeville at the tail end.

Here's something. I was working in Duluth. I was a child, working onstage when suddenly all the lights went out. Musicians couldn't read the music and the only lights came from the ushers who dashed down front and aimed their flashlights on me. It got a tremendous hand. Maybe I should have kept it in the act. Another time I was working in the Palace theater in Cleveland. Joel Grey's father was on the bill—Mickey Katz. I noticed while I was singing that smoke seemed to be filling the orchestra and the audience was shifting around, kind of nervous like. And I, too, was more than a little nervous. Suddenly the manager came onstage next to me and whispered, "It's all right," then a loud voice told the audience not to be alarmed. There was some paper burning in one of the ducts but the exhausts were being turned on and everything was all right. And it was. But for a time it looked like something was going to happen.

I was signed with Paramount people to join a unit to go out for three months. We opened in New Haven, then Boston, and the third week we came into the New York Paramount. You remember the *RKO Theater of the Air* on NBC? I was asked to go on it. When I came to New York two men came to see me from NBC. Every Friday night they wanted me. We thought it was a gag. The Morris office, my agents, pooh-poohed my hopes for radio. They said my voice wasn't good for radio. I believed them. After all, they were big agents. And who was I—a little singer. So I told NBC I had a three-month contract with the Paramount unit and they said to see them when I was through. I did. And I got on NBC radio with my own show, first sustaining and then with sponsors. At the same time I also did some commercials that were on CBS. Was the Morris office surprised! They had said I was no good for radio and I certainly wasn't going to pay them a commission for something they had nothing to do with. Oh yes, they had me going to some little old lady who was supposed to teach me how to place my voice—whatever that meant—to sing something like "I'm A'wearying for You" in round tones. It was disastrous.

The closest thing to vaudeville was the Ed Sullivan TV show. But that, too, is gone. Anyway, now I'm through with vaudeville and show business. I'm active in volunteer work and that keeps me busy. I have a good busy life, an active life. And while I sometimes miss vaudeville and all the friends I made and all the good times we had—well, it has passed.

LOU HOLTZ

LOU HOLTZ was rated as one of the funniest men in vaudeville. He made the name "Lapidus" synonomous with what was termed in vaudeville Hebe (Jewish dialect) comedy. He was also well known for his singing of a series of jokes set to music, each ending with a resounding "O Sole Mio." His singing voice was good enough so that he was hired by the Shuberts to substitute for Al Jolson in case Jolson didn't show up for a performance—an event which never happened.

Holtz was a great favorite at the Palace. He played there many times, sometimes acting as an emcee. Between vaudeville dates he sometimes formed revues, where he surrounded himself with pretty girls. One of them, Lyda Roberti, became well known in her own right.

Another of Holtz's trademarks was his "Maharajah" stories, a double-talk series with an interpreter translating the Maharajah's nonsense into English. Holtz did both parts.

I was born and raised in San Francisco. That town had the greatest entertainers I've ever seen. They worked in the cafés, of which we also had the best. There was one trio, the Hedges Brothers and Jacobson, who were terrific. One kid played a boogie beat on the piano with one hand and a hot saxophone with the other. All three were handsome and sang terrific harmony. They were so great—I'll tell you how great they were: Some guy came in and saw them and booked them into the Hammerstein Roof in New York for a week and they stayed there for ten weeks. Then a guy from England saw them, brought them to England, and they never came back to America. They were the biggest thing that ever hit England. Then there was a quartet here, Sylvester, Jones, Depringle, and Morrell. When they broke up and went into vaudeville as singles, each got $1000 a week. And that was in 1910. Figure out what that would be today. That was the class of talent we had here in San Francisco.

Do you remember Curly Monroe and Gus Chandler? You wouldn't know them, you're too young. Well, they sang songs and did those little steps that Jolson saw and took. Gus had a sister, Annette Chandler, who became a vaudeville headliner.

Anyway, I got a job on the beach, at the Crest, here in San Francisco. What happened was that the Crest didn't have a show. The owner, Eddie Perry, a great piano player, called me on the phone and asked me to go on. He used to let me sing there from time to time and let me keep all the throw money. He said to me, "You're going to be big someday." Anyway, he introduced me as coming from Chicago and I was a big hit.

The headliners at the Crest were George Whiting and Sadie Burt. They were as good as they could possibly be. Now George was married, but his wife was in Chicago and he was madly in love with Sadie Burt. Someone told George's wife what was happening in San Francisco, that Sadie and George were living together, or he was going with her—whatever the expression was then. So she hopped a train for San Francisco. A guy in Chicago knew she was coming so he called up George to warn him. George got Sadie Burt and grabbed a train for New York. He and his wife must've crossed each other. And that's the reason I came in—the Crest didn't have a show without him.

One night one of the biggest female musical stars in the business, Elsie Janis, came out to star at the Crest. She was with Charlie DeYoung, who owned the *San Francisco Chronicle*. He became a great friend of mine. He wanted her to hear me sing "Alexander's Ragtime Band," which I had learned from Gus Chandler, with the little moves, the shticks, etcetera. This was in 1919. When I finished, she said to me, "Lou, you don't belong here. You come to New York. I have an act written for a trio and you can be one of the trio. I'm also bringing in Ralph Doherty and Val Harris." Harris had a beautiful voice and was one of the owners of the Crest. He later had a place in the San Fernando Valley. He's dead now. Anyway, that's how I went to New York. Oh yes, I took Ralph Doherty and had to pay his fare. He never paid me back. He never had any money.

When Ralph and I hit New York I went over to the Irving Berlin music publishing office—Watterson, Berlin, and Snyder—to get some songs. Well, the manager, Max Winslow (a great guy), says to us, "So you're from Frisco, eh? Lemme hear you sing something." So we go into one of those small rooms with a piano and we give out with "Alexander's Ragtime Band," again with the little steps and shtickluh—you know—"When that midnight choo-choo leaves fro' Alabam/I'll be right there, I've got my fare . . ." Well, this was a new thing. He says, "Hold it a minute." Then he goes out and comes back with a little skinny guy. This guy listens and says, "You're great." You know who that was? Irving Berlin!

So Berlin says, "Listen, we're having a big thing at the Friars tomorrow night. It's a party for Enrico Caruso, and we want you to go on." We went on and we were a hell of a hit. In the audience was an agent, Marty Samter. He was then handling the Hedges Brothers and Jacobson. He asked what we were doing in New York. We told him we were part of a trio for Elsie Janis. He said, "You guys are crazy. You're going with me. You'll go where I'll tell you to go."

Now, we'd never been on a stage. We didn't know about makeup, walk on, or walk off. But Marty was a big talker. He said he was going to make us rich because what he saw in us was something great. So me and Ralph Doherty went out into a theater. We went on the same way we did in the cafés . . . and nothing. When we finished, the theater manager came backstage and said one word to us—"Out." Later he took me aside and said, "You know, I think you have a chance." In the meantime Doherty, apparently fed up, sent a wire to some girls in San Francisco to send him $250. They did and off he went, leaving me in New York alone. He wanted me to go back too but I refused. I told him that when I went back it would be to the Orpheum—that was the big-time vaude house in San Francisco in those days.

So now I'm doing a single. The first job I get is a hotel on 43rd Street —Miller's. I don't know what it's called today. It was the hotel where there was that big murder case—Captain Becker, Gyp the Blood, and the other hoods were involved in it, about 1913. Living in the same hotel was Harry Carroll, a great song writer; also Ballad McDowell, another great song writer, who had just finished the song "I'm Always Chasing Rainbows." I worked at the Miller Hotel about three months. One day I'm going uptown in the subway when I meet a beautiful girl, Rita Rowen. She's working in a theater with another girl. (By this time I'm through with Miller's. Harry Delson was the star there—a Jewish comedian, the funniest guy in the world. He had those parodies and material that Fanny Brice stole. Funniest son of a bitch you ever saw.) Now I have a job at the College Inn on 125th Street. Rita Rowen and I start going around together a few weeks and we decide to get married. I take her with me to the College Inn where I'm getting $45 a week—that's big money in those days—and they pay her $45 a week too. So we are living high. Hotel costs us $2 a day for both of us and everything's great. I tell her about Elsie

Janis, how she said to call her. Rita says I ought to call her now. So I call her and tell her I'm married and she wants to see my wife. She asks us for dinner in her apartment somewhere on Central Park West. She takes one look at Rita and says, "How the hell did you get such a gorgeous girl?"

In the meantime the San Francisco Crest had closed and Val Harris came east to rehearse at the Globe Theater where Elsie Janis was playing in the *Lady of the Slipper*. That was 1914. Montgomery and Stone were also in the show. Every night we would rehearse on the stage of the Globe after the show was over. The directors were Elsie Janis and Fred Stone. We opened in Newark. We got $250. We were booked for fifty weeks in vaudeville.

Our first New York date was at the Palace. Sarah Bernhardt was the big thing on the bill. Her leading man was Lou Tellegen, a nice guy who later went into pictures here. I'll tell you something funny. Another big thing on the bill was a new kind of talking picture invented by Thomas A. Edison. As I recall it, nobody thought much of it, one way or another. We played all over the country, all the theaters. The act was Val Harris, Rita Rowen, and Lou Holtz in an Elsie Janis sketch.

Rita and I got divorced. Time went on, and I started to do a single act again. I opened in a few places, but nothing much. My agent said, "Someday you'll make a thousand a week—but not today. You're twenty-two and you look like fourteen. You talk about a girl and that's no good. They don't believe it. Become a blackface comic and some of that material will stand up." So I blacked up. I got $125 in my first blackface single act at the City Theater on New York's 14th Street. Savoy and Brennan, a great, great act, were on the same bill. Sure, I know they were supposed to be fags. But who cared? They didn't bother me. I know women in this business who were lesbians. Again, who cared? So she's a lesbian one hour a day. The rest of the day she's charming, a great performer, and a pleasure to work with.

Let me go back here a little. I began improving and finally I got an Orpheum route. There was a song writer around, Arthur Jackson, who became my friend. A clever guy. He wrote a cycle of songs for some girl in vaudeville and she was to pay him $500 for them—a fortune. He played the songs for me and when I heard the third number I asked if the girl had heard the songs yet. He said no. I offered him $500 for that one song alone. I didn't have the $500. I agreed to pay him $50 a week for ten weeks. I was working then.

When Arthur Jackson was a kid in Pittsburgh the burlesque houses there always had a number at the closing where the comic and all the girls would come out. The comic would pick one of the girls in the "Pickout

Number," and she would say something like: "A horse and a flea were shooting dice . . . something something something/The horse slipped and fell on the flea and the flea would sing out 'there's a horse on me.'" Or the comic would sing, "Hinky doo—hinky dee," etcetera. The idea was to get four lines like: "I lost my dog the other day but I found him easy because/ I figured if I was a dog where would I go/ And there he was/ O sole mio—O sole mio." The O sole mio made it.

They always wanted to hear more verses, so all I had to do was to take any good joke, rhyme it, and that was more material. For example: "My wife ran away with a chauffeur last year/ Now I'm as nervous as I can be/'Cause every time I hear an auto horn/I think he's bringing her back to me/ O sole mio . . ." Here's one I always finished with and they loved it: "A fat lady tried to get on a streetcar/She didn't know whether to get in front or behind/The conductor said, 'Which end will you get in, madam?'/She said, 'I'll get them both in at the same time if you don't mind'/O sole mio . . ."

Well, that was the beginning and the making of Lou Holtz. I stopped every show. Wound up next to closing, where I always killed them.

A guy who is now dead, George White, opened a show called the Scandals. His leading comedian, Lester Allen out of burlesque, gets the flu. They call me. I'm working at the Colonial and I tell them they're crazy, I don't finish until a quarter to eleven. So they call Albee at his home. White tells him that he's got every nickel in the world tied up in the show and cries so hard that Albee, no soft touch, agrees to let me out. Of course, Albee is not so charitable really. I have to agree to play back for him for four weeks at $250 a week.

Jules Lensberg is White's orchestra leader. I don't have time for more than a quick talkover the first show before I go on. White has a bad show. The star is Ann Pennington, who's getting $300 a week. I am in for $250. The show is doing about $8000 a week and breaking even. Admission is $2.50 top. But there is no audience. We open September, 1919, in the middle of an actors' strike. The Scandals is the only show open and we don't do anything. We fold and that was that.

Looking back a little—I came out of the Winter Garden where I was hired to understudy Al Jolson. I got together some good songs and good jokes but I never got on. Then I went on the road again and when I got back to New York I opened at the Colonial. All my jokes were already being told by forty other guys. The songs were old and Al Darling, the house manager, who was the brother of the big Palace booker, canceled me—the bastard. I told him, "I'll be back here as the headliner and you'll be lucky to get a job in a gents' furnishing store, you dirty son of a bitch."

Left to right: Lou Holtz, Magda Gabor, Adah Lewis, Bess Myerson and Harry Hirshfield, at the Plaza Hotel in 1957.

And a few years later not only did I play as a headliner, but that bastard was out.

Originally I never did a Jewish gag. This "Lapidus" thing started like this: John Reber of the J. Walter Thompson Agency got me on radio Thursdays for $1150 a shot. His argument was that Rudy Vallee would be on for only twenty weeks and I'd be on for the rest of the year. But I ran out of material, so I went to the Friars to speak to Frank Tinney and Sam Bernard. We talked, but no ideas. Now, I used to do a story about this guy with long pants. It ran about six minutes. Reber said that it was the kind of story he wanted.

I was on my way to the ball game—the Giants at the Polo Grounds—cabbing up Central Park West when I saw a new apartment house going up and the architect was some guy called Lapidus. I said the name Lapidus to myself a few times, adding a little dialect, and it sounded good to me. The following week I tried a Sam Lapidus story, or tied him into several stock jokes, and they went. That's the story. The idea came from Gregory Ratoff—he had an accent or a dialect that killed them.

That Maharajah bit started with a dinner that was given in Washington for a famous maharajah at the Indian Embassy. It was a big dinner with caviar and stuff. I can't remember the gibberish I used to do exactly because there is no such language. It was all double and triple talk, with proper inflections. Cut in your own words, but they shouldn't make any sense, except a word here and there, so it sounds like something. At the end the interpreter would stand up and say, "Maharajah say you have a wonderful country, American women very beautiful, say hello," and sit down. The maharajah would get up again and again sound off in those long meaningless words. The interpreter would again rise and say something about "Sky very beautiful, music very good," etcetera. And that would go on until the interpreter would say, "Maharajah wants to know where is toilet."

Carmen Miranda was on the radio show. She couldn't speak English and I couldn't speak her language. But Reber wanted her on. The timer on the show—some kid, God bless him—said, "Why don't you do the maharajah bit here? But use 'washroom' instead of 'toilet' on the air." And you know, it became one of the biggest things there was. Only Eddie Cantor with his "Parkyakarkis" was even with me.

Vaudeville business was a good business. A guy would work all over the United States—be away for maybe four years perfecting his act. Now they're asking comics to be funny every Thursday night or whatever. It's impossible. Take Flip Wilson. I stopped looking at him. I didn't find him funny anymore. I see he was canceled. He should have pulled out after the first year, and then later, maybe, come back. I think Johnny Carson is good, particularly on ad libs. Jackie Gleason can't stand up in one but he's a great actor. Sid Caesar is also great, but not in one. Buddy Hackett and Don Rickles are great comedians. Bert Lahr was great in a scene. Alone—nothing. Bob Hope was nothing in vaudeville. He used to come to me and say, "Lou, I'm opening at the Bushwick—you got a joke for me?" And I'd give him one. It was radio that made Hope—and Benny.

When I was at the Palace and got $6,000 a week, Kate Smith got $1,000 and Lyda Roberti got $1,000. Too bad about Lyda. She fell for that big director—what was his name—Leo McCarey. She was stuck on him and he lied to her. Said he would divorce his wife. I got her from "You Said It." So one night she was on whisky and sleeping pills—and she'd never drank before, and that was that. She was Polish. A wonderful girl.

Now there's no place where a guy can be lousy and work his way up. But if he's any good, he removes the crap and has an act.

There's a dame around today who's as good as Bernhardt ever was—

Anne Bancroft. Great! I saw her sing and dance on the Perry Como show. And there's Shecky Greene—a great comedian—he's as strong as an ox.

But vaude isn't really dead. There was Judy Garland and her four, five acts. And Danny Kaye and his four, five acts. They went into the Palace and killed them. If I were a young man today I would come up with some top acts and we'd show them.

But today I'm happy doing what I'm doing. Taking care of my family, my wife, my two young sons. Little League etcetera. I have a lovely wife and two great boys and a lovely home. Work? What for? What'll I prove?

I don't know why Burns still takes dates—not me.

JACK HALEY

JACK HALEY *was a handsome comedian with an excellent voice. He started in Boston, his home town, and never quite lost his accent. In vaudeville he teamed up with various partners, whom he speaks of in his interview. His most successful partnership was with comedian Benny Rubin, with whom he appeared at the Palace and all over the country. Today Haley may be best remembered as the Tin Man in the Judy Garland classic,* The Wizard of Oz.

No longer active as a performer, he devotes his time to overseeing his vast real estate interests.

I got into show business as a song plugger. It was my first professional job. I'll tell you this—though I could sing and people would listen, I was also supposed to sell the sheet music. And when I couldn't do that, I was fired. I worked in Philadelphia for McCarthy-Fischer, a music publishing firm. Before that I was a bellboy and switchboard operator for the Philadelphia Club. While I was working there I would go over to a small-time choreographer, Eddie Kramer on Locust Street, to take some tap-dancing lessons. I think I paid him about $1.75 a lesson. Philadelphia was famous for its hoofers. And anybody who had visions of getting into show business one way or another would always learn hoofing.

Well, my song plugging was a flop and I was back running the switchboard and bellhopping when I got a call from Ed Kramer. He said, "There's a guy here who needs a guy just like you. He's got a girl act. He's got all his people. I'm rehearsing his six-girl chorus. He's got all his principals, but his juvenile didn't show. I think you'd be great. Can you get over here at two o'clock?" I did.

Jack Haley and Benny Rubin at the Palace. (Photo courtesy of Popular Press)

There was this guy, Huston of Whipple and Huston, who did an act with his wife. Now he had a job with George White's *Scandals* and he put his wife out in an act so they could have a little extra money. He had got Le Baron to write this small-time girlie act, and that was what I was joining. It was a tabloid musical—called simply a tab—about a drugstore, and I was the soda jerk who attracted all the girls to the soda fountain. Before I went to work, the store had been doing so poorly the owner had had to bring his daughter back from college because he couldn't afford to keep her there. But I increased business, and at the finish it was found out that I represented the United Drug Corporation and had been sent there to buy the store to add to our chain. Instead I fell in love with his daughter and we got married. That was the whole thing.

I dreamed about being able to go out on stage, working in one, without any story or girls, maybe with a man partner, capturing the audience. I loved the independence and the freedom that would give me. So I kept looking and waited until the opportunity came. I got another fellow, Charley Crafts, from Boston, and we had it made within six months. We first played a lot of small time—who didn't? That's where you learned your craft, and then you were selected to play the big time. What made vaudeville so wonderful was the freedom, the tremendous freedom. You could do whatever you wanted onstage, as long as it was in good taste. Managers would never bother you. They weren't creators, they were producers. You received immediate appraisal of any new creation you might think of. You'd get a funny idea and you tried it out. If it was any good, got audience approval, you kept it in. If not, you threw it out. Consequently, a perfection was attained because you could polish a bit, keep it smooth and make it part of your act. The field of artistic development was in vaudeville. It was probably the most ideal life for an entertainer.

If you finally made the big time—let's say you were playing Keith's on Chestnut Street in Philadelphia—you'd be there for a week. So you played golf in the morning. If you were a good act, you were on late in the bill, perhaps 4 P.M. You'd come in from your golf, shower, shave, dress, do your act (twelve to fifteen minutes), take off your makeup, go out, have a good dinner, and come back at ten-something at night. You did your act twice a day and the security was amazing. You could buy a house on your contract for a route.

If you had a good act, you got a good route. And I'm talking now of acts like Billy Gaxton and Victor Moore. Moore did an act with his wife for years and years. It was a beautiful life. Money was important, and remember, we are talking about pre-inflation days. Pat Rooney and his wife got $3000 a week. Rock and White were also in the $3000 class. There were plenty of others.

I remember Walter Huston when he was with Whipple and Huston. They did a comedy sketch. He was a shoe salesman and the entire stage was like a shoe store. This woman came in to buy a pair of shoes. There was funny dialogue. He got the laughs. They did a song and dance. The curtain dropped and they came back again in one to do more song and dance. Walter Huston later became a big dramatic actor. I think it was *Desire Under the Elms* that gave him his chance, and then he went into movies.

If there was security for the big-timer, the small-timer also had security. If he and his wife played instruments, they could hire a boy or girl singer and between them make out very well.

To get back to the Palace: Six months after Charley Crafts and I teamed up, we were in the Palace. Only a vaudevillian who has trodden its stage can really tell you about it. Audiences can tell you who they saw there and how they enjoyed them, but only a performer can describe the anxieties, the joys, the anticipation, and the exultation of a week's engagement at the Palace. The walk through the iron gate on 47th Street, through the courtyard to the stage door, was the cum laude walk to a show-business diploma. A feeling of ecstasy came with the knowledge that *this is the Palace*, the epitome of the more than 15,000 vaudeville theaters in America, and the realization that you have been selected to play it. Of all the thousands upon thousands of vaudeville performers in the business, you are there. This was a dream fulfilled; this was the pinnacle of variety success. Each week eight acts were chosen, fifty-two weeks a year. This meant that only about 415 of the thousands available could play it. And of these 415, many repeated annually. As you walked through the stage door, you sensed the distinctive air; the aura affected even the employees. After all, they were with the best. You were struck by the courtesies, the backstage amenities not experienced in other theaters.

Eddie Darling was the Palace booker. He knew what the theater represented and knew what the audience wanted. They were a hip audience. I'll never forget when I walked out on that stage with Crafts on my first appearance. I used to wear a funny little hat and I had a flower in my hand. We came out from different sides of the stage. We received a slight reception from some of the actors and agents out front who knew us. Instead of going right into our act, I looked out at the audience and said, "So this is the Palace!" It got such a laugh. You could not get that kind of laugh in any other place. But that audience was sharp. In it were the agents, the bookers, the gamblers—those who knew vaudeville and show business. My approaching it with such disdain—"So this is the Palace!"—got such a big laugh that we were home after that.

Crafts was my straight man. We did harmony, danced, kibitzed. It was a good act. We were the Martin and Lewis of the time. That was the kind of act we did.

Though vaudeville at the Palace was the epitome, we all dreamed of getting into a musical comedy—a Ziegfeld, a Shubert, or a Dillingham show. We were always on our toes, because, who knows, maybe they're out there looking us over. The reason we longed for a musical was because then we could have an apartment. Wouldn't have to live out of a trunk, as we usually did. Proctor's Fifth Avenue—it wasn't on Fifth Avenue, it was on 23rd Street off Sixth Avenue, or maybe Broadway—was where acts were watched closely by those booking either the Palace or a new musical comedy. Vaudevillians used to go back and forth between musical comedies and vaudeville. It might surprise you to learn that many dramatic actors, the stars of the legit who may have regarded vaudeville as beneath them, also played vaudeville when they could. And for good reason. If they were important, they could make as much money in a year of vaudeville as they could make in five years of legit. Here are a few: Ethel, John, and Lionel Barrymore, though not all together; Florence Reed; Mrs. Leslie Carter; Richard Bennett; Carter DeHaven; Henry B. Walthall; Walter Hampden.

I recall being at the Bushwick in Brooklyn on a bill with that wonderful dramatic actress Julia Arthur. She was doing a scene from *Hamlet* and she took the liberty of playing the title role. Finally she did a soliloquy, and her last line was the somber "Great is before and the last remains behind." Now I'm in the wings, waiting to go on. The music is very dramatic, the curtain goes down very slowly, but it's apparent the audience is not interested. The music finishes, our announcement cards go up, and the music also goes up very fast. We dash out and I say, "Did you hear that, about 'the last remains behind'—did she mean us?" Well, you never heard such laughs.

Oh sure, I got into musicals. That's how I got into pictures. I sang "Button Up Your Overcoat" the first time on any stage. Ethel Merman and I sang "You're an Old Smoothie" together for the first time on any stage. *Girl Crazy* was her first show. She came into the Palace after that one and we did bits together. Al Segal, a vocal coach, saw her in a little café, and seeing the possibilities, arranged an audition and she got *Girl Crazy*.

Talk about discovering talent makes me laugh. Once I was playing the Ambassador Theater, St. Louis, a Skouras Brothers house, for sixteen to twenty weeks. A little girl, about fifteen, came backstage with her lame mother. The mother asked me if I would try out her daughter and maybe get her onstage. We used to run neighborhood talent contests. So my wife and I went into the basement, got the piano player, and we tried her out. She could hoof like hell and she sang fairly well. So we rehearsed a number together, and I announced from the stage that the girl was local, brought her on, and that helped me too. While she was there the local *Daily Variety* guy—I can't think of his name—saw her. He had a thing going with Universal Pictures. They gave him a number of dollars if he could get them young talent. He got this little girl to go to Hollywood and she became a starlet with Universal. The girl's name was Betty Grable.

So the natural thing is for me to say that I discovered her. But that wasn't so. After all, you have to start some place. While I was at the Palace working with a girl, Helen E. B. Reck, Jack Benny was on the bill with me, doing a single. After that he worked at the Winter Garden in a Shubert revue with a girl, Dorothy McGuire, who later became Penny Singleton. Benny liked the idea of working with a girl so much he later put on his wife, Mary Livingston.

Vaudeville was an important part of the entertainment world. There was nothing else to touch it. Pictures didn't kill vaudeville, until the talkies. They killed it. A Sunday night concert, which was vaudeville, at the Palace was an event. People dressed. Not only for the Palace, but also for the Winter Garden and the other theaters that ran concerts. The Sunday laws forbade regular shows, so they called them concerts and everything was okay.

I worked with Benny Rubin at the Palace where we were twin emcees. We stayed together there for a few weeks and then we went around the circuit with the same act. But we weren't an act per se. We were the two headliners, we were the masters of ceremony. We did bits through the show, and that was all.

MACK LATHROP

MACK LATHROP *and Virginia Lee were considered one of the finest dancing acts of the late thirties and early forties. They first met at the Palace as members of different acts. Lathrop did a hoofing, tap-dancing act with a partner in a team known as the Lathrop Brothers. Miss Lee was a child prodigy and played the Palace as part of a "kiddie" revue. Later she joined a flash act.*

Lathrop's partner (they weren't really brothers) quit the business at the same time that Miss Lee wanted a change; an agent who knew them both suggested they team up. They tried it, rehearsed, liked it, and became partners. Later they extended that partnership to marriage. Always performing in full evening dress, including top hats, they were a smooth, top-flight tap-dancing team.

They have since retired to operate a successful dancing school in Connecticut.

We started in Chicago in 1927 in a little neighborhood movie house, only two shows a night, one of those nickel-and-dime joints. But these were the places where you had an opportunity to break in and learn and correct your mistakes. I don't know where and how they do it today. You have to start at the top now. Singers make it with a hit record, assuming they make it at all. But I don't know about dancers. Maybe if they're good enough they can get into a chorus line. I don't know how they're going to develop any Fred Astaires or Gene Kellys today.

The two-a-day was really show business, though we did five-a-day at the New York Paramount and we were there six weeks. We were on the bills with Gene Krupa and Tony Pastor—this was in the heyday of the name bands—and we were ready for a rest cure after that. It was no fun.

When I started in Chicago I was part of a team called the Lathrop Brothers. We weren't related. Chuck was trying to get a break and so was I, so we got together. We played all over, even the burlesque houses around Chicago that used to put on specialty acts. Then came Western Vaudeville dates and after that a showing date. The one other act on the bill told us we ought to go to New York. He called his agent-manager recommending us highly.

We got to New York and this agent, who we had yet to meet, got us a showing date in Jersey City, $62.50 for three days. We opened on a Monday, and that night, after the evening show, a man knocked on our door, came in, and said, "I'm Milt Lewis, your manager-agent." He said he liked what we did and asked us if we were ready to open at the Palace. We said no-no-no. But we closed Wednesday and he called us Friday and said, "You open at the Palace Monday." That was it. We almost fainted. We were scared to death. It was like winning a big sweepstake lottery ticket. Here it is our first New York date, and we get the Palace! On the bill were Ben Bernie and his band. He had Georgie Tapps with him. The headliner was Trixie Friganza, a big star then. We were on in two, following a six-person act of tumblers. They were so great and got such a big hand it scared us. Then we went on. Anyway, we got through and got the Orpheum route. We were in the unit headed by the Colleano Family. They did everything—comedy, song, acrobatics. The young son—I don't remember his name—became a big movie star in England. We also worked on the Orpheum time with Bob Hope. Jack Benny had a guy in the box who used to throw insults all through his act. Benny also had a girl with him at that time. We also played with Burns and Allen. But none of these people had arrived then. Later they all became millionaires.

When talking pictures came and acts were cut down to four I knew it was only a question of time. Our manager was also handling Virginia Lee. She was in a flash act. It was decided to put her in with us to get a little sex appeal into the act. She wore beautiful things and we wore tails. She stayed with us until my partner Chuck got out of the business. He was supporting a family and we weren't working too much. Virginia and I stayed together until we both quit. We met in 1935. We were married in 1937. It turned out to be a good thing. We did some TV. The best thing we did was on a Kate Smith show. The next day Charlie Yates called us to say he had booked us in San Francisco. I asked him to get us dates in Los Angeles and Chicago on the way back from San Francisco. He said

Lathrop and Lee

he'd get them while we were in San Francisco, but I wanted firm commitments before we went off on that long, long haul. So we turned it down. And for six months we laid off. It was then that we decided to open a dancing school here in Newtown, Connecticut. Nobody knew us here but we went into it anyway. It was a hard struggle. We didn't advertise and it took four years of hard-earned money and work to make it a success. And now it is.

In small time we worked on the Death Trail—that was the name for one-nighters in places you never heard of, like Missoula, Montana, places where nobody would go unless they really needed work—and we did. They weren't theaters, they were kind of stores, with benches instead of seats. When the show began, the baker, the laundry truck driver, and maybe the garbage man dropped what they were doing and jumped in to play the music. They were the band. They'd come in and they couldn't play. The first time we had our music played well by real musicians, we couldn't dance to it. We weren't used to it, it was strange. The conditions in these Death Trail theaters were miserable. We can laugh about them all now but they weren't laughable when we were going through them—that is, Chuck and I. Virginia wasn't with us then. But we got a lot of experience. The Bert Levy time was really awful. Their houses were often in the same town we were working in, but theirs weren't even as good as ours—which I've already described.

We also played the Paramount unit. On one, Borris Morros arranged a screen test for [Virginia Lee] and me. She got a picture out of it. It looked like we might get a break when she got a call from George White to audition, and she did—and that was that. Universal wanted to sign me for one of those nothing contracts. But it looked like I would be one of those second lead types—you know, the guy who never gets the girl—for which there wasn't much of a demand at the time.

Once I was going to send a wire to Charlie Yates, my manager. I got the book—one of those with blank telegram forms—and inside was a telegram already written. It was from George Burns to his agent: "We won't work anymore for $350 a week—Don't book us anymore."

We worked with Jack Benny several times. Way back then he was onstage in the hinterlands—good theaters, two-a-day, but the audiences didn't understand him. And he would be out there dying. And he would look off into the wings and make comments to us that would have us hysterical with laughter, but the audience wasn't laughing. We also worked with Barry and Whitledge, one of my favorite acts. They were so funny but they died all the time. Like Benny, they had the whole show screaming with laughter, but not their audiences. There was also Jack Carson, who used to imitate Laurel and Hardy—that was before he made it in pictures. Then we played with Abbott and Costello when they were just a small comedy act working on the Steel Pier in Atlantic City.

We were okay once we made it—there weren't too many dancers that made it. There was George Murphy—he became a Senator; Gene Kelly, Fred Astaire—the lead types. King and King were tap dancers—Nick Condos was one of the Kings. Later he was with the Condos Brothers and later still he married Martha Raye. Anyway, they became the Three Kings and they were an absolute sensation. We followed them into the Palladium in London, and we heard about their great success. London was at their feet. And then they played the Paramount Theater in Paris, and we followed them there too. When we got to the Paramount, we asked how the Three Kings had done. We were told they were terrible. Nobody liked them. We wanted to know why—they had been such a sensation in England. We were told the French had booed. They didn't like what was called tap dancing. Apparently it was new to Paris. And then we said, "That's what we do." Well, we rehearsed with the band—forty pieces, gorgeous. All of a sudden a man came on—the manager. He asked, "You make clickety-clack with the feet?" We said yes. He said, "Oh my God. The Three Kings— they booed, whistled"—and he went away shaking his head. We thought, well, this won't take long. We'll be canceled—that's show business. We went on—beautiful clothes, beautiful music. We were never better—except there was no reaction from the audience. We'd finish a number and not hear anything. We finished the act and walked off in a dead hush—nothing. And there standing in the wings was the smiling manager saying, "Good, good, good." We said, "What do you mean, good? They didn't like us at all. No applause—nothing." "Good, good—they didn't boo you at all." So that's how we became famous in Paris—they didn't boo us.

Then we played Holland. Some of the people we played with were coming up, as perhaps we were, but they went all the way up. We went just so far and that was it.

We worked with Bing Crosby at the Paramount. He was just coming off the Chesterfield Radio Show. These people wanted to work—not for the money, just to work. If they didn't have anything, they'd look for a benefit. In this day and age it's amazing how many performers make it with a record and then have enough sense to go out and learn their trade so they can actually entertain the people. There's Sonny and Cher, Elvis Presley. In most cases, it's once around for these record acts who don't learn their trade.

You know, I still get *Variety*. And I hate to say it, but the thing I look at first are the obits—who I lost who I knew.

CHARLES MOSCONI

THE MOSCONI BROTHERS—Louis and Charlie—were two youngsters who did dance steps that amazed and electrified viewers. They had a routine in which Charlie, in girl's clothes, did his steps opposite Louis' boy. In a less sophisticated era the audiences loved them, and no one ever called them gay. Occasionally the pair was joined by other members of the dancing family—pop, brother Willie, and sister Verna.

Their trick of dancing halfway up the pillars on the side of the stage has never been equaled. Audiences could be counted on to gasp and yell with excitement.

Louis died some years ago and Charlie, though he no longer performs, is still in one aspect of show business—he owns a theater ticket agency.

Dancing came naturally to us. We came out of a dancing family. We actually started as the Mosconi Brothers, then it became the Mosconi Family. That was my father, me, my brother Louis, my kid brother Willie, and my sister Verna. Later we again became just the Mosconi Brothers—just me and Louis.

As I said, dancing came naturally to us. My grandfather was a ballet master in Genoa. When we came to America he couldn't make any money with dancing so he opened a peanut and hot chestnut stand. My father would sell newspapers, and when he got home he'd sneak down the cellar to practice tap dancing. Then his father would come down and wallop him. He'd yell at him, "There is no money in dancing and you're wearing your shoes out."

In 1908 or so my father opened a dancing school at 4th and Market streets in Philadelphia. It was a big school with a big hall, something like the Roseland Ballroom in New York. The hall had a big slippery floor. It was so shiny, so beautiful, you could eat off it. We used to wax it regularly and we were taught to dance on that very slippery floor. This early training on a slippery floor was a very big help to us later when we went into vaudeville. No matter how slippery a stage was, we could dance on it. Very few people could. But slippery or painted floors made no difference to us. We could dance together, Louis and me, and bounce off walls like nobody has been able to do before or since.

We started out doing ballroom dancing onstage. We got to be very well known in and around Philadelphia, so we got ourselves an agent and he put us into theaters in town and in Germantown, Allegheny, South Philadelphia, and all around. We must've played fifteen to twenty small-time theaters. Then we got a three-day date in Reading, Pennsylvania, where we were caught by a Palace booker, a damn good booker. His name was George Gottlieb. I remember he changed his name to Godfrey during the war so people wouldn't think he was German.

Anyway, Gottlieb caught us and put us into the Palace. And luck was with us. It had to be luck because what did we know about vaudeville or how acts were routined? So we were slotted to go on right after the intermission. We came on in full dress. I did a soft-shoe dance. My brother put on Charlie Chaplin makeup, and while he was doing that, I put on a wig and a dress and did the girl that Chaplin used to work with —her name was Edna Purviance. Then we did a fast one-step, hit the wall, bounced off, hit the wall again, and the house went wild. We tore the house down.

There was a sign backstage that said "Two bows only." So we took the two bows. Now if you take two bows and they're still out there screaming you'll break the house down if you don't go out again. But we wouldn't break the rule until a man dashed backstage—we later found out it was Mr. Albee—and ordered us to take another bow. I said, "It says there only two bows." He said, "Never mind that sign. Go out and take a bow." So we went out, came off, went out again. Six bows. From then on, it was *Boom!*

Now one of those lucky things happened. Jack Donahue was on in two and very unhappy about it. He became that famous straight man who worked in so many Broadway shows. He was also a hell of a good dancer. So Jack Donahue and his wife—they worked together—pleaded with the house manager, Ragers, to put him in a different spot because the audience was still walking in when he went on.

The Palace shows started at 2 P.M. There was a short overture and a

Palladium and Palace billboards featuring the Mosconis.

Pathé newsreel that took maybe fifteen minutes, and then came the first act. We were listening while Donahue was arguing with the manager and Louis turned to me. He wanted to see some of the good movies that were playing around so he said, "Why can't we change? We'll go on in the two spot and let Donahue go on in our spot opening the intermission." The manager thought we were nuts, but he figured the office would go for such a layout. He called and got an okay.

Now the opening act was Lucy Gillette, a Dutch magician. She was great and she did twenty-six minutes and got a big hand. So when we came on they were already sitting down and ready for us. Instead of going on at maybe 4:00 or 4:30, as before, we now went on at 2:30, did four

142

numbers, and there was plenty of time for Louis to see his movies. So that's how we broke into the Palace and big time.

Our manager booked us right away for a two-year route on the Orpheum Circuit. Now, one thing I never made a mistake about in show business was in signing papers. When our manager told us about the Orpheum two-year deal, I was against it. I believed that if we went on the circuit for even six months, they would never hear of us anymore in the big time. In fact, I said we wouldn't even go to New Jersey with the act. I wanted to cash in now. The manager said he had already signed for us. I said, "You can't sign for us. Besides, my brother isn't even of age." He was sixteen then, I was twenty. So we got around that. Instead we signed with the Shuberts and played the Winter Garden for many weeks.

All in all, we played the Palace fifty-two weeks over a period of seven years. We hold the record for the most weeks played at that house. In 1919 we were back in the Palace—it was just after the war was over and they were showing the Pathé News in the intermission period, right ahead of us. We went on that afternoon, and jeez, nothing happened. We hardly got any applause. At night the same thing happened. No applause. I was worried. What was happening? I thought of many things but it all ended up that I was scared. Where did we miss?

So the next day I got down early and walked around nervously, and I heard this dum-dum-de-dum—the "Death March." And I looked at the newsreel and saw that they were burying the Unknown Soldier in Arlington. I went to the manager and said, "While they're burying that fellow, they're also burying us. Don't put that one in ahead of us." The manager laughed and said, "I was wondering when you were going to find that out." He took it right out.

We did well all over the country, except in Buffalo. We had a hard time getting over to them in that town—I still don't know why. We played all over Europe. We were with the *Ziegfeld Follies* for one season. We played the Winter Garden. We were with *Hitchy-Koo*, a big musical, for one year. We played with Julia Sanderson, a great singer. Jack Benny was on many bills with us. He was never more than a number-four act, a fair performer, until he hooked up with Phil Baker. That was the guy who later had that big radio show, *The $64 Question*. So it was Baker and Benny for a couple of years. Benny worked onstage while Baker did the boy in the box who heckled him.

Our beginning Palace money was $150, which sounds like nothing today. But when we got our first Palace date, $150 was real money. It was also twice what we got playing small time. And in small time we did three shows a day. In the big time it was two shows a day. Four shows a day didn't start until the picture houses began with their presentation shows. Those were murder.

We always carried our own conductor. You'd go nuts if you didn't. You'd miss the first two days because the guys didn't know your music. It would always take them a couple of days to get on to it. But our conductor would give them the tempo and that made it easier for us.

As our act sharpened and got smoother, we would do seven numbers in thirteen minutes. And when we came off we didn't have one dry spot on us. But we were young and could take it. Nobody has been able to do our style of dancing. The last time we worked was in 1934. It was at the Orpheum Theater on 86th Street in New York. It's now called the Loew's Orpheum.

We wound up shortly after and went to California and opened a dancing school. Louis has since passed on and I'm now back in New York where I have my own theater ticket agency.

Oh, before we finish, let me tell you about when we played the London Palladium in 1923. We split headline billing with Harry Weldon. He was very big in England, a big star. He had been sick for about six months and this was his comeback. We had our sister Verna and our brother Willie working with us. And do you know how they billed us there? They called us the "Eighth Wonder of the World." I hated that billing. Anyway, we were held over for four weeks. They were great weeks.

Yep, vaudeville was a great profession and audiences loved it. They must have, they lined up at box offices for the nonreserved seats. And they were so attentive and so wonderful if they liked you. Even if they didn't like you, they were still great. There's nothing like it today.

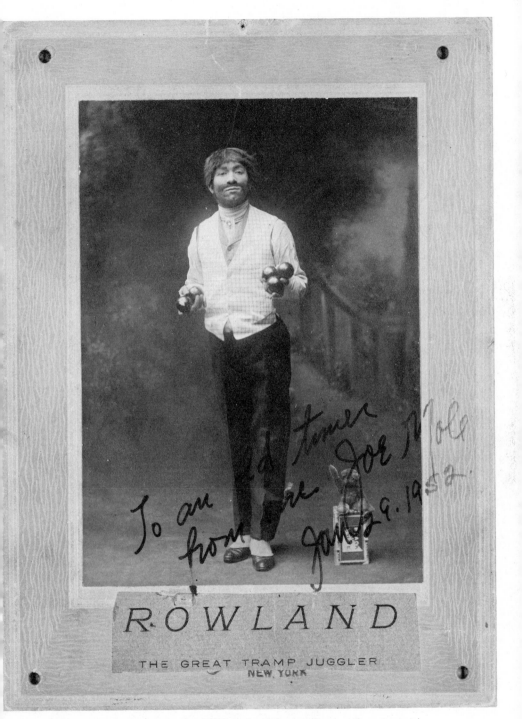

ROWLAND

THE GREAT TRAMP JUGGLER
NEW YORK

George Rowland, one of the few blacks who did a juggling act (most went in for comedy or dance routines). This photo was taken in 1904.

Jack Benny with his early vaudeville partner, Woods (on piano) in 1918.

Alla Nazimova, *famous dramatic actress of the 1920's, did sketches in vaudeville.*

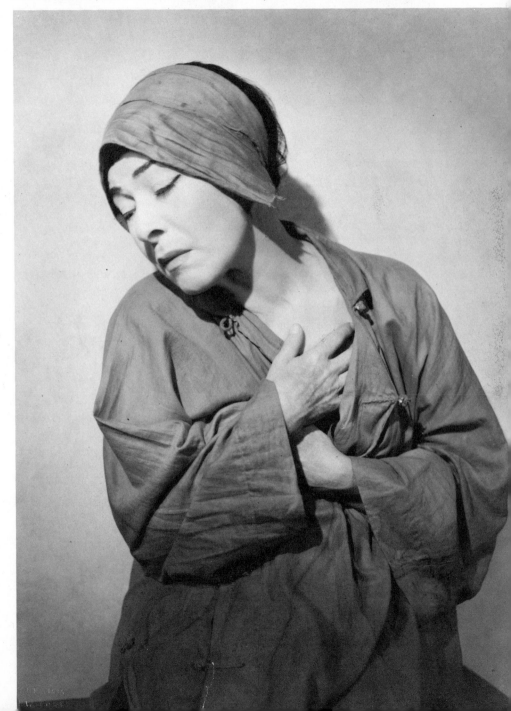

W. C. Fields in the 1920's.

From left to right: Mitzie Mayfair, Jack Pearl, Helen Morgan, Harry Richman, Ruth Etting, Hal LeRoy. All played vaudeville.

Jack Benny entering vaudeville, just prior to World War I.

Raymond & Caverly,
Dutch dialect comedy team,
in 1922.

Raymond and Caverly

Walter Huston, who as half of the comedy team Whipple and Huston (Whipple was Mrs. Huston) did a vaudeville sketch, "Boots," which later added a jazzband. Huston danced and told stories. He went into the play, Desire Under the Elms, and then became a famous movie star.

Jack Durant and "Fatty" Arbuckle at the Pantages Theater in Los Angeles in 1924.

Eddie Cantor and his family (circa 1928).

When vaudeville was King! Standing, left to right: Lillian Shaw, Fritzi Scheff, Fred Stone, Duncan Sisters, Eddie Darling, Rae Samuels and an unknown man. Seated: Sadie Burt, Charlie Dale, Joe Laurie, Jr., Lulu McConnell and Joe Smith (in the late 1920's).

Willie West & McGinty, a hot vaudeville knockabout comedy act circa 1928-1931.

Earl Carroll's Vanities: *Jack Durant, Lillian Roth and Bill Demarest in 1931.*

Mitchell and Durant in 1927, when they formed their partnership.

Ethel Merman, Benny Rubin, Jack Haley, Eddie Leonard, Patsy Kelly and Dave Apollon, as billed in the inner lobby of the Palace in the 1930's.

Shirley Temple and Jack Durant, in 1934.

At a dinner party in the late 1930's. Left to right, seated: Eve Sully, Ida Cantor, Eddie Cantor, Gracie Allen and Al Jolson. Left to right, standing: Benny Field, Blossom Seely, Harry Reiley, George Burns, Jesse Block and Mrs. Leo Spitz (whose husband was head of Universal International).

Mae West and Jack Durant in 1934.

*Alice Faye and
Jack Durant in 1936.*

*Gypsy Rose Lee and Jack Durant at the Palace Theater
in Chicago, 1938.*

The Paramount in the 1930's and 1940's. One of the major presentation houses, it no longer exists. A bank is now on the site.

The RKO Colonial in Dayton, Ohio, in the late 1930's.

The Palace's star-studded marquee in the 1940's, when it was attempting a comeback.

Blossom Seely and Benny Fields in the 1940's.

The Los Angeles Orpheum, another "presentation house."
Crowds are lining up for a free Chevrolet.

Gracie Allen and W. C. Fields in the 1940's.

Laurel and Hardy with Jack Durant at a Command Performance in London, 1947.

Typical vaudeville bill at the R.K.O. in Rochester, N.Y., in 1949. Left to right: Berk & Hollow; Two Chords; Pat Rooney (on mike), Kitty & Fannie Watson with mother in middle; acrobatic trio, Raya Sisters, Dolinoff. Standing in back: Wally Brown. Conductor Nick Frances is in pit.

George Burns and Jack Benny at a benefit show in 1950. (Photo courtesy of the Friars Club)

From left to right, back row: Joe Smith, Bobby Clark, Benny Fields, Charlie Dale, Murray Larkins. Front row: Mabel Smith, Lucille Clark, Blossom Seely, Mollie Dale.

Fanny Brice as "Second Hand Rose."

The Palladium as it is today. It is still the London home of "variety" (our vaudeville), but that is produced only occasionally.

Eddie Cantor and Ted Lewis

Lou Holtz in 1937.

Belle Baker

Bobby Clark and Fanny Brice, when they were both stars in the Follies.

Sylvia Froos

BENNY RUBIN

A SKILLFUL comedian with a talent for dialect comedy—Scotch, Irish, British, Jewish—Benny Rubin was a standout in the theater of the two-a-day. He also had great tap-dancing ability that always won added applause.

Raised in a Boston slum, Rubin entered show business as a straight hoofer, performing in the street, in amateur shows, and wherever else he could earn some money to help his family. He even tried amateur boxing because winners earned $5 or $10. His vaudeville-trained ability to change his facial expression and mannerisms to match his dialect added credibility and always drew big laughter.

In the early 1930s Rubin left vaudeville for Hollywood. He is sometimes seen on TV shows in dramatic roles.

I learned to dance watching the Soroka Brothers, two Boston guys, rehearse in a doorway near my home on Margin Street in Boston, next door to the Old North Church where Paul Revere did his shtick. All the kids on the block imitated them. I didn't know it was dancing—they called it taps. To me it was just a noise they were making, and we kids loved making noise. I tried it, liked it, and eventually I did better than the other kids on the block.

They told me I could take those taps to some of the neighboring amateur shows and perhaps win $1, $2, or $3—anyway, 50 cents. So from January, 1910, until December I was on every amateur show that would let me go on. Fifty cents in 1910 was real money. Here's the idea: If a person went into a fine restaurant in those days and ordered steak, potatoes, rolls, butter, coffee, and apple pie the bill would be about 35 cents. And when

I brought home a half a buck we didn't go to any restaurant. My mother would buy eggs at a penny each or 12 cents a dozen; bread was 6 cents a loaf. That half a buck fed our family of father, mother, and eight sons for some time.

I palled around with a fellow named John Francis Sullivan. In later years he, too, went into show business—you knew him as Fred Allen. One night I saw a kid get $3 for fighting. Well, I could fight and for $3 I'd fight anybody. My friend Johnny carefully explained to me that they were boxing, not fighting, And Johnny could box. He won about every boxing match he went into. So I, too, went in, and achieved an unbroken record —thirty-eight fights, no wins.

My acting was interrupted when the truant officer caught up with me and for the next fifteen months I was in the Industrial School for Boys in Shirley, Massachusetts. My wooden clog dancing shoes went with me.

The school taught me house painting and I followed that trade when I got out. I worked ten hours a day, six days a week, for $10 a week. I still hoofed nights in amateur shows.

Eventually my brothers and an uncle felt it was a disgraceful thing I was doing. To be an actor was disgraceful enough: a fighter was a real bum—and I was both. So they decided to make me a rubber heel salesman. My uncle put me to work and I got $20 and expenses. My first trip was to Providence, Rhode Island. I didn't accomplish much on the first day, but I did that night. I went to a burlesque show. During the show an announcement was made that because some boxer didn't show, anybody weighing in at about 125 pounds could get $25 if they went three rounds. I couldn't wait to go on. I got my brains beat out, winding up with a beautiful black eye. I didn't know that my uncle who had given me the job had come to Providence to see how his poor nephew was making out. He was in the audience and saw me get the shellacking.

When I got back to my hotel my uncle was waiting for me and fired me. During the bawling out one guest was an eager listener. He called me by name. And he took me into the kitchen and put a piece of steak on my eye. He amazed me by saying that he knew my name because he had seen me dancing in Boston's amateur shows. Then he offered me a job as soon as the eye got better. You know him as Lou Walters of Latin Quarter fame. His daughter can be seen regularly on NBC. Her name is Barbara Walters.

My first job was as a dancer with Billy Hall's *Revue* in Rhode Island. I think I got a fair hand for my first appearance. All this was in 1914 and I was fifteen. From then to 1917 there were two other tab shows, and finally I went into Zed Darrow's "English Daisies," also a tab show, but on a showboat. I got $15 a week plus food and board. That job was wonderful. Then came Hal Hoyt's *Gee Whiz*, where I got $27.50. I got into a crap game and won $150 and promptly gave my notice because I figured I was the greatest comedian and dancer there was and I was going to New York to take over the city.

When I got to New York I asked around about how to get into a burlesque show. This was July, and I was told it was the middle of a season, that they didn't hire until the winter. I was also told I would be smart to go back where I came from.

I heard that a Max Segal had a burlesque show in Brooklyn—*Cheer Up America*—and was looking for a comic to replace the one the show had. I went to the Strand Building, where Segal had his office, and said to him, "I'm your new comedian." He said, "Who the hell are you?" I said, "I'm the greatest dancer in the world." He said, "Dance." Well, you can't hear taps on a rug so he took me into the men's room. On the marble floor you could hear taps. So now he knew I could dance. "But how do I know you're a comedian?" So I told him some jokes. He took me to Brooklyn, introduced me to the manager and to Eddie Lambert, the comic I was to replace. They had me watch the show that Friday night, and then the Saturday matinee, and they threw me in that Saturday night. My salary was $60 a week and my name was outside on twenty-four sheets—that's the biggest billing you can get. I stayed with Segal's show for some time. Then I decided I had had enough burlesque. I wanted vaudeville.

I called on a Boston agent, Sammy Pane. He said, "You're a burlesque comic. How do I know you can do anything in vaudeville?" So I stuck stuff together and got an act for myself. I didn't know about writers. Anyway, I got booked and my first date was in Bridgeport, Connecticut, for $87.50.

When I made good there I figured I was again ready for New York. You know, I'm now the big vaudevillian. I showed my act in Proctor's Fifth Avenue and got myself jobs for $125. So I played around, mostly small time and gradually got better jobs. My money was now up to $350.

I met Jack Benny in 1923 when I was on the bill with him in Rochester, New York. To me, he didn't have much of an act. He was a monologist who got polite laughs. In my act I got belly laughs. And Benny used to stand in the wings and scream at my jokes. Later on, in the cellar where we dressed, he was still laughing. I loved a guy like that and we became friends. Now, I liked him because he was nice. He laughed at me and he was a decent guy. He liked me even though I used bad language and I was a rough guy, loud and vulgar. But he could see that basically I wasn't a rotten guy.

The Earle in Philadelphia, with Benny Rubin headlining. (Photo courtesy of Popular Press)

Benny Rubin, as a headliner. (Photo courtesy of James J. Kriegsmann)

The same year I was living at the Princeton Hotel, New York. I was also in a unit show of "Blackouts" for producer-agent Max Hayes. These blackouts were taken from George White's *Scandals* by Billy K. Wells, who wrote the scenes. This was long before you ever heard of Ken Murray or any of those people. We played the *Blackouts* throughout the country until about 1925, when I went back to doing a single. First time I went into the Palace I worked in four. The big comedy act was next to closing —I've forgotten who it was—but I was such a hit they moved me next to closing and from then on I was next to closing all the time.

As a single my salary went up to $750 a week until I got to California. I got a break in the movies then, signed with MGM for $2500 and decided that's where I'd stay. No more vaudeville for me.

Let me go back to the Princeton Hotel. When I stayed there I chummed around with Solly Ginsburg, who everybody in vaudeville knew as Violinsky because he played a concert fiddle and piano; Bert Hanlon, who did a single; and Benny Ryan, who worked with his wife as Ryan and Lee. Those three guys were also song writers and even wrote a song for me, one I could sing and dance to—"When Frances Dances with Me." Ryan's wife became ill and Ryan hired a girl to replace her in the act. She was a little dancer working with an Irish jig troupe. You know her as Gracie Allen.

Then Benny Ryan decided he didn't want to troupe and hired George Burns to do his act with Gracie Allen. So Burns and Allen played the circuit as a small-time act. Then Al Boasberg, a jewelry salesman who later became a full-time comedy writer, sold them a sketch, "Lamb Chops." They tried it, liked it so much they left Benny Ryan, married each other, and worked in their own act.

It is now 1931 and Eddie Cantor asked me to go back into the Palace with him as a team. I didn't want it. Cantor, who was supposed to play the date with Georgie Jessel, had a fight with him, so he wanted someone else. I didn't need Cantor. I could do all right as a single. Cantor pleaded, "Come in with me. I want to show that stinking Jessel." So we wrote an act together, made a deal.

During the period I was living in Hollywood I would pick up the vaudevillians I knew when they came to town, entertain them, and take them to the weekly fights at the stadium, where they could see the stars. When Block and Sully came through, I took them to my home, mentioned the Palace date I had with Cantor, and promised I would get them into the same show. A few weeks later Burns and Allen came through. I entertained them too, got them tickets for the fights, but told them I couldn't join them that night. I had to rehearse the act with Cantor. Just then the phone rang. It was Cantor wanting to know if we could do some rehearsing that very night. I said I had George Burns and Gracie Allen with me and he said, "Bring 'em along." I did.

While we were rehearsing, George turned to Grace and said, "Googie, how would you like to be on a show like that?" She replied, "Oh, my God—how could you wish for a thing like that!" Cantor, not knowing I had promised the spot to Block and Sully, said, "You want to be in the show? Easy," picked up the phone, called Abe Lastfogel, and said, "Benny and I want Burns and Allen for that bill we are going to do at the Palace."

Well, weeks went by. Cantor and I arrived in New York. We were met by the Bennys, Block and Sully, Ed Sullivan and his wife Sylvia, Blossom Seely and Benny Fields, Jack and Winnie Pearl. We all went to Cantor's suite at the Pierre where we had cold cuts, talked, laughed, and joked. All of a sudden Benny Fields said, "I have an announcement to make." Everybody became quiet. We all thought it was some kind of a joke. He said, "Blossom and I are rehearsing a show called *Girl Crazy* with Gregory Ratoff. Ratoff, who owns the show, was just offered a Broadway show by Jed Harris, called *Wonderbar*. Now if Benny Rubin would jump into *Girl Crazy*, he would save sixty people's lives, and our lives too." Cantor turned to me and said, "Why not? I'll make up with Jessel." And that's what happened. Cantor made up with Jessel and I went into *Girl Crazy*.

Now Cantor also had a radio show at the same time, the *Chase and Sanborn Coffee Hour*. He put on Gracie Allen and he did the material that George and Gracie did at the Palace. That made Burns and Allen headliners.

After *Girl Crazy*, where I took the Willie Howard part, I went back to California. Arthur Willi had been after me for some time to come back to the Palace, and finally I said I'd come but it would be with something different. Willi asked what I wanted. I said the first thing I wanted was a young Irish guy, specifically a tenor who could sing and of course talk, one who could play scenes with me. Al Melnick, my agent, said, "Send on the script of the proposed show and we'll see." Willi okayed it. All the other acts booked for the show were only those I wanted—Kate Smith, George Olsen and his band. Melnick got me a young actor as the Irish lad. I arrived in New York and Melnick and I went over to this actor's apartment. We handed him the script. He God-blessed me all over the place for taking him into the Palace with me. I said, "Here's the script. You've got all day to study it. I haven't slept much. I'm tired and I'm going to my hotel and sleep. But tonight you and I will rehearse." When

Melnick and I came to see the kid that night he was blind drunk so we took the script away.

This is too long to tell, but I hadn't spoken to Jack Haley for many years because I disliked him intensely. Never mind the reason. Melnick knew but insisted Haley was exactly what I wanted. The thing was that Haley had once been a big hit in Broadway shows, but he had been in two flops in a row and he needed a job. So Melnick convinced me. We went into the Edison Hotel where the Haleys, Jack and Flo, were living. They washed their clothes in the room. They were hung all about. They did their cooking on Sternos. I told Jack what it was all about. He said, "My God! This would be a Godsend for me." I said, "Okay. I'm going over to tell Willi about you being my partner. How much do you want?" He said he didn't care. "I've never played the Palace and if I get in, I'll take anything. How's about two-fifty?" I said, "Oh no that'll cheapen you. If I can get you five hundred, okay?" He said fine. As Melnick and I were crossing Times Square to go to the Palace building Melnick said to me, "You'd better ask Willi for a thousand and let him bargain you down." When we got to Willi's office I explained my idea and told him I wanted Haley. He said it was okay but asked how much he had to pay him. I said, "The same as me—twenty-five hundred." And that's how Haley was started on all those riches.

We went in for a week and were held over for six. We then went on the road and played every city in the country. I had an earlier commitment to make some shorts for Brynie Foy in Long Island. Jack Haley had a commitment to do a picture for Paramount on the Coast. We both finished our commitments, put the act together again, and went back into the Palace. I might add that between 1920 and 1932 I played the Palace twenty-six times. But back to Haley. I said I was going to do something different, something that's never been done before—write all new stuff.

I told Willi what Haley and I were going to do and that we were going to break in our new act at the Brooklyn Albee Theater. And we did. But right after the last show I got an attack and was taken to the hospital for an emergency appendectomy. And there went the Palace date. Haley couldn't go in without me. There wasn't anybody immediately available so Willi called Jack Lubin, who booked the Loew Circuit. He said he had a young punk in Syracuse. "I'll have to cancel him up there and bring him in." It was Milton Berle. And that's how he got his break.

I was in the hospital for ten days and by that time Haley had to go back to Paramount on the Coast. Melnick went after me. He said he could get me $2750 a week but I refused. I was tired. So I canceled all the dates and went back to Los Angeles. I got a radio show originating in San Francisco. The sponsor was Shell Oil.

One of the times Haley and I were at the Palace a man, Douglas Coulter, who was with one of the networks, came backstage and said, "Mr. Rubin, I have a radio show that fits you perfectly and I wish you would do it." I asked him if it originated in New York or Los Angeles. When he said New York I said, "Look, mister, I've got a family and a home in Los Angeles and after this is over I want nothing more than to get back to them and stay there." I told him if he wanted a comic, I would get him one. He said, "We don't want Mr. Haley." I said it wasn't Haley.

Now Jack Benny had been in Earl Carroll's *Vanities*, and when he closed and came to New York he wanted to do more vaudeville. His asking price was $1500 a week. The bookers said, "Fifteen hundred—for what? You've been away from vaudeville so long we don't know if you can still do a vaudeville act." He was advised to show his act. You know—take a showing date. And that broke Jack's heart. He wouldn't show for anybody.

When I told this Doug Coulter I would get him a comic I meant Jack Benny. Coulter wanted to know where he could see or hear him. I told him I'd call him.

We were all in Jack Haley's apartment in New York. There was Ed and Sylvia Sullivan and Dave Marks, the big toy manufacturer. I said, "Look, Jack Benny is in big trouble. I think I can get him a hell of a big radio show, Canada Dry, but you've got to help me, Ed." Sullivan said, "What can I do?" I said, "You've got the *Toast of the Town*. Maybe you can put him on it. We won't tell him I'm having somebody listening. You can tell Jack, 'So long as you're not doing anything, come on and do the show.'"

So Jack Benny went on the Ed Sullivan show and I called Coulter to tell him to listen. He then called me back and said he'd heard Benny. And that's how Jack Benny got his first chance on radio. The rest is history.

You may like to know that after 1932, when Jack Benny got his radio show, a writer named Harry Cohen called on me to sell me jokes—one-liners, etc. I didn't use that kind of material but I knew that Benny was looking for writers so I sent him over. Benny bought some jokes and after three weeks put Cohen on his payroll. Some time after, Cohen called on me again to ask me to persuade Benny to change his format—do a story format rather than depend on jokes. The reason was that Cohen was running out of material. He was afraid to make the suggestion to Benny because he might fire him and he needed the job. So I made the suggestion to Benny and he accepted it. But it was really Cohen who came up with the Mary Livingston character, Schlepperman, and Buck Benny Rides Again, etcetera. From then on, Benny never used the one-line jokes.

Cohen's wife was an ambitious lady. She convinced her husband that without him, Benny was nothing, and that Benny should pay Cohen half his own salary. Jack refused, so Cohen decided he would become a comedian himself. He got a radio show—I forget where—and then faded. I don't know what happened to him.

Do you remember Don Wilson? Well, I was on some radio program doing some fast commercials, for which I got paid handsomely. There was a guy there, an emcee or something, who laughed at everything I did. I told Benny about him and suggested he grab him. Benny did.

I mentioned Abe Lastfogel a while back. He's the top man in the William Morris Agency. I'm sure you know him. But what you don't know is that in 1921 we lived together on 92nd Street. We slept together in a double bed. And his sister Bessie cooked for us. On hot nights we would walk home from the office, going through the park. One particular night there were two kids playing the harmonica and dancing in the park and then passing the hat. The kid with the harmonica was Borrah Minevitch. The kid who danced was a Canadian, Ben Blue. We threw them some money and walked away. Abe stopped and said, "Why don't we take those

Benny Rubin in 1974.
(Photo courtesy of Popular Press)

kids up to Saranac for the show?" So back we went, got their names and addresses, and that's how they began.

I look back on my life in vaudeville: In the early days we traveled by train, often sitting up all night. We froze, though seldom roasted—theaters didn't run in the summer because there was no air-conditioning. When the presentation houses—those big theaters with movies—began using big names, it was pure murder for a comic. Not only were there four or more shows a day, but you'd work in front of a band—the bands were onstage. For the first show the musicians would laugh. The next show they would just look. And from then on they'd be yawning or whatever. Audiences watching them would think, if they don't laugh, why should we. And so it went. It was pure murder even though the money was big.

Big-time vaudeville—well, that was really something. I would go on say 3:30, do fifteen minutes or so, then out to a ball game or whatever. Maybe go home for a nap and dinner, or lunch. Come back at say 8 P.M., finish at 10 or so. Yes, it was show business.

HARRY RITZ

THE RITZ Brothers, Al, Harry, and Jimmy, were outstanding for their precision dancing. But it wasn't until they added knockabout comedy that they became vaudeville favorites. The burden of comedy was carried by Harry. A special material song, "The Man in the Middle Is the Funny One," became their trademark. It led to Harry's persistent bellowing plea of "Don't holler—please don't holler," as the brothers would argue as to which was really the funny one. Much of their comedy was physical. The brothers would push each other around while Harry wandered around the stage screaming, "Don't holler!"

We broke into vaudeville in the late 1920s; I think it was 1929—a hell of a time to break in. But what did we know about stock markets or whatever? Anyway, the stock market was busting wide open and there we were trying to become actors. It wasn't so much that we wanted to become actors as we wanted to make money—to eat, and maybe to meet girls. Our first break-in was at the Fox's Folly. I forget who our agent was, if we had an agent, but we got $50 for the week—that was for the three of us, Al, Jimmy, and me.

We worked joints, we worked wherever we could get a job. Our real name is Joachim and we changed it: Al got an extra's job in Brooklyn's old Vitagraph studio near Coney Island for 75 cents. They asked for his name and he gave Al Joachim. The guy said the name was too long. Al then looked out of the window and saw a truck marked "Ritz Crackers"— so his name became Ritz. When we started there was a kind of fashion in show biz for brother teams—there were the Slate Brothers, the Condos Brothers, the Reo Brothers. Now there was the Ritz Brothers.

The Ritz Brothers make a movie. Harry is in the middle, with Jimmy on his right, while the late Al holds the gun.

The Ritz Brothers' billing at a Miami Beach nightclub.

The most wonderful thing about vaudeville was the respect people had for actors. We had fans who would follow us. And if the early small-time days were bitter, and if sleeping atop radiators to keep warm and staying up many long nights on dirty trains to make jumps were tough, they taught us many things. Working to many different audiences also taught us our trade. Like most of the brother acts around then, we started as hoofers. We could dance, but who knew from talking? Sure, we picked up some jokes, but basically we were hoofers.

Well, about a year after we first broke in, we made the Palace. And was that a thrill. The headliner was Frank Fay and his wife Barbara Stanwyck. Fay was a star. She just came out for a little drama bit. Nobody on the bill, certainly not us, ever guessed that that girl would someday become a big movie star. But then again, why should we? We were interested in ourselves, our spot on the bill, our music, where we were booked next, etcetera. The sort of a thing that every actor was interested in.

Oh sure, between vaude dates we worked in Shubert shows. We had long routes, we played with the biggest headliners of the day. But that goes without saying. After all, we were the Ritz Brothers and there wasn't a big-time bill that we didn't fit and make better. We made a lot of friends. And if some of them copied us, what of it? Sid Caesar used to say that we were his idols. That was nice to hear. Our idol was Charlie Chaplin.

We have been credited with being the forerunners of many a comedy act—Jerry Lewis for one—but every actor learns from another. It isn't imitation so much as the acquisition of certain mannerisms. Later you develop your own abilities and somebody copies you. And so it goes.

JANETTE HACKETT

JANETTE HACKETT was a creative dancer whose costumes drew almost as much attention as her dance routines. At one time she was married to Harry Delmar, the dancer, with whom she produced successful revues. Later she used the knowledge she had gained to present a flash act.

Despite the appearance of delicacy, Miss Hackett was "well stacked," a fact not lost on male audiences. They may not have known much about interpretive dancing, but the lovely well-formed figure of the dancer was something they could appreciate.

Janette Hackett no longer dances but is active in the Ziegfeld Girls' Club by virtue of being an alumna of the Ziegfeld Follies.

I came out of a convent boarding school in Philadelphia. My mother, Florence Hackett, was in the movies. She played vamps. My biggest interest in those years—this was about 1916—was dancing, ballroom dancing. I would put up my hair to look older and go into the dance halls. When my mother lost her job we all moved to New York. There were my two brothers, my grandmother, my mother and I.

My mother went to work in the movies again, this time in Fort Lee, and I decided I was going to get a job in the chorus. So I got a job in the *Shubert Passing Show*. In that show I met Kitty Doner. I was about fifteen but I looked older. Kitty and I used to go into the corner and dance. She was teaching me dancing. One night she asked me if I would like to go into vaudeville as one of a four-girl group that would work with George White. I said yes, very much. So she said she would make arrangements for me to meet George White. But then she called me a few days later to tell me White had said no when he heard my age. He thought I was too young, I needed more experience, more glamor.

I then became interested in Hawaiian dancing. I thought it was fun. I must have looked ridiculous, a blond girl doing a Hawaiian hula, but I didn't care. Somebody told me that Nora Bayes was going to do a one-woman show. So I called, met her, and did an audition. She liked the idea of a silly-looking blonde doing a Hawaiian dance and put me into her act. There was another girl in the act, Faye Marbe, who created an Oriental routine. She was very good. Very good-looking, tall, slender, seductive, looked like an Oriental, and her family had money. I watched her and thought, if I can't get a job because I'm so young I'm going to change my image. I'm going to wear tight turbans, with jewels and things, a brassiere, a long tight skirt. I'll go barefoot and do Oriental dancing. In the meantime I was earning a salary as a blond Hawaiian.

I was studying Oriental art at the Metropolitan Museum and I used to practice my Oriental dancing after matinees. One of my plans was to join my friend in Gumps, San Francisco, when the tour got there. My friend thought I could do very well in the store's Oriental department. In the meantime Faye Marbe was given her notice and I was given her part as an Oriental dancer. This was quite a change—from a blond sixteen-year-old Hawiian to a twenty-one-year-old Oriental dancer. I went on tour with Nora Bayes. After some five weeks or so in Chicago Miss Bayes wasn't feeling so well and the tour didn't continue to the Coast. I wasn't stranded, I had earned enough money to travel back to New York.

I next got a job as a solo dancer in a nightclub. This was about 1920. I wanted vaudeville, but how to get in was the problem. Then a friend of Warren Jackson, a singer in our show called Billie Shaw (of Seabury and Shaw, a vaudeville act), came to me. Since I resembled her and danced very well, she wanted to know if I would join her husband, William Seabury, in a vaudeville act that had twenty weeks lined up. At heart she was a writer and this would give her a chance to retire to her writing and let me do the hoofing. I jumped at it.

So I joined the act, got recognition, newspaper notices, and we went into the Palace right away, followed by a tour of many outlying theaters. When I finished the twenty weeks Seabury and his wife put up the money for me to form my own act. I began looking for a partner. I found a boy, Harry Delmar, who looked good though he wasn't much of a dancer. But we got together. I gave him tips and we finally had an act. We were caught at Proctor's Newark by an agent who was there to see his clients, Whiting and Burt, who were also on the bill. Anyway, we got some dates on the

THE MAGAZINE OF
VAUDEVILLE
PALACE THEATRE

VOL. V   No. 7

Janette Hackett

184

Western Vaudeville Circuit. The jobs and the theaters were nothing to be proud of. It was awful. Then we were picked up by the Orpheum Circuit and got a route of forty-nine weeks. So now the act of Hackett and Delmar was in vaudeville and doing well.

It was about 1927 that we dreamed up our own revue, calling it *Delmar's Revels*. It was in this one that Ziegfeld caught me in a ballet, "Persian Garden," and became interested. Marian Spitzer and Walter Kingsley, who was her boss at the Palace, arranged a meeting. By that time, however, I was out of the *Revels* and off on a long vaudeville tour of my own. When I got back Mr. Ziegfeld had died. The *Revels* were basically my creation, but for reasons I needn't go into, Delmar and I didn't see eye to eye.

In 1929 or so I was headlining on the Keith Circuit, and when I played the 105th Street Theater in Cleveland I looked for my name as the headliner on the billboard, but found instead the name John Steele. My name was down at the bottom. I was very angry and took it out on Steele. I wouldn't talk to him. I ignored him. My mother, traveling with me then, liked him very much. He used to stand in the wings and watch me dance. We were together on the show, and when we came back from the Coast, Steele invited my mother and me to see *Sonny Boy*. The tickets came from a good friend of mine, John Royal, who was also a friend of Steele's.

From then on John and I got to know each other well. We had much in common and we had both been taken in the past. In 1930 we were married. I became pregnant and took a job with RKO, heading up the production department. When my son was born, my husband John was busy in various shows. Then things began happening. Martin Beck was suing the Orpheum Circuit, and he cut out everything, including my production department. I was fired. My baby was then a year old but I had to put an act together.

George Golden, a genius at producing acts, gave me an idea. It was to do a dance where the girl, at the finish of the act, would fall down a flight of stairs and meet her death. That's how I got the idea for "Bad Girl," which of course was from the novel of the same name. I would start out as a gay girl. This man would come in with a long cape, a hat, and a mask. I would figure someone was playing a joke—I was supposed to be drunk at the time—and he would come into my boudoir. The music would play as if it were a record, he would take off his cape and hat and pull me into this dance. There was a sinister feeling underneath, like something I didn't expect might happen. I would dance with him and reach for his mask, but I couldn't get it off. Eventually, in an embrace, I would pull the mask off and discover Death. Then I would scream and carry on, run to the top of the stairs—with him after me. When I got to the top I would reach out and pull a drape and then fall down the entire flight, the drape trailing after me and Death triumphant behind me. As Death would duck off the stage, the singer who was singing "Bad Girl" would come on to sing the reprise.

Well, this act was a sensation in vaudeville. It was great for me. I had no competition anywhere. I played it at the Palace and they went wild over it. My partner was a tall dark man who did well later in the movies— Cesar Romero. We had some funny experiences with this act. We broke it in in a small theater in Bergenfield, New Jersey, where the stage was so small we couldn't put up the stairs and Cesar had to pretend to choke me as I was lying on the floor instead. Then he was supposed to stand up for a breather after the curtain came down in front of us. But instead of coming down in front, the curtain came down behind us. The poor guy was getting madder and madder. And that dressing room! Ceilings were so low that Romero had to walk around hunchback.

Here's another incident that is funny looking back, but it wasn't funny at the time. It was at Loew's State. I was following an act that had chickens in it. I used full stage. My partner, Ivan Triesault, a ballet dancer, was to be the groom and I the bride in a very affectionate bridal scene. We came into this beautiful room and were dancing to this lovely waltz when out came the chickens, pecking at the footlights. The people were hysterical with laughter and the chickens were getting all the laughs.

Oh well, I know of other vaudevillians to whom worse things happened following animal or bird acts.

My brother, Albert Hackett, and his wife, Frances Goodrich, went to California, where they became quite successful as writers. They went out to do *The Thin Man* series and followed it with many dramatic pictures— *Ah Wilderness!*, *Diary of Anne Frank*. My other brother, Raymond Hackett, died some fifteen years ago. He was a fine actor and was married to Blanche Sweet.

Of course we played in vaudeville with them all. There was Belle Baker, Rae Samuels, Ruth Roye, Block and Sully, Bea Lillie, Milton Berle.

I told you I married John Steele in 1930 and it was one of the things I was grateful to vaudeville for. We've got a wonderful son. He's not in show business. He's six-foot-three and handsome.

Today I do chiefly the designing of "drop dead" dresses, those anywhere from $500 and up. I turned to that when vaudeville dates dried up and club dates also became scarcer and scarcer. In 1970 John became ill and I didn't want to leave him for more than a few days. As you know, John passed away in June, 1971, and I was hit by a speeding car and knocked out of this world for nine months.

I don't know what more to tell you. So here I am in this small room in a hotel that has long seen better days. And who of us hasn't?

RAE SAMUELS

RAE SAMUELS was billed as "The Blue Streak of Vaudeville." She had her own curtain that represented a silver flash of lightning against a dark background. Miss Samuels was one of the few vocalists of the period who did comedy-rube songs. The fact that she was always dressed in elegant gowns rather than in character costumes gave added zest to her performance.

She married her manager, Marty Forkin, who piloted her to stardom. She was a favorite at the Palace and all the Keith houses for many years.

Widowed, she now lives in quiet retirement, occasionally assuming a silent interest in an art gallery.

began in show business, I suppose, because my sister was in vaudeville. Actually, when I was a child I used to recite poems in my home town, Youngstown, Ohio. I used to perform—if what a child does can be called performing—in all those Irish Catholic halls, though I'm not a Catholic. We were Baptists and my people went to the Welsh Baptist Church. I'm Welsh. Anyway, I used to entertain every Sunday night. I liked to do that very much. People would applaud and tell me what a nice little girl I was. It was nice. There's a competition in Wales called *Eisteddfed*; choirs sing in competition. They held one in Gray's Armory, Cleveland, and I did very well. They had me do a part from Shakespeare. I was nine years old at the time. Imagine me at that age in competition against grown-ups who were real exponents of Shakespeare and had studied diction and elocution! I didn't win.

As a child I never thought of singing.

My sister could sing pretty good. She married a man who was a musician and he taught her. They formed an act and went into vaudeville. They called it the "Musical Hearts." I went along with it and I also sang. I didn't get along very well with my brother-in-law. He wanted me to practice the saxophone and I didn't like that at all. It wasn't a good act, as I remember it. It didn't amount to much, but my folks didn't mind me traveling with them and I liked it. I saw many new things and it was kind of fun.

When we got to San Francisco the manager of the theater we were in asked me what I was doing with a trick musical act like that. I was then singing something called "Wild Cherry Rag" that was like the "Grizzly Bear" in those days. "You're crazy," said the manager. "Why don't you get yourself three or four songs and go out and sing them?" I said I didn't know anybody who would book me. He said, "I'll book you if you get some songs together. I'll open you next week in Oakland."

My sister loved me, and when I told her I wanted to go out by myself, she said she didn't blame me and wished me well. So off I went to Oakland. I got $50 and all I had to do was go over on that ferry. When I came into rehearsal, the leader asked for music. I had no music. All I had was a lead sheet. My brother-in-law used to play for me in the act. That lead sheet was just for the right hand, no bass at all. Well, he looked at me as if I'd been in the sun too long. There were six pieces and these orchestra boys got together and made parts for the rest of the tunes and there I played for a week. I must've done pretty well because I was booked and toured all throughout California and down through Arizona. I didn't make much money, though, because I had my railroad fare to pay. But I learned a lot and got along.

Burt Savoy and his wife—it was Savoy and Savoy at the time, later it became Savoy and Jay Brennan—played all through Arizona with me. I went to Chicago with them. I didn't have any work. I didn't know any agent or anyone. I went to a picture show, the Alcazar, Madison, and Clark, where they used singers occasionally and I told the manager what I had done. He hired me and paid me $35 a week.

Actually, all I really sang were Irving Berlin's old songs. One day a man who was with the music publisher Leo Feist—his name was Jerome Wilson—came back and said, "I think you've got something, kiddo. My advice to you now is to learn every new song you can. Are you a quick study?" I said, "I can learn any song in five minutes if I like it." He suggested that with all the music publishers in Chicago I could go in to some of them between shows and learn their songs. It wasn't a bad idea so I followed it up.

There was a young cub reporter, Jack Lait, who used to come in regularly and we became friends. He was on the *Chicago American*. He was a man, a sweet guy. Anyway, I kept singing and all kinds of people would come in and offer me jobs. I was about seventeen then but I was still working for $35. One day a man who owned theaters around the South Side came in and offered me six weeks' work. He said, "I'll give you sixty a week and no matinees, and then keep you going around my other theaters." He was one of the Asher brothers. I went to my boss and told him I was leaving Saturday night. As I was picking up my music, he said, "Put the music back. I'll give you sixty."

My friend Lait had told me not to sign any papers without discussing them with him first. When I got a letter from a Mr. Charles Bray of the Western Vaudeville Circuit, he told me not to answer Bray's letter. Well, I got I don't know how many letters from that man. Then one day the manager brought a little woman backstage. She introduced herself as Mrs. Charles Bray. I said, "Oh yes, I have have had several letters from your husband." And she said, "Why don't you go and see him? I think he can do a lot for you." I said I'd been so busy I didn't have time, but I'd go. She said, "Come today." I said, "I'll come tomorrow." Before I went I wanted to see my friend, the newspaper guy, to tell him what was going on. He came in every day—the *Chicago American* was right near where I was working. He told me to listen to Bray and say I had to consider any offer, had to talk it over with my folks. (Now this was 1911 and my people weren't in Chicago.) Anyway, I met with Mr. Bray and he told me he wanted to book me on the Orpheum Circuit. I said to him, "Mr. Bray, you really don't mean that. I'm singing in a picture show. I've never been in a first-class theater in my life—a beautiful theater like the Orpheum." Mr. Bray said, "Let me decide. You'll probably be a lot better in an Orpheum theater than at the Alcazar, where you're working."

I went back and told all this to Lait. He said, "Now, here's what you do. You can't give him a definite answer until tomorrow. No matter what he offers you, tell him you want a hundred and fifty more and you must be placed not less than the bottom of every bill wherever you play. He must pay your fare and your accompanist. You must have an accompanist." I said I didn't think the man would take me seriously if I told him that. Lait said, "You tell him what I told you, and if he doesn't go for it, tell him to forget it. Oh yes, tell him the reason you need the hundred and fifty more is because your people and you have obligations." When I went back and made these demands, Mr. Bray looked at me as if to say, how did you get so smart so fast? But I wound up with $250 a week, fare to California and back, and Mr. Bray's promise to buy my clothes and pay for my piano player. My wrists were sore signing all those papers. I showed Lait all the contracts. He said, "You've just started. You'll make some money, kiddo."

I was to open at the Orpheum Theater in Duluth, Minnesota, in two weeks—could I do it? Mr. Bray wanted to know. I said, "Oh yes, I have all the songs, the material, but I'll need some new clothes." Lait was delighted.

Now, can you imagine closing at this nickel show on a Saturday night and opening on a Sunday afternoon in this beautiful theater in Duluth? All the theaters I was to play were the Orpheum. Well, I got more people in trouble that first week I opened. I was kind of shy talking to people offstage, but was as bold as a highway robber onstage. I did my work with authority. There were two men on the bill—I think they were Mack and Owen. (Frank Owen was in pictures later on.) They were on next to closing. I was on second. I did these crazy things. The best thing I did was an old man song; I played a rube in a beautiful dress. I had my tongue in cheek pretending to spit. The song was that one about "Giddyap, Napoleon, it looks like rain." Everybody thought it was very funny, with me dressed like that. When I came off, the bicycle act that had opened the show told me to go back on, the audience was applauding like crazy. So I went back out and I thought I took enough bows. But the bicycle act said, "Go back. You're killing them." I said, "I can't be that good." And they said, "Go back and tell the audience that." So I did. Then the manager came backstage and told the bicycle act to mind their business, that I knew what I was doing. He thought I was very wise and I wasn't at all. Well, when I went on again that night they put me next to closing and they put those two bicycle men on second. They wouldn't talk to me. They hated me.

One of the men was married to a beautiful Frenchwoman. He told her I was doing some kind of tricks onstage and sent her out to see what they were. The wife came back and said, "There are no tricks. No tricks at all. She's got a personality, so don't pick on her. She knows what she's doing."

I wound up the best of friends with these people. They even wrote a song for me before I left them. It was a rube song in which I played the mouth organ. Well, within a year's time from that nickel show I was back in Chicago headlining the bill at the Chicago Palace.

Before I got to Portland I was signed to open in the *Ziegfeld Follies*— and Ziegfeld had never even seen me! Honest to God. His man saw me. The Orpheum Circuit started in Winnepeg, or Duluth, then you would go to Minneapolis—or maybe it was Winnepeg, I forget—and out to the

West Coast. But before I finished the circuit I was signed for Ziegfeld and brought to New York. They put me in a theater on Broadway—I don't think it's there anymore—in a show called *Winsome Widow*. On the show with me was Bunny Granville; he did a drunk dance. We both did singles. We were there for a month while we were rehearsing for the *Follies of 1912*. The following season I was with Al Jolson in the *Honeymoon Express*. Jolson was, well, all right. He was a great artist. Other artists didn't like him so much but the audiences adored him. He was mean to his brother, who was a nice little guy. I played with him later on.

We had a great dancing act in that show, Doyle and Dixon. What pranksters they were. They could stop the show whenever they wanted to, have the audiences applaud longer than they should. And Jolson was very angry at that. My gracious, I wanted everybody to go good. If somebody goes good ahead of you, you have it all set for you.

When I played small time the rube song was the best thing I did. I also did character songs. I did Italian songs—anything you want. Even Jewish songs. My name is Rachel but I'm Welsh, Welsh as cheese my mother used to say. She was born right near where Richard Burton was raised in Wales. I can speak a little Welsh.

You know, it was easier to perform in the small time but it was easier to entertain in the big time. I was never nervous onstage. I didn't know what it was to be afraid. I never was envious of anybody else in my whole life. People would talk about Sioux City and Philadelphia—they're dead there. But for me Philadelphia was wonderful and I loved it in Sioux City, that crazy little town.

I played with Bob Hope many times. I was with him at the Orpheum in New Orleans when he didn't even have an act. He did blackouts. It was Bob Hope and Company. He had three other fellows with him and a woman. I'll never forget the trip down in an old open car, no top. When we passed, he would wave at us. Well, we got to New Orleans ahead of him —and the rain. It rained cats and dogs, and when Hope and his company arrived, they looked like drowned rats. One thing I'll say about Bob Hope. He was fine. He tried everything he knew. He'd change his blackouts every show.

I sometimes think back to the artists I worked with. In the *Follies* I was with Leon Errol, Bert Williams, Lillian Lorraine—she was a beauty —Fanny Brice—she was great. She could be serious and tear your heart out, or she could make you laugh till your sides ached.

Did you know that Milton Berle copies me? I used to play with him when he was a little boy in knickers. He was one of the finest boys I've known. When you see him, ask him where he got that gesture he uses. I used to do it. I'd walk up and hit the backdrop. I used to have my own drop. It was a material like turkish toweling dyed blue with big bubbles on it and a big streak of lightning that came down.

I knew Archie Leach when he was part of a stilt act. He became Cary Grant. His greatest ambition was to sing. I don't think he ever did. We were on the bill in Rochester or Detroit.

Phil Silvers was another nice kid. He worked in an act called Morris and Campbell. Phil used to sit in a box with Joe Morris and a bag of groceries between them, handing out celery. Very funny.

I'm rich in memories. I loved Benny Rubin. He was a very nice and very funny boy. The greatest rube song I ever did was written for me by Lou Brown, and what did he know about farmers? I'm not saying this to make fun, because I loved him. The one he wrote started: "I've got a farm about six miles out"—I forget the rest. Anyway, it's about this farmer who gives up his cow so he can have a wife and later is sorry.

Actually, I never sang published songs except when I worked in that picture show. Did you know I was the first one to do Irving Berlin's "Oh, How I Hate to Get Up in the Morning"? It was at the Palace and Berlin was at Camp Upton and the guy who was the manager for Berlin, came back and said I've got the greatest song you ever heard. If you put it on the stage tonight, you'll kill 'em." They played it for me and the minute I heard it I knew what it would do because the Palace was packed with soldiers. I learned the thing in five minutes. That night Berlin was in the box right off the stage and when I got to the line "Someday I'm gonna murder the bugler," the soldiers went crazy. Izzy Berlin came back and said, "Rae, that was marvelous. You couldn't have done it better if you wanted to."

I was asked to come to London to take Ethel Levy's place, but I was married and Marty and I were very close. Ethel sang and danced. She was great. You know she was married to George M. Cohan. I never kept company with a boy in my life until I met Marty. I was playing the Orpheum in San Francisco, and Marty—he was a prize fight manager— came to the stage door. It was a few days before New Year's. The doorman told me that this man had an introduction from an old friend. I didn't know anybody by the name Forkin. This was my first time on the Orpheum Circuit and I liked the people on the bill. We'd have parties—I'd play the mouth organ, someone would play the tin whistle—and I didn't want to be bothered with strangers. But Marty came the next day and I peeped out and said to myself, he's too classy for me—he was in a derby and a frock coat with satin lapels, carrying a cane. Not for me, I said. But he persisted. Finally I went to lunch with a couple of his friends—bookmakers I think they were, and they were nice but they could have killed him for bringing me. I wasn't dressed in fancy clothes and they were really dressed. I had on a sailor hat, and if my mother had known I paid $15 for it, she'd have killed me.

There were so many things and so many people. Marty ran into me in almost every city I played. It was always "accidental" he said. We married after six months. We were together over fifty years. I think of the old days when he was alive. They were good. We would talk and discuss things that happened every day. If we couldn't sleep, we'd talk until daylight. Oh well, God has been good to me. I'll be eighty-six on my next birthday. I've got good health and I've had happiness. I'm at peace.

KEN MURRAY

KEN MURRAY was a fast-talking comedian whose specialty was a speedy series of gags told in an obvious manner. Occasionally Murray used props, one of which was a small wind-up toy dog that would do somersaults. In print it doesn't sound very funny but when Murray used it and made remarks, the audience found it hilarious. He also added some clarinet playing, some dancing, and dramatic recitations, all done with a competent, authoritive air.

Perhaps he is best remembered today as the tall brush-haired emcee of the long-running Ken Murray's Blackouts, *which set a record, a seven-year run in Hollywood.*

I went into show business because my father was a vaudevillian—Jack Doncourt. He was part of a two-man comedy act—you know, a comedian and a straight man. I was brought up on a farm in upper New York State, though I was born in New York City. My father bought that farm in the Catskills and his idea was to go in for raising fancy chickens, like guinea hens and ducks. It never worked out, but that's a different story.

As a boy, Douglas Fairbanks was my movie hero. I used to swing from the rafter in the attic trying to do the same tricks I saw Fairbanks doing in his latest movie, which I had seen the previous Saturday afternoon in the Fireman's Hall in town. I was sixteen when we moved back to New York. I think that was about 1918.

Ever since I played at acting in our attic I wanted to be an actor. After moving back to New York and graduating high school I became a door-to-door salesman but hung around any theater where my father was playing. I got to know some of the acts on the bill. There was one particular fellow—Burt Carlell, who was in an act called the "Wyoming Trio"—who fascinated me. Between shows, while the organ was playing for the movies—they were silents—he taught me a waltz clog, a soft-shoe, a buck and wing, how to spin a rope, how to crack a whip and knock a cigarette out of someone's mouth. On my own I also learned how to play the clarinet. I figured if I was going to go into show business I would learn everything I could in case I ever did manage to break into vaudeville. In those days show business meant vaudeville. Besides, that's what my father was in. In the meantime my father was after me to get a steady job—not that door-to-door selling. I finally got a job in a department store's music department—this was before radio—and that's where I bought my first clarinet. It cost $30 and they took $2 a week out of my $15-a-week salary to pay for it.

It was about 1921 when one fellow on the bill with my father looked at me and said he knew some guy who was looking for a straight man. "Can you sing and dance?" Well, I didn't do much singing but I could dance. So I met Pete Curley—he was a burlesque comic now playing vaudeville—and I became his straight man. The act broke in out in Huntington, Long Island. From the beginning I apparently had the ability to do a comedy straight. You know, there are a great many of our comedians who are not really comedians. They are really good comedy straight men. Bob Hope is that way. Cantor was that way. Benny was that way. And that's what I was from the beginning. But when I worked with Pete Curley I sometimes got laughs on the questions—the straight lines—so I didn't last too long with him. Old-time comics didn't want their straight men getting the laughs. They wanted the laughs for themselves.

I had put up a notice, or an ad, at the NVA club, one of those "At Liberty" notices—straight man, sings and dances—all on the strength of that one job that I was fired out of. Charles Senna, who had an act called Murray, Senna, and Dean (his wife was Helen Dean), decided to hire me. Murray Morey was leaving the act and I would have to change my name to Murray to keep the billing intact. So I called myself Ken Murray. My father was all for the name change because he was working under Doncourt, his real name, and if I used it there might be a mixup. Besides, if I turned out to be lousy it would be under some other name than his. I worked in the act about a season, and when it ended, I started working, or looking for work, as a single. I played the clarinet and sang songs like "Barney Google," told jokes, and played the $2 and $5 theaters around New York. One theater was the Chanticleer on Tenth Avenue. I also did the Fally Markus dates. Fally was a theater booker who put all those break-in dates

Ken Murray

into theaters around New York. You know what he paid—$10. And it was big money.

Then I got another job with a unit as a straight man in a big act billed as "Thorr." It was there that I met a girl, Charlotte Rich, and we got married. We worked as a two-act for about a year and a half and we broke up. She was unhappy. I went back to working as a single. I started in show business in 1922, and in 1926 I was playing the Palace as a single. The headliner was Will Mahoney, the Australian. He was great. I was in the number-four spot.

Let me go back a minute. In 1925 I was playing straight to a great comedian in a big flash act. We were at Loew's State in the dead of winter. It was about show time and my partner wasn't there. The stage manager yelled at me to go and find him. I was all dressed for the act—white flannels, blue coat, etc.—but I dashed out in full makeup to the Somerset Hotel on West 47th Street. I found him, passed out on his bed. I got him up and we slipped and slid on the icy sidewalks, stepped into snow banks, but finally made it to the theater. The poor devil didn't know what was going on. I fed him straight lines and he gave me blank stares. He did an act but it was all ad lib. What a master he was. I remember he looked out at the audience and said, "I'm sorry I'm late. My wife stopped me on the street and said, 'Drunk again.' I said, 'So'm I.'"

On the same bill was Eva Tanguay, the headliner. She was still a great star but audiences didn't know that she was going blind. She had to be led from her dressing room to the wings.

I joined the Harry Carroll unit. He was a great songwriter. I did scenes in the unit. We played the Keith and Orpheum time. In 1927 the unit played Los Angeles and that was my first trip to Hollywood. I had a movie camera and a projector at home. Instead of taking pictures and sending them home, I took movies and sent them home. I stayed around Los Angeles for a while and then rejoined the unit in San Francisco.

When I got back to New York RKO—it was no longer Keith's—signed me for another route. Gave me a long-term contract and my own unit. I came out to the Coast and that's when I first met Bob Hope. He took over my unit when I didn't want to go on the road anymore. Bob was just starting.

Then we came into the thirties and I got on radio. Had my own show —"Hollywood Hotel." Vaudeville was falling apart in those days. I remember one of the last tours I did in vaudeville. Houses were closing in back of me as two-a-day was going into three-a-day, with pictures. That was 1929–1930–1931.

Even though vaudeville seemed to be through, I still took jobs in it if nothing else was available. In 1942 I played the Loew's State, and I thought back to 1926, when I was on the big time, playing the Palace when I was only twenty-three years old. In those days I was billed as the youngest comedian on the Keith time. I had all sorts of offers from the great musical comedy producers of the day, including Ziegfeld. Albee had signed me to a seven-year contract and wouldn't let me out of it. Albee was supposed to have said they—RKO—had big plans for me. So I did a talkie for RKO in 1929, something called *Half Marriage*. It starred Olive Borden. After that came a flock of movies.

By 1942 I was sitting on my hands. There were no radio offers, so when the Loew's State date was offered, I took it. One night before heading back to the Coast I stopped off to catch a new revue, *Priorities*. It starred Lou Holtz, Hazel Scott, and others. This was a great vaudeville show, and it gave me an idea. Out of what I saw that night Ken Murray's *Blackouts* was born. It made history, playing at the El Capitan in Hollywood. Actually it was a glorified vaudeville show with girls who didn't

Ken Murray and Marie Wilson, when they appeared in Murray's Blackouts.

just stand there. I worked with them—gave them lines, bits, etcetera. And if almost every night some big star, unbilled, would come onstage, that was so much added gravy.

You can see, however, that all of this came out of vaudeville. What a training ground that was! It was there you learned how to read lines, how to walk, stand, move. How to build a comedy bit, timing, etcetera. There is nothing like it today.

Now I have a boy, Cort, who graduated from Brigham Young. He sings and wants to go into show business. He majored in journalism and has been in the Navy. I took him on "The Merv Griffin Show." It was a father-and-son show—Burt Bacharach and his son, and Tony Martin and his son, and me and Cort. My boy sang. He sang fine. But I told him, if you want to be in show business, you want to be an actor, there's no shortcut, you've got to learn your trade. Now, when I started in vaudeville, I learned by playing dumps, but there are no places like that anymore. So Cort goes to school at night, and days he works on a small local paper. But he's learning.

I feel sorry because there are so many actors who would've been big

Ken Murray competing against himself: at the Palace in person, and across the street in a movie, Ladies of the Jury.

stars, with legs that would've lasted. The only trouble is they got their laughs and got there fast by taking their routines and styles from somebody else instead of developing their own style. Most of them fade out. For example, watch some of them on television.

George Gobel is an excellent comedian. There's no reason why he isn't on top. But what he did in his act ate up so much of his talents and facets of his personality that he came to the end much, much too soon.

On the other hand, take Hope and Benny and Burns. They know what they're doing. There's a longevity to it. It wasn't an accident. They learned their craft. One learns from experience or one goes to a school. One can't be taught to be a comedian, but one can be taught the fundamentals, the rudiments of acting. In the old days the studios nursed and took care of their contract players. They saw that they learned their craft and slowly built them to stardom. But there are no studio systems today. A Paul Newman, a Steve McQueen, a Marlon Brando, learned their craft the hard way. They learned their business.

A certain type of comedian is virtually extinct today. There are no more W. C. Fields or Laurel and Hardys. It's very simple. If you have two sons, one goes to West Point, the other to Princeton. It is certain that the West Pointer will not become an actor. There is only one man in the arts who came of there and that was Whistler, the painter. But out of Princeton you can easily come up with a Jimmie Stewart, Hank Fonda, or a Josh Logan.

The point is that if you can't develop a certain type of comedy, because there is no place to develop it, then you can't have that kind of comedian. So there won't be any more W. C. Fields. The only comedian around today who has a little smidgen of it is Jerry Lewis, and he had a little vaudeville (very little is true) with his father when he was young.

You see, comedy has changed. People still say that vaudeville will come back, but vaudeville doesn't have a chance of coming back. You can't have major league baseball unless you have bush leagues—and there are no vaudeville bush leagues.

I had a chance to learn. I played the $2 and $5 dates. Long before there was a Borsht Circuit I played Ellenville, Monticello, Liberty, and Ferndales. I had a chance to find out what I could do and not do.

Nightclubs? You don't try out in nightclubs. The few nightclubs left today want finished performers, box-office attractions. Fortunately a Frank Sinatra will give a comic like Pat Henry a chance, and such a comic will start to emerge. But on the whole comics today must learn their trade in small nightclubs and there aren't too many around.

In the past comedians were taught to have audiences laugh at them.

The Vaudevillians

Today the comedians laugh at the audiences. Now, it's a good thing to have a Shelley Berman, a Bob Newhart, a Dick Gregory, pick our foibles apart. But they are not comedians. To me they're caustic commentators. Funny and good. The veteran comedians, the vaudeville comedians, were clowns. One of the funniest of the present-day comedians is Dick Van Dyke, and the Lord knows he's no great example because he's not that broad. But he moves with his body as well as with his lines.

For the most part our comedy today is cerebral. The other was physical and broad. One can say that the old comedy was corny and the present generation doesn't want it. Yet when there are those film festivals showing whole series of Marx Brothers pictures, or W. C. Fields pictures, they attract large crowds—and those were all broad comedians.

PERCY OAKES

PERCY OAKES managed to move into vaudeville because the famous dance team, Irene and Vernon Castle, fell out of a Chicago date. He was perhaps the first dancer to do the overhead spin, twirling his partner high overhead in what was then considered a daring stunt. Later he added a hat and cane and some singing to his act. He married Pamela DeLour, who was then his partner, and billing was changed to Oakes and DeLour. The dance team became known for their speed and amazing tricks. Later Oakes added two more girls to the act.

Oakes is now semiretired, though he still does some work as a theatrical agent.

I got into show business because some of the people I knew were in it and I admired them. I was brought up in West Virginia and was educated in the schools there. We were taught to read and write. We also had to learn a trade or our education wasn't complete. I learned two trades. I learned telegraphy—you know, da-da-dit-da—and also worked in the printing business. When I came to Chicago I got myself a job with R. R. Donnelly, night work, that gave me days and weekends to try to get into show business. I rented a room on the North Side of Chicago. I got it out of a newspaper ad. It said, "A single room—$1.50 a week, including two guitar lessons." That was for me. I wanted to play the guitar and sing. The room was the worst hole, no heat or nothing. Who cared about heat? I was young and in Chicago.

I got to know Donald Kerr, who was driving a taxicab in Chicago, and we used to meet at the dance hall regularly. He also wanted to go into show business and he became Kerr and the Kensington Sisters. They came to New York before me. He used to do acrobatics and taps, that kind of stuff. In Chicago we both went scouting for jobs. You see, back home I had been in a minstrel show when I was ten or twelve, and that was so much fun I wanted to do it again but not as an amateur. The fellow who really started me off on it was Ray Jackson. He was my next-door neighbor. He was one of the most unforgettable persons I ever met. He was a fellow who made a million three different times. He first made comedies in England. In later life he married—his son was Freckles of the Our Gang comedies. He was the creator of the marathon dances.

Well, anyway, back in Chicago, 1913, I read in the *Tribune* there was a call for chorus boys. I was a pretty good dancer. I had been taking lessons at the auditorium for 50 cents a lesson, and with my guitar lessons that came free with my room, I thought I was pretty good. I was one of the first singers who could strum a guitar and sing. So I went over and said, "I have a friend, Donald Kerr, and we both want to get in the show." So a fellow played the piano for us. (He was the musical conductor, I learned later.) He said, "I can't use them. They sing like bullfrogs." A girl standing by came over and said, "What are you people talking about? You don't know music." And she went over to Harry Asken—I think that was his name—the producer. He had the LaSalle Theater in Chicago. Anyway, after talking with the owner she came back and said to the conductor, "You take both these guys." That was the first time I met Sophie Tucker. She was the star of the show.

I went on the road with this show and I picked up every step I could. I created a lot of Russian steps. When I got back to Chicago I decided I'd be a juvenile. We had played all one-nighters—New Orleans, Atlanta, all over the South. We never came East. Anyway, I wasn't going to be a chorus boy. Donald Kerr was living out in the suburbs. He had teamed up with his two sisters and now had a vaudeville act and that encouraged me greatly. He had also married and had an act with his wife, Effie Weston. He told me about agents and I went to one agent's office and said, "I'm a juvenile and I'd like a job." He said, "Don't bother me, I've just had a big disappointment. I'm supposed to have a ballroom team opening here. The Castles are setting the world on fire in New York. They're the biggest thing in the East. I had them booked to come out here and they've fallen out on me." So I said, "I'm a dance team." He said, "You just told me you're a juvenile." I said, "I'm a juvenile dancer." So he said, "where did you dance?" I told him in New York. I hadn't been to New York yet. I put up a big bluff. He asked me if I had a partner and I said of course. Well, I had met my wife—who wasn't my wife then—but I knew her as a

The dance team of Oakes and DeLour, who got their chance when Irene and Vernon Castle fell out.

girl who spoke French fluently, Pamela Delour. She was French-American-Indian, some sort of a distant relative of William Jennings Bryan. I had been dancing with her every Saturday and Sunday at the dance halls. She thought I was a big actor. I didn't tell her I worked in the printing business. So I went to her and said, "I've got a job as a dance team. I want you to be my partner and we'll start rehearsing Monday." This was Saturday. I hired a hall and I told her when I called, "Number One," I was going to do a certain trick, and I showed her the trick. She was scared at first but later she got the hang of it and liked it. I was the first fellow who did the overhead twirls with the girls. Then, I told her, I'd say, "Number Three," and she was to stand still. This was where I'd go into a routine of floor stuff with all this Russian dancing that I did to American music.

We went over to this restaurant in Chicago the agent had told me about—I think it was Rector's—the afternoon after we had rehearsed for two days. When we got there they were clearing the floor so the public could dance. Up until then they had never had ballroom dancing in a restaurant. It was always in ballrooms. I told the manager, "I'm the dance team, and you've got to take that chandelier down." I had a lot of nerve as a kid. I said I did tricks overhead. I really did—they were what got me the job.

I spent two years in Chicago, 1916–1917, and then I came to New York. We played a nightclub, the Boulevard Inn on 40th Street and Broadway. We were there eleven months. Each night the same three people came in and sat at ringside. One night the headwaiter said that trio would like us to come over and have a drink with them. We thought that was nice and we also wanted to find out who they were. One fellow gave me a card with his name—W. I. Passport. I found out later he was the German representative of the Orpheum Circuit. His card gave the address of the Palace building, sixth floor. He asked us if we did any other numbers besides that terrific fast spin. I said yes. He said, "I don't care what you do as long as you finish with that number." In the meantime there was a show, *Florabella*, at the Cort Theater and they asked us if we would like to go with the show. It meant going on tour for about six months, but the salary was very good, so I said yes.

Then I went to see this Passport in the Palace building. In those days it was like a bank up there on the 6th floor. It was hard to get into. But they let me in right away. It was then I found out that one of the men who had been at the nightclub was Martin Beck. He asked, "When are you closing?" So I told him my story. He said, "That's better. You go with the show, and when you're through, let me know and I'll pick you up." So we went with the show and we closed in the Midwest. This was about the end of 1917.

We went to my wife's folks (Pamela and I were married by now). They had a small farm in Illinois. One morning I went to the RFD mailbox out in front and there was a bundle of newspapers. I said, "Somebody's sent us a bunch of newspapers. Shall I throw them in the wastebasket?" My wife said, "Let's open them." So I opened them and they were the Orpheum contracts for the vaudeville circuit.

I had never played vaudeville up to then so I didn't know how the hell I was going to get my money if I played Winnepeg, or Milwaukee, or whatever. I don't remember what the salary was but it wasn't bad. Well, we did it. I opened in one with a cane and straw hat and sang—oh very fast—"Every attraction that requires pep and action by some to distraction," set to the "Hungarian Rhapsody." If I had missed a word, I would have been a dead duck, but I never did, thank God. And then the curtain opened and I introduced the two girls, my partner on one side and Jane Moore, who later became Moore and Ravell, on the other side.

Well, we played about every vaudeville house there was. We played the Palace five times. It was a great life. And we had all sorts of adventures and met all sorts of people. One time we were in New London, Connecticut, breaking in a new act when a little girl, about five, came into our dressing room to sell us a chance on an alarm clock. She was part of a family act on the bill, "The Red Hooper Revue." It was the father, mother, brother, and little sister in the act. This little girl, Margery Reed, and her brother used to dress as a tiny bride and groom. The mother played the piano and the father, Pete, did a song and dance. Well, we bought three chances. The little girl grew up to become a well-known star —Martha Raye.

Oh, we played plenty of small time before we made the Palace. I recall the freezing winters throughout Montana and Idaho when we played the Ackerman and Harris Circuit. The one- and two-night stands were awful. The long jumps—if you got a three-day job in one spot, you lost the rest of the week making the next jump. Looking back at it I know it was all part of learning your trade.

There was the time a stagehand told me there was a fellow on the bill (he didn't say who he was) who wanted to play golf with anybody who played. Well, the man turned out to be Hayakawa. He was the headliner on the bill. I was pretty good at golf. I didn't know he was pretty good too. He had been captain of the Yale team. We became friends and I told him I was figuring on going into the agency business. And he said, "Why

*Martha Raye, when she was
Margery Reed. She met Percy
Oakes while she was part of
a family act, "Red Hooper
Review."*

don't you manage me? I'll be happy to have you." He got $2500, and
that's the story how I started off with him.

I worked with many people. I split the billing with Elsie Janis; Jack
Norwood and I became good friends. We played in Keith's, Philadelphia.
There was Frank Fay and his girl stooge—Patsy Kelly. Her brother was
Fay's chauffeur. I played probably a half-dozen times with Fanny Brice.
Another girl we played with was Rae Samuels, she was Marty Forkin's
wife. Marty handled Bill Robinson. That reminds me: We were in Seattle,
closing the show, and I came out and there was Bill Robinson standing

by the mailbox. He said, "Perc, do you want to borrow two hundred dollars." I said, "No, I don't need anything." My wife thought that was a peculiar thing. The next morning I came back to the hotel before the matinee to see if there was any mail and there was Bill standing in front of the mailbox. He said, "Perc, can you let me have ten dollars?" I said, "Ten what—didn't you want to give me two hundred dollars last night?" He said, "Yes, and I wish the hell you would've taken it. I gambled last night and lost it all. I'm broke. I don't even have enough for breakfast." So I gave him the ten. He was a big gambler.

It was about 1922 when we got down to Los Angeles and started back east. In those days the shows used to assemble in Winnipeg, play the Coast up through Vancouver, and go down to Los Angeles. Then we'd start back to Salt Lake, Denver, Omaha, or Kansas City. We'd then disband. Some would go to Memphis, maybe others to the Palace, Chicago, Cleveland, etcetera. When we got to Denver on our way back, Cooper's wife got sick—it was Cooper and Robinson then, before Bill became a single—so Cooper had to leave the act. Bill had never done a single. The manager said, "Bill, do whatever you can for the matinee. I'll get an act out of Chicago to fill in for the rest of the week." Bill went on and did so well the manager said he would keep him if he could make it a little longer.

Percy Oakes today.

So Bill stretched it out with some gags and stories and that was the start of Bill Robinson as a single.

We played Lincoln, Nebraska. My wife had corresponded with the governor's wife, who knew about our coming and would be there for the evening show. The following day they were going to send a car for us. Emma Carus, a very big star, was the headliner and we followed her. It was a great audience. All dressed and all in reserved seats. As part of my routine I would spin my partner, throw her on my back, and then spin like lightning all over the stage, all split-second timing. The music cue was to go into the last chorus when she got up. I always did a whirl in the middle of the act that brought the house down. I did an extra one this time and the roars of applause encouraged me so I put on more speed and hit the footlights and then went head over heels out into the orchestra. We were going at top speed, as fast as the music could play. I grabbed my partner around the waist, she fell on top of me, I lifted her back to the stage, and then grabbed hold of the edge and pulled myself up—the trombone player gave me a boost with his trombone—the music still playing. I then did the spin, threw her on top of my shoulder again, and went into my last spin. The whole house went into cheers and screams. Next day I'm in a barber shop and the fellow says, "Gee, they tell me there's a great act here. The dancers go clear out into the orchestra. I think I'm going to see that show." Everybody thought it was in the act. My partner wasn't hurt at all. I was her cushion.

Well, in 1930 I quit performing and became an Equity agent and also handled some vaudeville acts. I had my office in the Palace building for thirty years.

SAMMY LEWIS

SAMMY LEWIS *owed much of his show-business fame to his talented wife-partner, Patti Moore. Sammy was a dance originator and choreographer. He joined Patti when she played the Palace. One of his innovations was that symbol of the twenties, the Charleston.*

Patti, a wonderful clown and dancer, became his wife, and as a team they performed all over the United States in England. Though a competent vaudevillian, Lewis preferred being backstage to performing onstage. He became the successful owner of a nightclub in Hollywood—Slapsie Maxie's, fronted by ex-pugilist Maxie Rosenbloom. The club presented many performers who subsequently became big stars in many entertainment fields.

I joined Patti Moore's act about 1923–1924. She was going into the Palace and had a dancer with her by the name of Buster Brown. He was sort of an offbeat dancer. He never danced in tempo but in a kind of freaky offbeat way. Oh, he was good in the act but Patti felt that she wanted more of a legitimate dancer. I was in Atlantic City with the Murphy's Minstrels. I worked in blackface and I got a lot of experience there because I did dialogue and comedy, acted as the end man, danced, and did the olio [interim act while scenes are changed]. I was getting $50 a week. Naturally when I got a telegram from Sam Kesler, who owned the act—it was Aaron and Sam Kesler, they were big agents in those days—asking me to open at the Palace with them, it was a big thrill and I grabbed it. You know the Palace was THE PALACE in those days. It was the biggest theater in America.

Up to then nobody had ever done the Charleston at the Palace. And I was doing the Charleston. I had learned it from the black dancers in *Running Wild*, who were also working in Atlantic City. The dance came from Charleston—that's where it got its name, I guess. So I joined Patti. I did some bits with her and for the finale I produced and choreographed the Charleston and we were a tremendous hit. From then on we were on the Orpheum Circuit. We arrived in Chicago to play the Palace theater. The headliner was Richard Bennett. He was a very big legit actor. Very big. Our show, "Patti's Revue," was an extra added attraction. Also on the bill was a girl singer, she was in number two—Ruth Etting. Patti was number three. I'm talking about 1925. Bennett closed next to intermission. Usually the comedy act was next to closing, so we were a very big hit in Chicago. There was a band onstage and Patti Moore in her songs and dances featuring Sammy Lewis. We weren't married then. I was just working for her and the Keslers.

A funny thing happened. Richard Bennett was kind of stuck on Patti Moore. He was taking her out, and it was none of my business, we were just working together. She was my boss. Anyway, on opening night he sent her a bouquet of flowers. Ruth Etting was in the two-spot and that opening night all the people you could think of were there to see Ruth Etting. The man she married—you know, the Gimp—had everybody there, the governor, the mayor, and you never saw such flowers as came up. Basket after basket. Ruth was a big hit too. Among the flowers that came up were a dozen or so roses that Bennett had sent Patti. They got mixed up in Ruth Etting's flowers, so they went to Etting. She didn't know they were for Patti. She didn't look at the card. She just took the roses and threw them to the audience and the orchestra and then she looked at the card and said, "Oh my God—these were for Patti Moore—what am I going to do?" We followed her on the bill. I was offstage at the time (Patti did the opening number alone) so I asked her, "What's the matter, Ruth?" Ruth said, "I did a horrible thing." She told me what had happened and I said, "Don't worry. There are about eight or ten roses left. Give them to the boy and send them up to Patti. It'll be all right." And she did that. Now when the boy brought the flowers up to Patti, she looked at them. She looked at the audience and she made the crack of the evening. She said, "Who's the butter and egg man?" In those days "butter and egg man" was a big expression. So it got a tremendous laugh. Anyway, we were a big hit. Patti was wonderful. She sang and did acrobatic dances; then we did double dances.

Paul Ash was opening at McVicker's Theater the same time we were at the Palace. And his manager came to catch our show and saw me in the

Sammy Lewis and Patti Moore, billed as "Dancing With a Sense of Humour."

act with Patti. He sent an agent around to ask me if I would open with Paul Ash. My salary with Patti was $125 or $150 and he offered me $350. I had to give notice and pay another's boy's fare in to replace me.

From Chicago we went to Minneapolis to pick up a couple of weeks. And when we closed, it was over Labor Day and I was busted. I didn't have two cents. I had already given my notice and they had deducted the transportation for the boy plus a little advance salary, so there I was, dead broke. Everybody on the bill seemed to be busted and I couldn't borrow. Then Ben Blue came through. He was with the Brown Derby Band. Ben Blue and I were raised together. We both came from Washington and I taught Ben to dance and got him into show business when he was a clerk in a haberdashery store. I'm talking now about 1920–1921, before I started to work alone. I was trying to work around New York, starving. I

213

brought Ben to New York and we all lived together—Ben, Dave Blue, and me. And all three were starving. We had nothing. If one got a job, we split the money. We lived together in one room. Two slept in the bed and the third slept on the window sill. We took turns. The Automat was across from the Palace—is it still there?—and on the corner was a Liggett and Myers drugstore. I remember we used to buy a bottle of malted milk tablets there, go in the Automat, get a glass of water and put a tablet in it, and that's what we lived on. We used to sit around where Duffy's statue now stands. Dave and Ben went to audition for a fourth or fifth company of *Irene* or *Mary*—I don't remember which show it was—and they got jobs in the chorus. That's how Ben and Dave left New York. Dave became a choreographer for MGM and Ben Blue wound up here as a solo dancer.

But getting back to when Ben Blue came through Minneapolis—here was my old pal, so I got a hold of him and said, "I need money to get back to Chicago because I'm opening with Paul Ash and I can't raise any. The offices are all closed for the holiday." I had sent wires but they were under doors of agent's offices. Ben said not to worry, but I never heard from him about the money. When I did catch up with him I asked what happened. "What happened?" he said. "I lost money shooting crap." I said, "That's a fine thing. You could have borrowed money from somebody." Anyway, to make a long story short, Patti gave me the money to come back. Here I was leaving the act and she still gave me the money.

I opened with Paul Ash and stayed with him for quite a long time. That's where I first started choreographing numbers. I also did solos and worked in the presentation. We did a number a week. We'd open the show with the girls. Patti was doing well at this time. She came back to Chicago and headlined at the State Lake theater. I saw the act and naturally I went back to see her and paid her back the $50. I said, "I was reading in the papers that you're going to marry Richard Bennett." She said she wasn't sure. I had a feeling she liked me and I knew I liked her. Well, she went back to New York and when I got back there we saw each other, had some dates, and after six months or so got married. The first year we were married Patti had a baby and we lost it at birth. When she got well again we opened with Paul Ash at the Chicago Oriental as a team. Of course we worked all over wherever there was vaudeville. This is now about 1927. We worked the presentation houses. I don't know if they could be called vaudeville, because in presentation houses you did one number here and another number there. Nothing was put together. We finally got to the New York Paramount. Jennie Jacobs, a famous Equity agent at the time, wanted to handle us. We were then with the Morris office. Jennie called us and made us an offer to go to England—this was 1929. We had never been out of the country. A fellow, George Brach, who owned the London Palladium, saw us at the Paramount and wanted us. We said we'd go if we could go on the same boat with him. We wanted to go with somebody who knew England.

We were the only act that Brach caught at the time. But he bought a lot of scenery and lights for the Palladium even though we were the only act. And remember this, we had never done a vaudeville act together. But we had chutzpah and guts enough in those days. Anyway, we were signed to open at the Palladium, featured under Louis Armstrong, and that was our first vaudeville date. We never worried. We were in England two and a half weeks before we opened, so we had plenty of time to get an act together. We opened and we did a stair act. I was dressed as a butler and Patti as a maid. When we put the act together I didn't realize we would have to make so many costume changes. I danced while she changed and vice versa. Anyway, we got through the act. We were a big hit—I still don't know how—and it was a good thing or I think George Brach would have killed us. Everyone in London was kidding him about Patti Moore and Sammy Lewis. Who were they? Where the hell did you get them? You mean you went to America and that's all you brought back? And he was telling them they never saw this type of dancing and comedy—a boy in a sailor suit and a little flapper. Anyway, like I told you, they loved the stair dance, comedy and all. You see, Bill Robinson hadn't played in London by 1929, so naturally our stair dance was a revelation. We stayed at the Palladium for two weeks, played a few other theaters, and then went to Germany to work in a show called *Zwei Craveten*—that means Two Ties. We were in that show seven, eight months. I did the choreography. Marlene Dietrich was the ingenue, but she only stayed six or eight weeks when they replaced her. During that period she made the picture *The Blue Angel*. Patti used to help her rehearse. My gosh, Marlene was beautiful. She was just gorgeous. You never saw a more beautiful figure or a more beautiful face.

We worked all over the Continent because we could take the dialogue out and just do the dancing. About a year or so later we were in that restaurant next to the Palace where all the actors hung out when in comes Marlene Dietrich. She had just made her first picture for Paramount. The rest is history.

When we were in London George Burns and Gracie Allen were at the Coliseum. We were very good friends and they joined us on the Continent before we opened at the Palladium and I never had so much fun in my life. If you see George, ask him about it. A million laughs. We were often

Patti Moore and Ben Lessy, partnered in a nightclub comedy act.

on the same bill because we never conflicted. They did a talking act and we did a comedy dancing act.

Our last performances were in Australia. That's where I met Slapsie Maxie Rosenbloom. I loved Australia. We were ten weeks in Melbourne and five weeks in Sydney. We had the time of our life. I love horses and betting, and I could do both in Australia. We landed back in California in 1931 and by then we were doing a new act, "South Sea Sadie." Barney Dean was in the act with us. We brought Barney out to California and he stayed on. He became a writer for Bob Hope and Bing Crosby. Anyway, to go back a little, we went to Australia from California and we came back in 1936. We loved California and wanted to stay there. We had a little money. I was going to go into pictures, or direct, or something. And Patti would play parts. It turned out that we opened a nightclub instead —Slapsy Maxie's—and you know it became the most famous nightclub in California. There wasn't a star or a comic that didn't play it. There was Jackie Gleason, Danny Thomas—I paid them $150–$200—all of them played it. I had it for eleven years and sold it in 1947.

In the years we were in vaudeville, it was great. You'd come in at 8 and go home at 10:30. Bills had eight or nine acts, all different: acrobats, roller skaters, animal acts, great comics, great singers, a sketch with Richard Bennett or the greatest actress of them all, Sarah Bernhardt. There was so much work in this country. You had the Orpheum Circuit, Loew, Pantages—oh so many that if you did only one act you could do it for twenty years and not change one word. And I think that's what helped to kill vaudeville. There was no initiative to do anything new. And then came radio. The acts that had the intelligence to go into it like Burns and Allen, Eddie Cantor, and Jack Benny, went into it for little money. I didn't have sense enough. Patti and I didn't know anything about that medium. We were happy. We had all the work we wanted. I loved to bet horses, play golf. Had we gone into it at the time, we would've been successful because Patti had tremendous talents. She was a good singer and talker. You know she was a great dancer. Jack Benny thought Patti was the best straight woman in show business. As radio developed, more and more actors stagnated. They didn't think radio would last, just like they didn't think talking pictures would last. And of course the radio people didn't think TV would last either.

Well, you know what happened to vaudeville. I think if it were to come back the kids would love it. They could see the rock groups, the country westerns, the offbeat numbers. Today you go to a concert and you get four rock acts.

Las Vegas is doing the same thing today that vaudeville did. They're repeating the same acts three or four times a year. I was a Vegas producer at the Riviera and the original producer at the Flamingo. I took chances. I brought in *The Pajama Game*, *Guys and Dolls*. The only hotel in Vegas today taking chances is Caesar's Palace. And the producer there was one of my assistants when I was at the Frontier.

The Vaudevillians

When Patti passed on my heart was no longer in the business. I was an agent for a few months but I really didn't work at it. I didn't have my heart in it. To be a good agent you have to believe whatever you're selling is great. But being a buyer all those years I just couldn't believe that a certain act should get $50,000 a week, when I knew he wasn't worth $10,000. So I kinda eased out of it.

ARTHUR TRACY

ARTHUR TRACY *made his reputation as the "Street Singer." His best-known song was his theme song "Marta." Just the opening notes of the song were enough to send audiences into wild applause.*

The tall, well-built, blondish baritone chose songs that allowed him to display his clear voice to the best advantage. Tracy was originally a product of radio. His reputation brought him to England where he became a stage favorite.

He became so popular that Variety *reported the following on May 13, 1932:*

> *They called the cops out at the Capital [Theater in New York] today, and believe it or not this statement is meant literally. There was a cordon of cops to straighten out the mobs. Tracy did excellently, with the customers hanging on to the notes of "Chloe" as if he was a Caruso come back to life.*

I could always sing, even when I was only eight. But it was my father who taught me voice, how to love music, and how to play violin. It is funny thinking about the violin because when I became a pro I used an accordian. But that's another story.

We came from Philadelphia and it was while I was in grammar school that I made my first public appearance. I sang in a school play. When I reached high school one of the instructors who taught voice coached me on whatever songs were to be sung at the assembly. I would sing them first alone. The second time the assembly would join in.

Singing was now in my blood. I would sing anywhere. A friend who had moved to New York said, "Everybody knows and loves you here in Philadelphia. But why don't you come to New York where nobody knows you?" So I came to New York, a rank amateur. I had no money so I moved in with my friend. He already had a boarder so we split the rent three ways.

One night we went to Keith's on 14th Street. A notice was flashed on the screen of a coming amateur contest—applicants to apply at B. S. Moss's Broadway Theater. I went down and talked with big Fat Harry Shaw who was in charge. Amateur contests were regular things in those days. In fact, they became circuits. You entered contests in different theaters every night. First prize was always $5. I won every time. Whenever the emcee put his hand over my head, the applause was deafening. This went on for two, three weeks, and believe me, I could use the money.

One day Harry Shaw called me in and said, "Look, kid, you and I know your winning is legit. But winning every time, some of the public might think it's a fix. So instead of going into the amateurs, why don't you take a show out for a week and you be the emcee. I'll pay you twenty-five for the week."

Now, as the emcee, whenever I put my hand over some kid's head, the audience would yell for me to sing a song. They didn't know my name but they remembered my singing. Of course I was happy and finished the shows with my singing.

Then followed a number of years of club dates, concerts in Atlantic City, in hotels, always singing solo. And then it happened. I was caught by Lawrence Shubert, the cousin of the young Larry Shubert who is now in charge of the Shubert theaters. He caught me in a Philadelphia night-club. With him was the manager of the Winter Garden in New York. They called me over to their table. I was asked to come to Larry's office as soon as possible, and told that the man and he both liked my voice.

Of course I went. I was given a letter to the top producer in the Shubert office, a Mr. Simmons. I sang for him and was immediately given an important role in *Blossom Time*. And when that was finished I went into another Shubert operetta, *Student Prince*.

When that wound up, I went into vaudeville. I joined the act of Eddie Kopps and Loretta McDermott. I was put into the act by a booking agency. I was to sing. Loretta had been married to Joe Frisco at one time. She and Eddie were doing a dance act. It was beautiful. And she was beautiful. They were both fine dancers. I was to come onstage and do a song while they changed their costumes. I didn't get any billing or anything. We played the Keith Circuit and the Loew Circuit.

Arthur Tracy, in costume as "The Street Singer," November 1931.

When that ended, it was back to club dates. I even did some singing in burlesque shows. I would come out between the set shows or whatever, and do a song in front of the curtain.

It was Frank Salt of Salt and Pepper who saw me perform and advised me to call on Ralph Wonders at Columbia Broadcasting. "Tell him I sent you," he said. (Did you ever catch Salt and Pepper? That was really their names. Frank Salt and Jack Pepper, a wonderful song-and-dance act. Jack Pepper was Ginger Rogers' first husband.) Anyway, I called on Ralph Wonders and he set up an audition for me. That was in May, 1931, and everybody from Bill Paley down was listening. I came through with flying colors. They called me to Paley's office and I was told the committee was satisfied. I was to be given six weeks on CBS radio. I was to do eighteen shows and the first program was to go on in about six weeks from that date.

While I was preparing my program, gathering music, practicing, I was wondering how I could create some kind of identification, some kind of a title. I would have loved to take the "Vagabond Singer," but Rudy Vallee had "Vagabond Lover" for his title so that was out. I finally settled on "International Balladeer" because of the international scope of my work. I could sing in ten or twelve languages. Sure the name was a jawbreaker but it was the only one I could come up with.

Three days before I did my first show I picked up the newspaper and there in the amusement section was an item that Freddy Lonsdale had just arrived from London to do a show for the Shuberts called *Street Singer*. That was it. I grabbed it but added "of the Air" so I couldn't be accused of plagiarism. I called myself "Street Singer of the Air." This went on for a few weeks until a lawyer friend said I didn't have to worry about plagiarism because you couldn't copyright the English language. "Street" and "singer" were just two English words.

I did my eighteen shows in six weeks and I was asked by CBS to do two additional weeks so they could sell me. They finally sold me to Pillsbury Flour. I was paid $625 for each shot, so I got $1250 for the two shots a week. It was then that the Keith people booked me on their circuit with star billing. When I played Baltimore, a 2800-seat house, we had to do five shows a day. (They normally played three or four a day.) The business was so big it was SRO. We were such a draw that Bill Sexton, the general manager for Loew's in Baltimore, caught me at the Keith house and telephoned Louis K. Sidney in New York to grab me.

When I came to New York I signed with the Loew organization to play for them thirty-five weeks. Of course there was a problem because of the competition between Loew and RKO. But so long as you allowed a certain lapse of time before playing a competitive house in the same area it was okay. Besides, Loew's with its pictures-and-vaudeville combination was offering top headline acts more money than RKO and it was going after the acts that were getting heavy public following due to their radio shows.

I was now being handled by CBS's Ralph Wonders. I had just come off the thirty-five weeks of Loew's. I had worked very hard because I also did the four radio broadcasts a week. I did concerts and benefits and I was anxious to take a rest. Then I got a call from Ralph to come to the office. I went and Ralph said, "The Palace wants you." I said I was tired. Ralph said, "They've got to have you. There's a war on Broadway and they need you." I said no, I wanted a rest. Ralph called the Palace booker in front of me and told him I was too tired. After hearing that the booker raised his salary offer to $1000. Ralph put his hand over the phone and said to me, "They're offering a thousand." I said, "Ralph, money is not my god. I want a rest." Ralph turned back to the phone and said, "I'll have to call you back. I have to talk to him." He hung up and started hammering at me: "He's offering you a thousand more than you've ever got." I still said no. Eddie Darling then raised the price to $2000. Well, Ralph Wonder beat me over the head telling me I had to do it, that it would establish my new salary as $2000 from then on. I was too tired to argue any more and said okay. Well, the Palace people were very understanding. They gave me every leeway. It wasn't the work. Actually, it wasn't as hard as I was used to working. I had microphones and I could take it easy. I was quite young and my voice was quite flexible. I just put a little more smaltz into my songs and I got away with it.

I did big business in all theaters. There are certain houses where I set records that still stand. For instance, the Michigan Theater in Victoria, where I was followed by Mary Pickford, if you please. I set the record. And she was already big in pictures. She did a sketch. While I didn't see the figures, I'll tell you that Clark Gable played the New York Capitol, as did Ramon Navarro, and my gross was bigger than theirs.

It is difficult to sit here and indulge in self-praise, except that I'm just stating facts. I actually used to get a minimum of three big receptions— and I mean *receptions*—at every appearance. The first was when I did "Marta," my theme song, behind the curtain. The second was the minute my name was flashed, or a number referring to my name appeared on the electric flasher. And when I came on there was the third big reception. This happened all over the world.

Ed Sullivan is a witness. On his show, you know, the audience was always egged on by the announcer and the applause sign telling them when to applaud and when to subside. Ed said to me after the show was over, "You are the only artist in all the ten years I've been on who got applause without the urging of a sign or an announcer." The minute they would hear "Marta" offstage—because I started offstage and walked on with it—I got an automatic hand.

Once at the New York Capitol Ken Roberts was the announcer. The show was designed to create a radio atmosphere. He would announce, "Ladies and gentlemen, Columbia Broadcasting Company presents the Street Singer." One time Ken was jammed up in traffic and couldn't make the show, so I announced it myself. I didn't mind. It was quite a thing.

I once did a show for the Merchant Seamen and Madeleine Carroll was on it with me. The hookup was a peculiar one. The orchestra was playing in London. Ben Grauer was the announcer. He worked from here, as I did. We all used earphones—you know, cans. Grauer announced about the orchestra playing in London. To the listener it made no difference. But it was quite a feat. Maybe a first. The show that was heard around the world. It doesn't sound so important now, but during the time it seemed so.

Later came another first—a broadcast from a blimp, or rather a balloon. It was a small blimp with a basket below which didn't have much room. The basket was jammed with a Fox News cameraman, his assistant, the pilot and his assistant, one or two others, and me with my accordian. Anyway, we flew over the city for a fifteen-minute broadcast. Paul Douglas, who later became a movie star, was the announcer. The whole thing took about two and a half hours. It, too, was a first. The same blimp went up in flames a short time later, and all the occupants were killed.

Many, many years later I went to visit Judy Garland when she was at the Palace. I was in the wings when she finished her act, came off, and fell into my arms. I thought she recognized me. But she didn't. I said to her, "Judy, you were wonderful." She said, "Thank you," so meekly. I realized she didn't recognize me. I said, "Don't you remember me, Judy?" She said, "Why? Should I?" I said, "I'm the Street Singer." She said, "Oh— Arthur Tracy—I was one of the Gumm Sisters who was on the bill with you at the Michigan Theater in Detroit." I didn't remember the Gumm Sisters but I did remember we had a chimp. And Judy said, "Do you remember the chimp on the bill?" and laughed. Me and the chimp were the only things she remembered of the bill.

Do you remember the act Anthony and Rogers? Anthony's identification was his yell, "Hey Botcha Galoopa . . ." It was like my "Marta" was to me. He used to play a violin and with each stroke of the bow his pants would drop a little until they reached the danger point. He would then pull them up and start over again. It was a very funny act. I'll tell you why I mention the act. When I was playing around in Philadelphia I met George Jessel and he said, "If you want to make it, you have to develop a personality. You sing great but you must also do a little talking. Tell a story." I remembered the advice so I learned a few gags though I was not a gagster. Today, I will say with pride, I tell a terrific story. In fact my stories today are probably as well known as my singing. But in those days it was different.

I was playing a theater and Anthony and Rogers were on the bill as the stars. I did my act, got tremendous applause, and thought this was the time to tell some gags. I told a few and all I got were polite laughs and courtesy applause. I knew I was slowly dying. So being inexperienced, I said, like a fool, I was going to ask one riddle and then I'd go back to singing. I asked, "Where does the wind go when it isn't blowing?" I don't remember the answer but I remember somebody hollering, "You've got it!" I stood there petrified. I knew enough not to leave the stage but I didn't know how to answer. Out of the corner of my eye I could see the house manager running down the aisle, through the pass door, whispering something to me from the wings. The other acts were standing around feeling sorry for me and whispering instructions but I stood there petrified. When suddenly I hear this "Botcha Galoopa," and that broke the spell. Everybody knew who that was. The audience loosened and the tension went down. But I still stood there. Out came Fred Anthony. He bowed and milked the audience for applause while he whispered to me, "Do another song, kid—quick! My senses returned and I whispered back, "I'll do 'Vesti La Giubba' from *Pagliacci*." Fred stopped the applause and said, "Ladies and gentlemen, I wuz allus standa in the wings. I listen to da kid. He's great, no? I'm gonna ask with your permish—I'm gonna ask for heem to do an Italian song. Hey, professor, you got an Italian song?" I got my chord and I went into "Vesti La Giubba," finishing to tremendous applause. That was my first lesson in learning how to develop a personality.

My first appearance in England came about in a curious way. My record "Marta" had become very popular in that country, sold about two million, and there were inquiries about my availability for that country. Tommy Rockwell, who was then the head of General Artists Corporation, a large talent agency, was in London at the time with the Mills Brothers. Val Parnell, the talent booker of the Palladium, said to Rockwell, "Europe is full of street singers. I understand you have one in America, could you bring him here?" Rockwell said, "I don't stand to make a nickel out of this deal because I don't manage him, but on my say-so play him and you'll have a big hit on your hands. Just give him music, lights, and an audience, and get the hell out of his way." And that's how I got to England—on the strength of Tom Rockwell's recommendation I was booked for the Palladium. I got to London a week before my opening date and Val Parnell asked me to play that week in Manchester. I was relieved because I was nervous about the Palladium and liked the idea of working a week in another English city to sort of get used to the country. On the same bill with me was Dick Oliver, and he was a great support to me. He comforted me and helped calm me down. Dick later became the son-in-law of Winston Churchill when he married Sarah Churchill. Dick was a very good comic. A sort of Jack Benny type.

My reception was phenomenal. Yet when I went into the Palladium the following week, I was more nervous than ever. That was July 22, 1935. Everybody from royalty down was in that opening audience.

Sigmund Romberg had just written "When I Grow Too Old to Dream." He gave me a copy and an arrangement and said he'd be grateful if I introduced the song in England. I did. All in all I did fourteen songs at the Palladium and was on for nearly an hour. When I finished, the applause was tremendous. I told the conductor I might not do the Romberg song, but I did. When I tried a beg-off speech thanking everybody, including the heads of the Moss Empire theater chain sitting in the boxes, I just blacked out. The manager caught me. Now, the curtain at the Palladium doesn't drop, it closes in from the sides. Somebody held me and somebody else threw cold water into my face. I got up and went out again and told the audience what happened and thanked them again. I couldn't find words to thank them. I said their applause was music to me like I hoped my singing was for them.

Here's another one: I was appearing at the Moss Empire—this was second only to the Palladium. I used to finish my act with a little speech of thanks and wind up with Noel Coward's "I'll See You Again." This one night the reception was so tremendous and I was anxious to get off. I started to sing the first line and I stopped. I forgot the next line. I nodded to the conductor who gave me an arpeggio and I started over again and stopped. Then I told the audience, "Ladies and gentlemen, your reception was so tremendous it just knocked the lyrics right out of my head. I'll try once more." I tried again and when I got to the second line I was still blank. A woman sitting in the first row stood up and shouted, "Sing it, Arthur—I'll sing it with you," and gave me the line and sang the thing all the way through with me. When I finished, there was pandemonium in the house. Of course I threw the spotlight on her. That theater never heard such applause and such screams as I got that night.

Arthur Tracy, 1975. (Photo courtesy of James J. Kriegsmann)

One of the greatest thrills was an incident with my father, God rest him. He and other members of my family came to New York to the Capitol theater to see me perform. After my performance they asked me to come down to get some orange juice. It was very cold. I'll never forget it. My sister suddenly said, "Look, look up there," and there was that big electric ribbon moving sign and it said, "Radio's Latest and Greatest Sensation— onstage—Arthur Tracy, The Street Singer." My father stood there with tears in his eyes. He wouldn't move until he saw that message repeated four times.

Yes, I was a vaudeville performer but my fame came from radio. It was radio that brought me before the public but it was vaudeville that gave me the opportunity to appear before them in person.

I remember when radio first came on the scene all performers thought it was a joke. No established performer ever wanted to go on radio. They would argue—"What, sing or tell jokes into a machine without an audience? Never!" Well, you know what happened. It was vaudeville that gave me the experience, the finesse, the know-how, while it was radio that gave me an opportunity to learn in the beginning.

People ask me all the time, "Why aren't you back—why don't we have vaudeville?" But that's another story.

RUDY VALLEE

WHEN RUDY VALLEE *entered vaudeville with his band, The Con-*
necticut Yankees, he was already a radio favorite. Preceding his initial stage
appearance, he kept reminding his radio listeners that he was to appear at
the RKO 81st Street on a certain date. This constant plugging drew
an amazing crowd to the theater.

    The RKO bookers were impressed by this newcomer and put him
into the Palace early in March, 1929, and he did well. Then came movies
and a long-running show, the Fleischmann Hour, *which was a radio vaude-*
ville show. Vallee did so well as the emcee that he was offered what later
became the Toast of the Town, *the Ed Sullivan show.*

    Today he lives with his wife on one of Hollywood's highest hills,
overlooking the city. Following a very long Broadway run in How to Suc-
ceed in Business Without Really Trying, *he began to lecture and occasion-*
ally perform before college and fraternal groups.

I always loved music and as a child I sang myself to sleep. I was also
always fascinated by any facet of show business, whether lugging water
for the circus, the 161 Ranch, or any carnival that came to our little town.
I recall getting the water for the man who ran the Oceanwave Show. I
promptly threw up my dinner when I took my first ride on it.

    I had one of the first roll-up curtains in our little barn where I would
have shows like *Down East* or just pictures projected on a sheet. Admission was pins of various sorts.

    After a fight I had with the chief clerk in my father's drugstore in
1917, I took a job in the Star Theater in Westbrook, Maine. I swept out,

took care of the furnace, helped to project the films on the hand-driven projector, took tickets, etcetera—all for a $1 a day—and enjoyed doing it. Did it for one and a half years until I moved over to the Strand Theater in Portland, Maine.

The Strand was a beautiful deluxe house, 1800 seats, beautifully tiled lobby. I was the head usher in one of those bellboy outfits. I left to go back to high school. When I came back I became the assistant projectionist—again at $1 a day. The machines were two big Simplex, both motor driven. I used to watch the stage enviously, never dreaming that someday I would appear on it and play a saxophone solo.

I was looking at the Wurlitzer catalogue wondering what instrument to buy, a picollo, ocharino, or even a xylophone, when the head projectionist, I think Dick Farr was his name, came in carrying a saxophone. He said his teeth and mouth were hurting and he couldn't play it anymore. He was renting it for $5 a month and asked if I'd like to take it off his hands. I did and four years later, 1921, I had taught myself to play it well enough to do a solo on the stage of the Strand.

I had a great admiration for Rudy Wiedoeft, the king of saxophonists, I would listen to his records for hours, emulating and imitating his wonderful tones. I didn't have Rudy's technique. I missed entire passages and whole cadenzas. Yes, Rudy Wiedoeft was my idol. It was his name Rudy that I took for my own, dropping the Hubert.

When I graduated high school I entered the University of Maine. My ability to play the saxophone made me a campus hero. Anybody who could play the saxophone was looked up to with awe. I was almost as popular as the football captain. I continued my college education on the advice of my idol, Rudy Wiedoeft. I had thought of transferring to a band school in Ithaca. It was Wiedoeft who urged a college education instead.

I worked my way through Yale and was a Spanish major. I got my meals free by playing with a student band in the college dining hall. I was also part of a small unit, the Dance Five, with whom I played at Yale. We had about three to five jobs a month, all one-nighters. In addition I played for weekend tea dances in and around New York and Boston. It was as part of the Yale Collegians that we obtained and took vaudeville dates during the summers that followed.

Our first date was in Baltimore where we followed Fred Waring. We observed, fascinated, that they used a Stein grease stick which looked like a big phallus. They made dabs all over their faces and then smoothed these dabs out. The result was a paleface Red Indian! In Lancaster we played a broken-down small wooden theater. The heat outside was 110 in the shade, and as we peeked out of the small window of the cellar in

Rudy Vallee in front of the Yale Football Band before the Yale-Princeton game, 1926.

which were our dressing rooms, we could see the heat waves rising from the hot sidewalks.

We played the Strand Theater in New Britain, Connecticut. We were on the same bill with three comedy acts. They became very famous in later years. They were Will and Gladys Ahern, Jed Dooley and his wife, and Fred Allen and Portland Hoffa. Gladys Ahern was a knockout. She was a black-haired Irish beauty. She's probably a grandmother today. Jed Dooley's wife was a gorgeous, gorgeous thing. I don't think Portland Hoffa was too attractive. Fred Allen preceded us and I memorized his entire act including his nasal tones. He had a big piece he called "Disappointment of 1926." The years obviously were changed as they changed.

We played some nice theaters and some awful dumps. On one bill I met Freddy Martin. He was just a tenor sax man in a band. We became very good friends. We also played the Capitol, Washington. We played Pittsburgh theaters; there was the Albee, the Grand. It was in that city that we were stranded. We lived in some vaudeville boardinghouse. We managed to pay our way out and headed back to either New Haven, New York, or Boston, I don't recall which.

We were picked up again by the agents who booked the Fox Circuit and we worked at the Academy of Music, the Audubon, Fox Jamaica, Folly, and others. I was in the doghouse here a few times. I came late because I took the wrong trains but everything was straightened out. There were some amusing incidents, and some not so amusing, but it was all part of what we learned was show business.

In Davenport, Iowa, we arrived too late to set up for the opening show, so we set up in the dark while a South American pianist, Don Zelaya, was waiting to go on. As he came in to do his act he fell into our bass drum and for a while refused to go on but was finally mollified. It wasn't funny then. We were afraid we'd be canceled. But looking back at Zelaya struggling and screaming, it was funny. I later worked with him at

Rudy Vallee in 1929.

the Brooklyn Paramount in 1929. Later, out here in California in 1946, he made a color short of his performance. He used to talk about the effect of music on various parts of the body. He was fat but a good comedy musical act.

Yes, vaudeville was fun—rough at times, but still fun. Later, when I played the Keith houses after breaking in at the 81st Street Theater, it was a different kind of vaudeville—but more of that later.

I graduated from Yale in 1928 but late in 1927 we heard of a new New York supper club, the Heigh-Ho, near the site of the then fashionable Stork Club, that was looking for a new band. I had formed a partnership with Bert Lown, and we went after that job. The club was in a two-story building owned by Bruce Brisbane, a Hearst editor. It had opened New Year's Eve and Lipstick—that was the name Peter Arno's wife wrote under—gave it a bad review in *The New Yorker* magazine. John Dickerman, who owned the club and three others in the Village, was partnered in the Heigh-Ho with George Putnam, the publisher. He wanted the club to be very exclusive. Formal dress necessary. Herbert Hoover couldn't get in in a gray suit and Otto Kahn couldn't get in in tails. It was for the Park Avenue, Gentile elite.

We tried out on the night of January 8, 1928, and got the job. The Sunday night before I was one of some twenty musicians hired to play for the big Jewish Theatrical Guild dinner for William Morris, Sr., at the Commodore Hotel. No dancing, just a big dinner. George Jessel and Lou Holtz were the emcees. A number of rabbis, military, and other distinguished guests, including Mayor James J. Walker, were present. The musicians were from the Lopez, Bernie, and Whiteman office. We all got $13–$14 for the evening. There were many big acts and I sat there with my mouth open looking at the celebrities. In my vaudeville career up to then I had never played on the same bill with such big names. Some became big later but not when we saw them.

So there I was at the Heigh-Ho with my Yale Collegians. I took on the singing chores, using my small megaphone. I would announce, "Heigh-Ho everybody, this is Rudy Vallee and the Yale Collegians." Two, three months later, March or April, the Atlantic Broadcasting Company (call letters WABC) arranged to do remotes from the club, seven nights a week, from 7 P.M. to 3 A.M. We also played for Saturday afternoon dansants. When WABC said they couldn't afford an announcer, expecting me to drop dead, I said I'd be happy to do it.

I started with little talks about the songs we were to play, little tidbits about the writers, composers, etcetera, which I had prepared. And the letters started to come in by the thousands. "Who the hell are you? You're

233

so different, different, different." Sure we were different. We had only two sax, two fiddles, and four rhythm. So we couldn't play the stock arrangements, otherwise we would've sounded like everybody else. My approach was also different—from my "Heigh-Ho everybody, this is Rudy Vallee announcing and directing the Yale Collegians" to my limiting tunes to choruses and my little introductory talks.

Some of my brother alumni objected to the "Yale Collegians" title so I changed it to the "Connecticut Yankees," taking the name from the musical then playing on Broadway.

I could always talk easily. I inherited this ability from my father but the greatest influence upon me was Dr. William Lyon Phelps, Professor of English at Yale. Billy Phelps, as he was affectionately called, was a most brilliant man. I observed his way of taking mundane subjects and making them glow with interest and light. I owe everything I've written to Dr. Billy Phelps.

Do you remember Sammy Smith, the song plugger? He believed in me. He brought in Earl Carroll, hoping to interest him to use me in one of his revues. Carroll wasn't impressed.

Then he got Bill McCaffery—I really put it on for him. Funny hats, novelty tunes, bits, etcetera. Apparently he, too, wasn't impressed. Listening to the pleading of Sammy Smith, about how great I was as a radio personality, he decided to check this radio reputation with some of the secretaries working in the Keith office. Their screams of enthusiasm must've convinced him for he offered us the 81st Street house for three days, two shows a day, for $400.

Two, three weeks before we opened, I plugged my opening over the air so that anybody who listened to radio knew I was opening at the 81st Street theater, the date and time. Come opening day—for Christ's sake, you couldn't get near the theater. Lines around the block, a jammed lobby, ushers and manager helpless to stem that mob. And when we came on—there were six other acts on the bill—they screamed and bellowed. Years later you were to hear that sort of thing for Sinatra and then later the Beatles.

Before that night was over George Godfrey, one of Keith's top bookers, came backstage and called me over. He asked me what I wanted to play the Palace and about twelve weeks of full-week stands at other Keith houses. Stupid, *stupid me*—if I ever needed a smart agent!! So, scared a little, I swallowed and said apologetically that I knew $1500 was a lot of money but for eight men—I stopped. I was ready to back up. Godfrey looked down and then looked up at me. Hid a little smile and said maybe they could afford it. Afford it! If I'd of asked for $10,000 with the business I proved I could attract, they'd of paid it!

We packed the Palace as we packed every other Keith house we were booked into. All this was a far cry from my earlier valudeville jobs when as a part of the Yale Collegians we worked summers in whatever theater would have us.

We opened at the Palace March, 1929; the hallowed Palace Theater on Seventh Avenue and 47th Street. As every vaudevillian knew, to have played the Palace was to have reached Mecca. Though not a vaudevillian in the deepest sense of the word, I played enough vaudeville to have acquired an awe and respect for it as a symbol of greatness. We played on the full stage with the curtain coming up on us, including me.

I mention this because I never had to learn some of the basic rules of vaudeville—how to come on and how to get off. As a band sideman occasionally coming down front to sing through a megaphone, entrances and exits didn't concern me. I was always part of a musical group.

Rudy Vallee in front of the Star Theatre, where he worked for seven dollars a week. On Rudy's right is Fred Eugley, who hired Rudy in defiance of the singer's father, on Rudy's left. This photo was taken in 1930.

The Heigh-Ho Club where we made our first radio broadcast didn't think too highly of radio or us. Management didn't think radio brought in any increased patronage, and what it did attract wasn't what the management wanted. Furthermore it objected to the clutter of microphones, etc. One thing led to another and we were let out.

Losing the Heigh-Ho didn't faze me. Another nightclub, the Versailles, then on East 60th Street, off Fifth Avenue, much later to become the Copacabana, wanted me and my band. This is as good a time as any to point out that the relationships between vaudeville and nightclubs, and vaudeville and radio, and vaudeville and the movies, were close. There was hardly a vaudevillian who saw it slowly dying who didn't try radio and aim for the movies. If he could tailor his routine to suit the intimacy of a nightclub, then into a nightclub he would go.

I had the best of all three. I was on radio (by this time WOR, NBC, and WMCA were broadcasting my voice weekly). I was doing a Keith tour and NBC Artists Bureau set me and my band for a picture to be called *Vagabond Lover*. I was to get $11,000 a week for five weeks, for me and the band. RKO was producing. The less said about the film the better. It was pretty bad.

After the movie and after the Keith dates were played, I was offered the New York Paramount, where I played for four weeks, and then came the Brooklyn Paramount, where I stayed for a year and a half.

Vaudeville veterans knew that vaudeville was rapidly being replaced by the presentation theaters in most of the major cities. These were large, luxurious theaters that played four or five shows a day plus a movie. That's what the Paramount was—a presentation house.

In October, 1929, I went on the air for Fleischmann's Yeast. It was frightening. Here the stock market was breaking wide open, a depression was in the making, and we were engaged by Standard Brands for its Fleischmann's Yeast to start what was eventually to become the Thursday night broadcast over NBC for many years.

My first show was broadcast from the organ loft of the Paramount theater between our stage shows. For the first two years my radio broadcasts consisted of my band, my singing, and perhaps one or two guests. In 1932 this was changed. It became a variety program, a vaudeville radio program, and many a vaudevillian got a new start on my show or was given a new market to show his wares. At the time NBC was the only coast-to-coast network, so talent appearing on the "Fleischmann-Rudy Vallee Show" were glad of the opportunity we gave. We used legitimate actors from the Broadway stage. We had Fanny Brice on for many weeks as "Baby Snooks"; Lou Holtz; Bob Hope; Red Skelton; Bob Burns of bazooka fame; Joe (You Wanna Buy a Duck) Penner. There were so many it is difficult to recall them all. We used all sorts of personalities. If I'm not mistaken, Eddie Cantor's first coast-to-coast broadcast was on my show.

After much probing and searching for a theme song we finally chose "My Time Is Your Time." When you rang my front door bell, the first three notes you heard were "My Time Is."

I was so busy I no longer had the time to write introductions to my songs. A brilliant young man, George Faulkin, who could write pretty much the way I thought, did all my little introductions exactly as I would say them—just the way Carroll Carroll wrote every word that Bing Crosby ever spoke.

One time I asked Carroll Carroll and another man who were doing the "Kraft Music Hall Show" to come to my Thursday night preview particularly to see and hear Victor Borge warm up. He'd been turned down by every agency here, every network. Nobody could see this man's genius. Harry Mazur, who was running KFWB, called me on the night of November 21, 1941, just before Pearl Harbor, to tell me he had this young Danish pianist and nobody wanted him. I put Borge into a little nightclub I owned—I and 1500 other celebrities—the Pirate's Den on La Brea and Beverly, and let him do everything he wanted. When he did that punctuation routine of his I damn near fell off my chair.

The story of how that song "Vagabond Lover" became associated with me started back in 1926 when I was part of the touring Yale Collegians and we were playing the Circle Theater in Indianapolis. One night we visited the Savarin Hotel Roof where Charley Davidson's orchestra was playing. Charley sang this song "I'm Just a Vagabond." That was the first time I heard it. Two years later, the summer of 1928, we were playing the Milton Point Casino in Rye, New York, and two girls asked if I would play "Vagabond Lover." I jotted it down and did it over one of my radio broadcasts. In later years many people claimed it as their song. By then I was signed with Feist Music. They were publishing everything I put out. Suits were started but nothing ever came of them. The one man who claimed authorship died of tuberculosis and it turned out he didn't write the song at all.

Poor Joe Penner died after a heart attack. Nonsense, it wasn't a heart attack—it was heartbreak. First time I saw Joe was at the New York Paramount watching Bing Crosby singing "Mississippi Mud" and Joe Penner saying something about raising corn beef and cabbage with a knife and fork. Then in 1931, at the Brooklyn Paramount, I played straight for Joe, as did Paul Whiteman years before. I knew his routine. It was in a corner of our rehearsal studio atop the New Amsterdam Roof from where we were doing the "Fleischmann Hour" that I saw Joe studying something. I asked what it was. And he said it was a song called "Flies" that they'd written for him. I asked, "Aren't you going to sing the 'Pussy Willow Song'?" and he said, "They don't like it." I went to Gordon Thompson, no relative to J. Walter Thompson, he was producing the show. I said, "Gordon, what is this? Don't you know Penner is a worrier? He's the type of guy if anything happens in front of that microphone he's going to run right off the stage. He's been working for over thirty years doing the same damn thing, and if you walk on the wrong side of him, he's gone. Throw him a cue he doesn't expect and he's gone. And you're asking him to memorize a new song even if he can read it from a paper. You crazy?" So he said, "Okay, let him do the 'Pussy Willow Song,'" and that made all the difference. Three months later Penner had his own program and was a sensation. What do you think his signature was? The "Pussy Willow Song." He was a big star. He was up there. And suddenly he was no longer big. And he couldn't take it. His whole life was what he did. And when nobody wanted him, they wore him down.

About Jack Benny: I didn't think he ever thought of me as a personality worth presenting. You must understand there's a typical Broadway type of character best epitomized by most of the performers who came before I came along. I was the first to speak beautifully, intelligently, with good grammar. So I suppose there was some resentment.

I perform on occasion when I'm asked. I can please them, make them leave talking about Rudy Vallee. Unfortunately I can't bring them in. But I'm content with what I've done. I can sit up here and look down on the world and smile that my time is still your time.

JOE SMITH

JOE SMITH *and Charlie Dale became legends through their classic comedy sketch, "Dr. Kronkhite," which became known in virtually every branch of show business. Joe played the bluff, aggressive patient consulting the gentler, more retiring Dr. Kronkhite (Charlie). Their routine was based on malapropisms and word play. In the exchange between doctor and patient Joe asked, "Are you the doctor?" When Kronkhite replied in the affirmative, Joe countered with "I'm dubious," and Kronkhite returned a polite "I'm glad to know you, Mr. Dubious." When the doctor questioned his patient about his diet—"What do you eat? What kind of dishes?"—the patient indignantly answered, "Dishes—what am I, a crocodile?"*

Smith and Dale started their partnership at the turn of the century. They performed on the Bowery and before Presidents. After they had been together for some time they formed the Avon Comedy Four, a unit which was considered one of the funniest acts in the business. With the advent of microphones onstage they couldn't dash about as madly as before, so they became a two act. At least two of their routines are described here by Joe Smith himself.

Charlie Dale died some years ago. Joe lives in an actors' retirement home.

Charlie Dale and I met by accident. It was on the Lower East Side, Eldridge and Delancey, one Sunday afternoon. We were both on bikes and we bunked into each other. We started an argument about whose fault it was and people standing around kind of pushed us together.

They wanted a fight. Anyway, we took our bikes back to Harry's bicycle store—we both rented from him. He heard us yelling, looked at the bikes, and said not to worry, there was no damage. He also said the way we argued reminded him of Weber and Fields. He said we should be friends and offered us a tandem to ride for a half-hour for free so we could get acquainted. And we did. And that's how Charlie and I met.

So we became friends, though he was two years older than me. I was working as an assistant shipping clerk. Charlie was a printer's apprentice. Sundays we played ball on the lot where P.S. 20 was built, at Eldridge and Rivington streets. P.S. 20 became a famous school. Edward G. Robinson, Paul Muni, Irving Caesar, Senator Javits, George and Ira Gershwin, and Charles Silver, the president of the Board of Education, went to that school. Some years ago that school had a fiftieth anniversary. A lot of famous people attended, including Cardinal Spellman. And the school made Charlie and me honorary members.

One night we went to Tony Pastor's. There were nine acts. We sat in the gallery spellbound watching Montgomery and Stone. We left the theater talking about how we could also dance, recite, and maybe sing. So we began practicing a buck and wing, we picked up a song popular then, "The Gambling Man." When we thought we could do it we went around to places on the Bowery that had shows and boxing exhibitions. We saw the manager outside one place, a tall heavyset man with a big cigar. We asked him to put us on. He laughed at us. Put his arms around us and said, "Sweethearts, you kids are too young." I was about thirteen, Charlie was fifteen. "See me when you grow up." That was Al H. Woods. He later became a big Broadway producer. We went around to all the Bowery saloons, where we danced and sang for throw money. And we didn't do badly. These weren't really saloons. They were kind of amusement halls.

We both took jobs working in Childs' Restaurant for 50 cents a day plus one meal. At night we danced wherever we could get on. That is we danced, sang, and kind of told jokes. We were both in blackface. This was around 1898.

My brother was a bouncer working for the Palace Gardens, it was on 13th Street and Third Avenue. It was a kind of family saloon with tables, a stage, and booths. My brother talked the boss into letting us perform. He did and he finally hired us for $24 for both of us. We were so proud, though we still kept our part-time jobs at Childs'. After all, a big free meal every day plus 50 cents—and we could eat in those days—for only a few hours' work wasn't something we could drop like that. The first night at the Palace Gardens our hearts dropped. Outside there was a sign saying, "A new act, Smith and Dale." We thought we were fired before we even

Smith and Dale, in their famous Dr. Kronkhite act.

started. I got a hold of my brother and he said, "Don't worry—you are Smith and Dale," and showed me a bunch of calling cards saying Smith and Dale. He'd gone to a printer to order some cards for us and the printer said he had cards with Smith and Dale, that the guys who ordered them changed their names to Moran and Mack, and my brother bought the cards for very little. That's how Joe Sultzer and Charlie Marks became Joe Smith and Charlie Dale.

It was while we were working at Childs' that we got a letter from Will Lester, an agent, who said he liked us and wanted us to join the Imperial Vaudeville and Comedy Company in Roundout, New York. That was Christmas of 1900. We bought second-hand suitcases and two one-way tickets. We joined up with Jack Coleman, he used to sing "The Sunshine of Paradise Alley" with song slides. Will Lester did a sailor-and-captain routine and also a monologue. Charlie and I did a blackface burlesque bit and then all of us did an afterpiece, " 'The New Schoolteacher.' " It was a kind of travesty on night school on the East Side. We all lived at Zeis' Boardinghouse. He owned the large dance hall, catered to weddings. He boarded us. Our deal allowed us to play neighboring towns Monday to Friday. But Saturday we had to do a show at Zeis' and also tend bar in return for our room and board. After the show we did some square dance calling. But when it came to getting paid, it seems that all the money was always used up. We managed to get back to New York. We got some work at an Odd Fellows Hall. We even tried some boxing when we got caught in a police raid. We were fined $5 and my brother paid it. We then learned that Will Lester and Jack Coleman were singing waiters at the Avon Café, a saloon on 116th Street. So we joined again but this time we took the name from the saloon. We called ourselves the Avon Comedy Four. Our first job was at the Atlantic Gardens, on the Bowery. The act got $60 a week for four. We became a big hit and an agent, Al Mayer, got us a job at B. F. Keith's Union Square. Charles T. Aldritch, a quick-change artist and comedy magician, was the headliner. From there we went to Boston, then the Park Theater, Worcester, Massachusetts, Fall River, Massachusetts, Lynn, Salem, New Bedford, Lowell, Lawrence, Keith's Providence. Then we worked in the Midwest. We stayed for ten weeks in Hyde and Behman's Music Hall, Chicago.

We were now doing "School Days." We worked the Orpheum Circuit for eight weeks. That included San Francisco, Los Angeles, and Denver. About the San Francisco Orpheum: That was a big date. We played there for two weeks. The first week's bill had eight or nine acts. We played in our regular position, next to closing. The second week we were moved ahead because four different acts would come in. They were foreign acts, from Australia and all. The Orpheum that I remember—this was before the fire of 1906, we played it in 1904–1905—had about six rows in the orchestra, and the rest of it were tables and chairs where you could sit, eat, and drink while watching the show. We had two matinees a week, so you can see what kind of a theater it was. I don't remember that there were any other theaters like that in the United States. And as far as the audiences were concerned, they were like Continental audiences. They came all dressed up with their reserved-seat season tickets.

It was while at Hammerstein's Victoria in New York that Leo Edwards, the brother of Gus Edwards, called on us with a new song that he said would be for us. We listened and liked it. It was "School Days," which became a national hit.

It was also while at Hammerstein's that we became a test case. This was in 1909 when Sunday vaudeville shows were against the law. Actors could talk, maybe sing, but they couldn't move or dance. So Hammerstein decided on a test case and we were going to be it. We did our school act and Hammerstein told us he wanted us to do our full act that Sunday night. "You're going to be arrested," he told us. "We want a test case." So that Sunday night we did our full act and a detective came backstage and arrested us and took us to the 47th Street station. The next day we had our trial at the 54th Street court. It was the City of New York against the Avon Comedy Four.

The judge asked the detective to come up and explain the act. So the detective—what the hell did he know?—said, "A guy comes out and rings a cowbell. He's on the stage. He wears a chin piece and a high black hat. He rings the cowbell and on walks a fag. He's got on red stockings and says he's taking charge of the schoolroom while his brother is sick in bed. So he asks the feller in the red stockings, 'Do you belong in the class?' And he answers, 'Yes.' Then he asks, 'Where are the rest of the children that belong here?' He says, 'They're down in the yard playing pinochle.'" The judge looked confused. "Then," went on the detective, "you hear somebody singing and then three of them run and the teacher grabs hold of a cane and wants to hit one of the fellers but they finally sit down and the teacher says, 'I'll now call the roll.' And one of the fellers gets up and gives him a roll. Teacher, or whoever, says, 'Name two of the principal oceans.' One of the fellers says, 'The Atlantic and the Pacific.' And the teacher says, 'That's a tea company.'" The judge looked angry, knocked with the gavel, and said, "They have no act. Case dismissed." That's how we established a precedent of Sunday night concerts.

During the years we appeared with almost everybody who was in vaudeville. We were on the bill with Weber and Fields in 1914. We

243

worked with Lillian Russell too. I'll never forget one of her monologues where at the finish she said, "May you live to be a hundred and die young." She was married at the time to a fellow who owned a Pittsburgh newspaper. There was one guy Charlie and I used to laugh our heads off at. He did a Dutch monologue and twisted up the English language. He was among the first of the topics-of-the-day talkers. He'd start off slowly and by the time he got to a point, he'd be so excited everything would be twisted. He was great. He was Max Gordon's brother.

We worked with Al Jolson when it was Jolson, Palmer, and Jolson. It was in New Orleans where they started. Harry, Al's brother, was in the act. Palmer would sit in a wheelchair and Al would push it, sing, and whistle.

I knew Will Rogers, and when he first went into show business, he was just with a horse and rope. He lassoed the horse and the fellows. I don't remember any talk. He was always chewing gum. He used to lasso one of our boys when we worked on the bill with him and it got laughs, though the boys lassoed didn't like it.

We worked many times with Fanny Brice. She was a very funny girl, but a good actress for only about fifteen minutes. In one sketch one of the fellows played her lover. She put her arms around his neck and with her face to the audience she stuck out her tongue. Of course the scene fell apart. I roomed with Eddie Cantor one week while we were working in Boston, I think. Charlie was with his wife. It was Cantor and Lee at the time.

Georgie Jessel? He must've been about twelve when we played in St. Louis. I was having ice cream and he'd come into the ice cream parlor and sit next to me and I know I held him on my lap and gave him ice cream.

Our routines were always developed from incidents that happened to us. Sure they were built up and tried out in out-of-the-way theaters before we brought them into the big time. There was the "Firehouse." It was a kind of travesty. Charlie did the chief. I did the lieutenant. And we had another fellow running in yelling his house was on fire. As the scene opens, we are sitting and playing cards and the alarm goes off. Charlie says, "There must be a fire someplace." He deals the cards and we are still playing and then the fellow runs in to yell his house is burning. He finally stands behind us while we are playing. We ask him, "How big is your house?" He says, "Three stories." "Is it brick?" "Yes." "Then you've got a lot of time, brick takes longer to burn." He stands behind Charlie and is looking over Charlie's hand. I say to the feller, "You got any mortgage on it?" He says, "No. It's free and clear—play your jack—it's everything I've got in the world. It's my life savings. Play your jack," he says to Charlie. There were a lot of pieces of business here. I say to him, "Your house must be down to the ground right now." And give him a can of gasoline to help him.

Actually we wrote this one with Billy K. Wells. It was supposed to be a sketch of a community that was losing money, not enough taxes and all that sort of thing, so it leased out all its utilities. I called the Fire Department "Joe Burns' Fire Department." The scene opens and Charlie and his wife come into the room. She says, "The superintendent called up and says there's smoke coming and there must be a fire." Then Charlie says, "All right. I'll write to Joe Burns' Fire Department and give him the information." She says, "Don't write, call him up." So Charlie calls me up. And I say, "All right, I'll be right over." I come over carrying a briefcase. I'm wearing boots, a cutaway coat, and a chief's hat. And we sit down to talk. I ask, "Is it a big fire?" He says, "Well, I don't know. Let's look." We open the door and flames come through. I say, "Not a bad little fire. What kind of ladder do you want? I've got all samples here." And I take out my briefcase and show him the covers for the furniture. In the meanwhile his wife comes running in, going crazy, and says, "What are we doing with furniture covers?" And I say, "It's the wrong briefcase." Charlie asks his wife to make a cup of tea and we sit drinking tea and figuring the cost of this and that and she's going crazy. Later we find there's a fellow in the next apartment whose wife is on vacation and he's making a steak and burning it. And that's where all the smoke was coming from.

The Dr. Kronkhite bit—I'll tell you how it came to be Dr. Kronkhite. We used to do a school act in one and then I did a series of imitations. One was an imitation of a friend of mine going into a delicatessen store to buy something. I'd be the friend and Charlie would be the proprietor. I'd say, "Good morning." He'd say, "Good afternoon." I'd say, "Good evening," and he'd say, "Good night—make a day of it." I'd say, "I've only got five minutes to spend a nickel. Gimme five cents' worth of that salmon." Charlie would say, "That's not salmon, that's ham." And I'd say, "Did I ask you what it was?"

Then I'd do more imitations and finally I had one on going into a doctor's office. This one began in 1906 at Hammerstein's Victoria. One of our boys would say offstage, "Oh you butcher." And I would look and he would come out with a handkerchief over his eye. And I'd say, "Did you holler inside?" and he'd say, "Yes." "Did the doctor pull out your eye?" He said, "No, five dollars is what he pulled out of me." "Five dollars? What does he charge for a visit?" "Five dollars for the first visit, three dollars for the second, and one dollar for the third." Charlie would come

245

out and I'd say, "Well, doctor, here I am again, for the fifth time. If I come again, you'll owe me eight cents." He would say, "Continue on the same medicine." That's how it took off.

One time I said, "Well, doctor, I'm here for the fifth time," and Charlie broke in with, "What's the trouble with you?" I was flabbergasted. Finally I ad-libbed. I said, "I don't know but every time I eat a heavy meal I don't feel so hungry after." He said, "What do you eat? What kind of dishes do you eat?" And I said, "What do you mean, dishes? What am I, a crocodile?"

So we kept adding. One time I ad-libbed, "Are you a doctor?" and when he said he was, I said, "I'm dubious," and he said, "How do you do, Mr. Dubious." Then we called it "Dr. Kronkhite" and we had a sign on the drop that said, "Dr. Kronkhite, M.D.," and that's how it was established. Later we used a nurse.

We did a Dr. Kronkhite for TV, using Barbra Streisand as the nurse. But for some reason they never put it on. The nurse bit went like this: I walk into the doctor's office and I'm greeted by the nurse. I say, "Excuse me, is this the doctor's office?" She says, "Yes, I'm his nurse." "His nurse? Is the doctor sick too?" She says, "No, I'm a trained nurse." "Oh, you do tricks?" Then I ask, "What are the doctor's office hours?" She answers, "Twelve to three, three to six, six to nine, nine to twelve, twelve to three." I say, "With such hours he must be a horse doctor."

Charlie would come out with a funny little walk. One time I said, "You walk like you're in the State Department." When we played Washington we were told not to use that line. So instead I said, "You look like a new congressman looking for a seat," and that got a big laugh.

We changed around in vaudeville. For example, in Pittsburgh, a very tough town, we were careful of what lines we used. When we first did the "Hungarian Rhapsody" there was a line where one of the waiters used to say, "I'd like to have some corn." I'd say, "We don't have any corn." Charlie would come right out and say, "I have two—one on each foot." We had to cut that out in Philadelphia. We also had to cut it out at the Palace. In fact, we had to cut it out in so many places that we finally dropped it.

Occasionally we would add this to the doctor bit: I would say I had the Asiatic flu and I took so much medicine that I was sick for a long time after I got well. Charlie would say, "Who recommended you?" I'd say, "A friend, Jacob T. Sonnevitch." "Sonnevitch?" I'd say, "Yes." Charlie would say, "I had a patient—Sonnevitch—he lost me twenty-five dollars."

If we had to lengthen the doctor sketch we would put in an insurance routine: "Are you insured? No? Well, you should be insured." "What do I get in your company?" "Well, for two dollars a week, if you lose your head, two hands, or three legs, you can get seventy-five dollars a week for the rest of your natural life." "Two hands, three legs—what am I, an octopus? I could pay two dollars a week for a whole year and never get hurt." "Well, maybe the following year you'll have better luck. And they've got their own cemetery—and it's wonderful, it's right near the golf course." "A cemetery next to a golf course? That must be the last hole."

You see, we had different finishes. In some places you changed things, or in different shows you switched things around.

In 1909 when we played in England, Ireland, Scotland, and Wales, our opening performance in Liverpool, at the first show they didn't get us at all. We worked hard. It was on a big stage on an apron in one and in front of that was a lot of water. So we were about thirty-five feet or so from the orchestra. And when we did our school act in two, add another twenty feet—so we died at that first performance. In the dressing room we started to talk about the ships leaving for the United States, and I said, "Wait a minute, fellers, let's work this out. We'll work slow. We'll work in one instead of full stage." That's what we did and we turned a flop into a hit. We played England a number of times. In 1929 we headlined at the Palladium; the billing was Joe Smith and Charlie Dale and their Avon Comedy Four. The act took thirty-five minutes and we were a big hit. We played there for two weeks. We played the Hippodrome in New York, which held 6000 persons. The old Sixth Avenue El used to pass by regularly, and still we could do an act and get great hands. We stayed there for twelve weeks.

We played to two Presidents in one day. One was an ex-President— that was at Keith's, Washington. At the matinee we played to Warren Harding, and in the evening we helped Woodrow Wilson from his limousine to enter the exit door in the stage alley. He was crippled but he loved to watch vaudeville from an orchestra seat near the exit door.

Now we get to Harry Truman. When I was invited to the UN in Flushing Meadows to listen to the voting for the partition of Palestine, we all had a voting chart. My friend, Aaron Fishman, who invited me, sent his voting card to several UN dignitaries for their signatures. It took several years. He needed one signature and that was Harry Truman's. So he phoned me to get it, as he knew we were appearing on the "Ed Sullivan Show" with Truman's daughter Margaret.

I phoned Truman at the Waldorf Towers and his secretary said, "Just a minute." After a minute the President came on and asked me to come to the hotel at a quarter to four. When I went into the Presidential Suite I had two copies with me. I handed them to the secretary. He said to go into the other room. I did and there was Harry Truman.

He got up from his desk and I said, "My name is Joe Smith." He said, "Yes, all right." And I put the paper in front of him to sign. And he signed. I said, "Thank you, Mr. President, it is a pleasure and an honor to meet you." And he said, "What's your hurry? Sit down."

Now what are you going to say a President when he says sit down? You are going to wait for him to talk? I knew he came from Missouri so I started to talk about the Orpheum Theater in Kansas City. I spoke about Pop Lehman, the manager, and his son and the gambling in the dressing room and other incidents that happened while we, as the Avon Comedy Four, played there in 1905. When I mentioned gambling, he smiled a bit. "You know nobody could ever stop gambling," I said. "Either playing poker, which you have done, or crap shooting, which I have done." Truman laughed and I got up. We walked to the door and shook hands. I said again it was an honor to meet him. And he said, "Just a minute, you know when you fellows played the Orpheum in Kansas City I was an usher in that theater." Wasn't that something!

Oh yes, we also played with Ethel Barrymore and she was a sweet girl. There were other girls on the bill and they all got her picture and her autograph. Finally one of our boys went over and said, "You're giving the girls your picture—how about us?" She said, "You know, I was just waiting for you to ask." She was a great performer.

The school act was our standard. We did it from 1902 to 1913. Then Charlie and I sat down one night and said let's look for another kind of act. Maybe a saloon act or a restaurant act. In a restaurant next to the Palace we talked about it some more. Sime Silverman (he was the editor of *Variety*) said, "Make it a restaurant—a Hungarian restaurant—because it hasn't been done before." And that's how that one began. Remember Lindy's? It was a kind of travesty on Lindy's. We used to eat there a lot. I was the chef in the sketch. Charlie did the boss. Irving Kaufman and Harry Goodwin were the waiters. When I made my entrance I said, "Well, I just had a good meal in Lindy's. I wouldn't eat here. It's terrible." So Lindy got the plug. That was the opening.

I'll never forget how we broke in the act out of town for about a week and a half, I think it was in Newark. We got the scenery, the props, and everything. Max Hart was our agent. I said to him, "We need another week to break it in." He said, "Okay, I got the week—it's the Palace." I said, "Wait a minute, Max—are you kidding?" He said, "No, it's the Palace." I said, "We're not ready yet. We haven't got all our props yet." Max said,

Smith and Dale's billing at the Palace.

"Everybody was over here to see the act and they liked it." So we opened at the Palace.

Now, we were right on after the intermission. I told the stage manager, "Don't open until I got all my props, a table, a stove, and other things. Now please, don't open until I give you the signal." So what does he do? The music starts and up goes the curtain and there I am onstage fixing the props. Now what the hell are you gonna do?"

The fellas playing the waiters, Kaufman and Goodwin, start giving orders. I'm looking for this and that, fumbling around, juggling eggs—

"Two fried eggs, one should be from the country, this one's from the old country"—and I'm looking for a frying pan to put the eggs in and all that stuff. Irving Kaufman comes on to sing. He does a solo in the middle of the act. I'm offstage and boiling. I keep talking loud: "Here's an opening. We've got a new act and they ring up before I'm ready." Martin Beck, who happened to be backstage, comes over and asks what's wrong. "Mr. Beck," I say "I told the stage manager not to ring up until I'm ready. And there I was in the middle of setting up my props and up goes the curtain."

Mr. Beck laughs and says, "Take it easy. I like the act."

We had lines when they were firing orders at me. I'd say, "Catch me a glass of water." And the waiter would say, "Where's the water?" and I'd say, "In the milk." We did the Dr. Kronkhite in the "Hungarian Rhapsody" act. I'd say, "I'm sick," and somebody would say, "Go see a doctor—go see Dr. Kronkhite, he's just around the corner." Then the curtain would come down and I'd be in one and we'd do the Dr. Kronkhite bit. It was really two acts in one that we did. It ran about thirty minutes.

One time when we were playing Billy Gray's nightclub in Hollywood, Garson Kanin's brother Mike came backstage and said, "Garson and I should pay you." I wanted to know what for and he said, "We have been doing your Dr. Kronkhite act in the Catskill borscht circuit." Mike wanted to write a motion picture story on us but I think the lawyers frigged it up.

I saw Jack Albertson and Sam Levene in the hit show *Sunshine Boys*. Everyone who saw it thinks it's the story of Smith and Dale. I saw it a few times and it's a paraphrase, but I think Neil Simon really had us in mind when he wrote it. Naturally when they did the "Doctor" sketch from the play on TV, people's minds went back to Dr. Kronkhite. I told Jack—who is a dear friend of mine and who does the bit of Charlie Dale—I said, "Jack, don't try to live it down, live it up."

You know that Jack came from burlesque. He also did a little vaudeville. He did a straight for a lot of performers. A nice fellow.

I told you about Al H. Woods when he was manager of the Bowery Nickleodeon and told us we were too young. Well, we met again sixteen years later and he engaged us for his show *Why Worry?* that starred Fanny Brice and George Sidney.

We were the Avon Comedy Four there. Harry Goodwin, Irving Kaufmann, and Smith and Dale. People never knew our first names; at times they called me Charlie and called Charlie Joe. One time a fellow gave me $10. He owed it to Charlie. I laughingly took it.

I know many two acts used to fight and argue a lot. But never Charlie and me. Oh yes, we argued but it was always about the act. When

Charlie died, November 16, 1971, the headstone I put up says, "Smith and Dale." And when I go, I'll be next to him. So how long can you be partners? Sure, we were lucky. But we liked each other and respected each other. And how many show-business partners can say that after being together over seventy years?

JEAN CARROLL

JEAN CARROLL *was one of the few successful comediennes of the 1940s. Her major vaudeville appearances were in the presentation houses. She was what in show business is called a "stand-up comic"—that is, she stood up in front of a microphone and did her act.*

Her observations on current customs, her domestic life, and her experiences buying a fur coat—"wholesale"—were hilarious.

She began her show-business career as a child singer-dancer. Later she met, teamed up with, and married another dancer, Buddy Howe (see pages 18–22). When he retired to become an agent, she continued to do a single until her own retirement. A grandmother today, she is still a very funny private person.

My professional career started when I dared to go and audition for a play. Everyone thought I was a cockeyed genius. And in those days they used to have talent scouts from theatrical agencies. A man came to our home in the Bronx—I forget his name, but he was with MCA and we knew that was a big agency. Anyway, he spoke to my mother and said he had seen me in the amateur shows, thought I was very talented, and would she be interested in having them, more or less, take me under their wing. I was still going to school. He said they would treat me as their own daughter, they would see that I didn't make any wrong associations, and they would train me. They'd show me how to walk on the stage and how to walk off. That I already knew. I had two legs. I could walk on and walk off. Sometimes I ran off.

Then I entered another amateur show. It was in a burlesque theater on 149th Street and Willis Avenue—Joe Somebody's Girlie Show. Rex Weber—you know him—he was in it too.

Oddly enough, my Mom agreed to let me go with MCA—which floored me because there was nothing more important to my mother than my education. But everybody agreed I was smart so it didn't matter whether I went to school or not.

By that time we had moved to Connecticut because my father was working there and I skipped three times in the first term. You know why? I knew where I lived. I was then about eleven, and that made me smart. I knew my full name and they immediately decided I should get out of school altogether. Go to college. It was easy in those days. If you were bright, ahead of your class, they put you ahead. Sometimes it was unfair because I ended up a punk kid in a class of much older kids.

I'd like to just skip over and say that things just happened, because that's the way it was. I never looked for things to happen. But I'd be getting ahead of myself so let's go back.

I was always crazy about jiggers. That's what we called them—you know, the tap dancers, we called them jiggers. I would aggravate my mother to give me 5 cents or 10 cents so I could see the jiggers. I used to look at the pictures outside the theaters, and if there were fellers who wore spats, I knew they were jiggers. Eventually I learned how to jig. And I was good too.

Now I'm in show business. We have a kind of teacher backstage who is supposed to teach us school work so we can satisfy the Gerry Society that says kids of school age can't be onstage unless stage teachers are provided. I'm now about fourteen and we now have a four-person act. Pearl Saxon, two fellows whose names I won't mention, and me. I was appointed the manager because I could talk longer. We came to the theater every morning and rehearsed because we were going to do a good act. And since they appointed me manager, I decided I would really manage. During a show I saw one of the fellows flirting with some girl and carrying on a little conversation. I was angry. You can't carry on a conversation doing unison dancing. So when we came offstage I told that guy, "I don't want that to ever happen again." It wasn't fair to the three of us. I guess he became angry. I don't remember now. Anyway, come pay night and instead of going with us he said, "You girls go ahead to the next stop"—it was some small town in Pennsylvania, I don't remember the name— "We'll be there tomorrow morning." His excuse was they had something to do. So Pearl Saxon and I went ahead. We checked into a small hotel we had been told about and went to the theater and waited for them to show up. They had the music and the wardrobe. When they didn't show,

I did what any normal American girl would do. I bawled. The manager, a very nice man, asked what the trouble was. I told him, between bawls, "We have no music, no money, no nothing. Our partners were supposed to come with the music and wardrobe for rehearsal—and nothing." And I bawled again.

The manager asked, "How good are you?" I forgot my tears and said, "We're really two great hoofers. We dance as well as any two men." He said, "I'll tell you what we'll do. Can you manage without music?" I said, "Sure—if you have a good piano player." In those days they had the greatest piano players in the pit. They knew every song that had ever been written. "But," I said, "we don't have any wardrobe." He said, "There's a little store a few doors away. I'll let you have the money. I think you can buy dresses for about twelve dollars." So we did.

We opened as a duo, she and I. I did my "five-foot-two with eyes of blue" with just the piano, and we managed to do six numbers. We really did a fine act. We never saw the fellows again. I don't know what happened to them. I think they put on our dresses and went away.

So that was the first time I was stranded. But there was another time. I was working with a band act in New Jersey, and the band leader absconded with the money. I did a flip. Suddenly out of nowhere I saw a face, a familiar face—it was my father. He had been notified by the agents, Al and Belle Dow, and he came to Red Bank to collect me. But even that didn't shake me. Nothing shook me. I'd have taken a job washing dishes to make enough money to get back home.

I was on a bill working with a man, Saranoff, and in those days some theaters used to have what they called Green Rooms. This theater we were in had one, a sort of lounge where the performers could sit, read, and play—they had a piano. I had a ukelele. I used to love to strum that uke and sing. Make up songs. So we are sitting there one day, all of us, kibitzing, and I'm playing the uke, and this chap, Marty May, he was the star on the bill, says, "You know something, you're really a talented girl and you're really funny." I used to do imitations of the Kentucky Colonel. I'd stick a pillow on my belly underneath and do the fat colonel and stuff like that. So May says to me, "How would you like to work with me?" I say, "Aw, come on." He's a star, and how would I like to work with a headliner? I say, "You're joking." He says, "I'm not joking at all, I mean it. You're one of the cleverest girls I have ever seen and you're funny. I could use someone like you."

I went to Saranoff and I said I had an offer to do a double act with Marty May. He told me May couldn't mean it. I said I wanted to take it and Saranoff became angry because he also wanted me. He said, "Why

Jean Carroll, when she and Buddy Howe were partners. (Photo courtesy of
James J. Kriegsmann)

don't you stay in my act and we'll also do some talking?" but I said no. That is how I really started doing comedy. It was with Marty May. Nothing was written. Nothing was ever prepared, which was crazy because how do you know how many minutes you can do? Anyway, Marty used to talk to me on the stage and I would answer whatever came into my head and this developed into a little style of naïveté, I became a little bit of a patsy. Then one day we worked on a bill with Buddy Howe, who was doing an act with Jack E. Leonard. They used to call him Fat Jack, except he wasn't fat then. Anyway, I watched Buddy and I liked him right away because he looked like my brother. Of course I knew Jack for a long time. I got friendly with Elise, the little girl who worked in the act with Buddy. She later married the Andy of Amos and Andy. Buddy and I hit it off right away. There was no romance. We knew each other quite a while before we really became serious. I decided one day when I saw him doing a dance onstage. My heart went blip-de-blip and I thought, my God, I'm in love with that boy, but he won't know it because he's not interested in me. Later I discovered that he had also found himself strongly attracted to me and had told Jack that I was the kind of a girl that he'd like to have except I was too young. So, it was meant to be. We ended up dating. We

(Jean) Carroll and (Buddy) Howe in London, 1937.

were in love and we wanted to be together. So I sat down and wrote an act and that's how the act of Carroll and Howe began. You know it well enough. Lord knows, you must've caught it many times.

Milt Berger—he was then with Jack Davies—got us booked into Loew's State when Sid Piermont was the booker. Then came the RKO theaters, the Pantages, there was so much work. Then finally, the Palace. Oh yes, I had worked the Palace before, when I was doing a single. On the bill with me was Ben Blue and Lauritz Melchior.

Well, the act of Carroll and Howe was doing okay. We worked the London Palladium. On the bill was an act called the Crazy Gang, comics, very big in London. The headliner was George Formby, a very big English star. We were just a little number-two act. But we were an instant smash and we became headliners. We were supposed to stay in England four weeks. We stayed there three years. We played all the provinces, nightclubs, made a couple of little movies, some shorts, and we became the big thing. After Burns and Allen, we were the big thing. We loved the people there and they loved us. We were amazed that they grasped our kind of humor, which, as you know is very personal. We didn't Anglicize it. We knew that if we tried to use their slang they would resent it. But who understands the spoken word and can appreciate it more than the British? Nobody. We never worked in other countries, though a lot of places wanted us—South Africa, Australia, all English-speaking countries. For a time we even considered learning enough French so we could go to France. But there was so much work waiting for us in America, what was the point?

So we came back, and of course since you covered us time and again, you know that we always came in with something new and different because I wrote the act. We saved our money and we were doing very well. In those days I'd say we were getting more money than any other man-woman comedy act around. We also did a lot of radio work.

You remember that dress thing we did? Well, here's how it started. We had just returned from England and I needed a new dress. I was looking in some window on 42nd Street, and I saw a pink blouse I liked. I went inside and said to the salesgirl, "What's the size of the blouse in the window?" She said, "It'll fit you." I said, "You don't even know what size I wear. Just tell me the size. Is it a twelve?" She said, "A twelve—you could never get into a twelve." I said, "I didn't come in for a figure analysis, all I'm asking you is do you have that blouse in a twelve?" She said, "I wouldn't sell it to you." Then she brought something out and said, "Now this is you." I said, "What do you mean, this is me? Is it me because it's the only one you've got?" When I came home I told Buddy about it

257

and he laughed and said, "That would really be a funny routine. Why don't you do it?" And that very night I tried it. Oh, I built it up a little. I said, "I tried on a dress and the salesgirl called Mrs. B. from out the back and she said, 'Look at her—isn't that her?' You know, they convinced me that it was me and I bought the dress."

And you remember that routine about buying a mink coat wholesale? That too was a true incident. A girlfriend of mine said, "You're crazy if you buy a mink retail. I have connections. I know a fellow in skins." So at three o'clock in the morning on a Friday we sneaked up, because nobody's supposed to know you're there. We got up there and the place was filled with people. They all knew him. They all came for the same thing. The funniest line in that routine was "Feel the pooh." Now, I don't know what "pooh" is (it's the pile under the fur) so, I say, "I'd feel it if I knew where to find it. Give me a clue." So that too became a trademark.

I always used to use Buddy as the butt of many of my jokes and you'd be surprised how many people would resent it, especially people who knew Buddy. They'd say, "How can you say that! He's such a wonderful guy." And I would say, "How can I say the things about myself that I do? I'm a wonderful girl." I used to do that routine about my daughter being a hippy with the dirty sneakers and dirty blue jeans, but why a beard? And you know people would actually come to me and say, "Does your daughter really have a beard?" I'd say, "No, I made her shave it, but I let her keep her mustache." When I did the thing about my mother living with us and how I lost my father nine years ago—"He's not dead, he's hiding"— people would say, "Why do you say things like that?" And I'd say, "Who should I talk about?" I also used to say I was fat. And they'd spin me around on the street like a top and say, "You're not fat, why do you say you're fat?" I'd say, "Because I want to say it. I can't say I'm fat, I can't talk about my mother, my husband, my child. You know, there is really very little left to say."

Did Buddy tell you about that guy at the Red Apple Rest? When Buddy and I, our daughter, and the collie dog came in, there's this guy who says to me, "You're really a good-looking broad. I can't get over it. Hearing you on radio and things. You're really a good-looking broad. You should stay off TV." I said, "That's odd, you look like a bum." Buddy kicked me under the table. He went to school to learn how to kick in the right places. He always said, "Don't antagonize a fan because they'll write letters."

I remember that in my day there were neighborhood theaters. Every small community had its own vaudeville theater and you had to almost know your audiences. If they liked you, they would follow you from theater to theater. They took an interest in you. It was almost as if you were part of the neighborhood. The rapport you had with these people you never had in any other medium of show business. The audiences were kind. Nobody ever heckled you. You were important to these people, who worked hard all week, and to the kids, who did their chores and went to school. The relationship between the performer and the audience was something you don't see any longer. There was a common courtesy that was extended even if you weren't terribly good. The audience would find some redeeming feature and they would make you feel that you had done your job.

Traveling from town to town was thrilling and exciting because I was always interested in people. People in various areas of the country were not all alike. I always sought what incidents made people, different people, laugh. Obviously I couldn't bring sophisticated New York or so-called metropolitan humor to people in small towns. Not that they were stupid. They were not. But big-city humor was alien to them. They would just not have understood it. So I would make it my business to listen in on conversations in local restaurants, stores, etcetera. I learned that in certain parts of the country you had to speak slowly—their ears were not attuned to the fast delivery and the jargon of a New York City person.

You could see the joy audiences in many parts of the country used to get. If they liked an act, they would mull over its jokes. They would feed on such things for weeks. They would pick up phrases. I know because when we came back they used to greet us with such enthusiasm when they heard material they remembered from the previous time we had appeared in that theater.

It was always a thrill for Buddy and me to have someone come up to us in a drugstore or anyplace and say, "We saw you onstage and enjoyed your jokes," or whatever. Their receptions were so genuine it made you feel that aside from the fact that you were getting paid a salary, you were bringing a little something into people's lives.

It was a good life. A very rewarding life. Oh sure, there is television, radio, pictures—but none of this is vaudeville. Too bad that present generations had to miss it.

ROSE MARIE *began in vaudeville as "Baby" Rose Marie but didn't appear in New York until she reached her late teens. Even as a child she had a husky voice that intrigued listeners. She is one of the few performers in this book who never played the Palace, though she appeared in virtually all the RKO houses and later the presentation houses.*

While her voice continued to fascinate long after she dropped the "Baby," it was her free-wheeling comedy that made her popular. Her "Jimmy Durante" imitation became a classic. Her "Butcher Boy," a special material song, was always in demand.

Today she is best known as the glib-talking girl of the old Dick Van Dyke shows and "Hollywood Squares."

I got into show business because I won amateur contests. The first one was when I was three and a half and it was at the Mecca Theater on 14th Street. My mother used to take me to the Academy of Music, also on 14th Street, and to other shows not too far from home.

How come a brat of three and a half goes into amateur contests? Well, at home I would mimic everything I saw, so when we went to the theater—my mother, a neighbor, and me—it was the neighbor who entered me. She thought I was cute, but my mother was scared, she didn't know what I would do. It was one thing to sing at home but in front of an audience—well, she was scared. I wasn't scared. I didn't have sense enough. To me it was fun.

Anyway, I won—what, I don't remember. But the audience then,

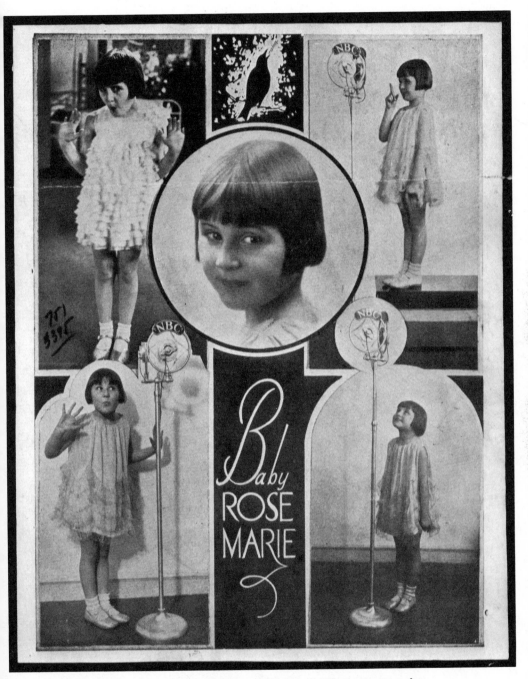

Baby Rose Marie singing "The Old Covered Bridge." (Photo courtesy of Shapiro, Bernstein, and Rose Marie Guy)

and many since, liked my kind of voice—it was kind of husky even as a child. Who knows why, maybe nodes or whatever they call them. I remember that winning one contest got us a trip to Atlantic City.

I was singing on the beach, just for myself and family, when a representative from radio station WPG, Atlantic City, heard me and put me on radio. And right away mail started to come in. Well, I was on that radio station for about a year and a half when a New York station, I think it was WMCA, heard about me and put me on the old Ohrbach hour. Now I'm going back a few years. Then NBC entered the scene and signed me to a seven-year contract. So there I was, six years old, and I had my own radio show on WJZ Sunday mornings at 12:15. It was coast to coast and Julius Grossman was the sponsor. I think my theme song was "Baby Shoes." It was a fifteen-minute show—a piano player, an announcer, and me.

Letters began coming in saying it wasn't a child singing, I must be a forty-five-year-old midget, no child sings like that.

NBC was part of RKO at that time, and I was signed to NBC's artist bureau. They laid out a tour of fifty-two weeks of theaters, the RKO houses, to prove I wasn't a midget. This NBC artist bureau also represented Amos and Andy, Rudy Vallee, Graham MacNamee, Leo Reisman, and Vincent Lopez.

So I played theaters all over the country to prove I was a child. On Saturday afternoons the theaters would hold kiddy contests in which everybody imitated Baby Rose Marie. At that time the big song was "Springtime in the Rockies" and everybody sang it. I did songs that were popular but I never did the deep love songs—you know, I love you—my heart breaks for you. I used to change things around so some of the songs became mother songs, like "I Love You Mother." Today of course "mother" is a dirty word. But anyway, that's what I did and that's how I did vaudeville.

Did the other acts resent me? I'm sure they did. They resent all child stars. You know that old saying: "Never work with kids or dogs." But all the people I worked with were very nice to me. They taught me all kinds of things like juggling, walking on wooden balls, and working on a trampoline. So I really got a hell of an education and vaudeville was wonderful for me.

On my fifty-two-week tour we ended up in California. We stayed out there for a month or so to try pictures or whatever. Nothing happened so we went back to New York. I did a picture back there, something called *International House*, which funnily enough was about television. This was in 1935. You can see it now on the Late, Late, Late Show. It was with W. C. Fields and Rudy Vallee. I did a number, "Why Blue-birds Are Singing the Blues." I also did records which were popular at that time.

The almost two years of vaudeville I did was about at the tail end of vaudeville. The vaudeville I remembered was the vaudeville that had been. The Palace was over with. The last vaudeville date I did was probably the Chicago theater in Chicago. I think it was 1939 or something like that. Oh yes, Mike Douglas, who was just a struggling singer, was on the bill. There was the Lou Breeze Orchestra plus a couple of other acts that I don't remember. But I remember Mike trying to get going. Also Irv

Baby Rose Marie with Milton Berle, at the Palace Theatre in Chicago, Illinois.

Rose Marie today, no longer a "baby."

Kupcinet—he had the Harvest Moon Dancers or whatever he called them.

I played in almost every town you can mention. They were all RKO theaters. Oh here's something: I was working in Rochester and they had a child labor law. You know, no child could work, even sing or dance. Well, everybody had come to see Baby Rose Marie because they had heard her on radio. Then the Gerry Society—somebody had called them in Rochester—came in and said I couldn't sing.

Joan Davis and her husband Si Will were on the bill. They were number two. Si came over and said to my father, "Do you have any of her records?" He said, "Yes," and Si then turned to me and said, "Do you know the records?" and I said, "Yes." So he said, "Okay," went on stage, and told the audience of my situation, that the law didn't allow me to sing. But the theater had some of my records, and they knew the audience wanted to see me, so they put a phonograph onstage. They played the records and I lip-synched them. So I did the first pantomime act and I was only seven.

As you know, I was married to Robert Guy. It's been years since I lost him but the pain's still there. He was a fine musician but never really my manager. He didn't want to be. Performing is a rough chore. It's the roughest form of entertainment because it's just you and God out there and nobody else.

Today you see a Las Vegas show, you see a small musical comedy. You see eighteen boy singers, as many girls and more. I used to walk on with just a piano player and do my act. And in those days I was a performer, I had a name as an entertainer. Rose Marie the performer. Television has changed all that. I've become an image to people, and if I do anything, even do a play, it has to be something that they want to see me in. When I do a play I have to pick out something that is not dirty because they don't expect it from me. It must be something they can associate with what they have seen on television.

I can't go out and just do an act anymore. I have to talk about the "Doris Day Show," the "Tonight Show," "Hollywood Squares." I have to talk about all that before I can get into the art of performing and showing that I am a performer. Every show I've done had production numbers. I did a couple of numbers on the "Doris Day Show." But these were just thrown in. They didn't really count.

Totie Fields keeps telling me, "You're the best goddam act in the business. Why the hell aren't you working? Wadda ya mean, sitting on your fanny?" Berle got after me about a month ago and said, "Why aren't you working? What do you mean, sitting on your fanny?" I said, "I haven't the material." He said, "I'll write your material. You should be working. You should be up there making money." And I said I just don't have the interest—or the attitude, if you want to say that. I enjoy doing a play and whatever play I do I wind up doing twenty minutes with the audience afterwards. I sort of kibitz around and ad-lib with them. I don't have anything prepared. I do very well on TV. Let's say I get by. I'm not going to retire tomorrow. I do "Hollywood Squares." I've been doing that for seven years. I do other shows, like "Honeymoon Suite," which Morey [Amsterdam] and I did as a pilot for a new series. Bill Loeb is my manager, has been for years. If I wanted nightclubs I'm sure the Morris office would want me and keep me on the road for ninety-six weeks. But I don't want that. I've done the road bit. I've been through all that. I'm in a position that every act wishes the hell they could be in. I'm on TV. I can't walk down the street that people don't recognize me.

So what do I need? Baby Rose Marie? I didn't mind that billing until I was about twelve. That's when it became *Miss* Rose Marie. Now that I'm an old bag I just use Rose Marie . . . understand?

When I look back at vaudeville, it wasn't so much what it taught me as what I learned working with some of the people in it. There was Milton Berle. There was Georgie Jessel, Rudy Vallee, Dick Powell, and so many.

So let me go already. I'll let you buy me a cup of tea. Come on!

GLOSSARY

Big Time	Theater that played straight vaudeville, no movies, only two shows a day. It usually had reserved seats.
Blackouts	Comic bits in which lights are blacked out right after a punch line is delivered.
Blue	Bordering on the obscene.
Break In	An out-of-the-way small theater where a new routine can be tried.
Chautauqua	A summer lecture circuit, sometimes produced in tents. Sometimes vaudeville performers were added.
Civilian	Anyone not in show business.
Death Trail	Small-time vaudeville tours in the Midwest, where jumps were long and performers sometimes did five or more shows a day.
Dumb Act	An act that doesn't talk; i.e., an acrobat, a juggler.
Emcee	Master of Ceremonies.
Fally Markus	A small-time theater booker who paid very little. Actors used "Fally Markus dates" to break in new material.

Flash Act	A man and woman act, a line of girls (and/or boys), singers and dancers who have their own scenery and often their own conductor. The act makes a "flash."
Gerry Society	The Society for Prevention of Cruelty to Children, which was headed by Elbridge T. Gerry. Children were not permitted to perform on the New York stage unless a permit was granted by the Society. The movement spread to many other states.
Gus Edwards	The best-known producer of children's vaudeville units, e.g., "School Days" and "Kiddie Kabaret" acts. Many famous stars came out of the Gus Edwards units.
Hype	To stimulate interest in a product, song or act. "So-and so is being 'hyped.'"
Jumps	Distance between places where the entertainer was to perform, usually traveling by rail.
Lay Off	Between jobs; actor out of work.
Legit	Legitimate theater.
Next to Closing	The next-to-last act, usually given to the chief star of the vaudeville bill.
Number Two Act	An act, usually unimportant, that is slotted second on a vaudeville bill.
Playing Time	Total weeks (or days) of employment.
Routine	Material used in an act, usually belonging to a specific vaudevillian.
Routining a Show	Laying out the running order of a vaudeville bill. A typical big-time eight-act show might run as follows: Overture 1. Acrobat (dumb act) 2. Girl singer or minor comedian 3. Tab show or flash act

4. A good comedy team or a top singing act
5. Knockabout or tab show (depending on what is slotted in number three)

   Intermission

6. A solid dancing team
7. The star of the bill
8. Closing animal act, juggler (dumb act)

Small Time   Vaudeville, sometimes with movies, usually general admission with three or four shows a day.

Song Plugger   A singer hired by a music publisher to help popularize and sell sheet music of specific songs.

Standard Act   An act thoroughly familiar to managers and bookers.

Steal a Bow   Bowing too often and too long.

Stooge   A foil, usually planted in the audience, to assist the comedian.

Tab Show   Tabloid version of a longer show.

Two-a-day   Big-time vaudeville, which only ran two shows a day.

Working in One   Performer who appears in front of the curtain. Comics usually "work in one."

INDEX